THE
COLORADO
TRAIL

NINTH EDITION

THE OFFICIAL GUIDEBOOK OF
The Colorado Trail Foundation

The Colorado Trail
Foundation

Early morning light in the Weminuche Wilderness.

THE
COLORADO
TRAIL

NINTH EDITION

The Colorado Trail
Foundation

THE OFFICIAL GUIDEBOOK OF
The Colorado Trail Foundation

THE COLORADO MOUNTAIN CLUB PRESS
GOLDEN, COLORADO

The Colorado Trail: The Official Guidebook of The Colorado Trail Foundation
Ninth edition

© 2016 by The Colorado Trail Foundation
710 10th Street, Room 210, Golden, CO 80401
(303) 384-3729 • ctf@ColoradoTrail.org • ColoradoTrail.org
Please alert the CTF to any errors or outdated information at the address above.

PUBLISHED BY:
The Colorado Mountain Club Press
710 10th Street, Suite #200, Golden, CO 80401
(303) 996-2743; (800) 633-4417; email cmcpress@cmc.org

Founded in 1912, The Colorado Mountain Club is the largest outdoor recreation, education, and conservation organization in the Rocky Mountains. Look for our books at your local bookstore or outdoor retailer or online at www.cmc.org

Bill Manning, CTF Executive Director	*author, updates to maps and elevation profiles*
Jerry Brown, Bear Creek Survey Service, Inc.	*GPS trail data*
Tim Burroughs	*developmental editor*
Takeshi Takahashi	*design, composition, and production*
Sarah Gorecki	*publisher*

COVER PHOTO: Descending into the Elk Creek drainage, Colorado Trail Segment 24. Photo by Ben Kraushaar
Title page photo by Lori Brummer

DISTRIBUTED TO THE TRADE BY
Mountaineers Books
1001 SW Klickitat Way, Suite 201, Seattle, WA 98134
800-533-4453 | www.mountaineersbooks.org

We gratefully acknowledge the financial support of the people of Colorado through the Scientific and Cultural Facilities District of greater metropolitan Denver for our publishing activities.

Warning: Although there has been an effort to make this book as accurate as possible, some discrepancies may exist between this guide and the trail. Before beginning an excursion on The Colorado Trail, users should be capable of independent backcountry travel and be experienced in relevant mountaineering and orienteering techniques. Failure to have the necessary knowledge, equipment, and conditioning may subject users of The Colorado Trail to physical danger, injury, or death. Some routes described in this book have changed and others will change; hazards described may have expanded and new hazards may have formed since the book's publication. For updates on trail changes and reroutes, go to ColoradoTrail.org.

ISBN 978-1-937052-33-1
Ebook ISBN 978-1-937052-34-8

Printed in USA

CONTRIBUTORS

This book is a collaborative effort by The Colorado Trail Foundation (CTF) and its volunteers, the builders and stewards of all 567 miles of The Colorado Trail. To find out more about the CTF, or to join in preserving and m intaining The Colorado Trail, visit ColoradoTrail.org.

Many people helped the CTF develop the ninth edition of The Colorado Trail guidebook and we thank every one. Jerry Brown surveyed the trail, completing it six times, gathering accurate trail data with professional survey-grade GPS equipment. Sam Parks hiked the newly added Collegiate West alternative and recorded detailed information at each mile point. Tim Burroughs donated his professional expertise and authored the five new chapters for this western alternative. Aimée O'Malley compiled trail features data for the guidebook as well as *The Colorado Trail Databook* for improved consistency. Morgan and Robyn Wilkinson refined the guidebook's trail descriptions. Paul Magnanti used his "triple-crowner" experience to write about lightweight backpacking. Dean Krakel utilized his expertise as former *Denver Post* photo editor to revise the photography sections. Coordinating the entire effort was CTF Executive Director Bill Manning.

A volunteer works to clear the trail. Hundreds of fallen trees are removed every year by CTF volunteers who maintain The Colorado Trail.

Many other volunteers assisted, including George Miller, Steve Staley, Gudy Gaskill, Dan Cohen, Tom Easley, Ron Davis, David Dolton, Jodie Petersen, Dave Peters, Georgia Hoffman, and Cindy Johnson, as well as CTF Office Manager Victoria Klinger and Field Operations Manager Brent Adams. This edition relies, in part, on earlier editions developed by Terry Root, Merle McDonald, Marilyn Eisele, Suzanne Reed, and others. Also contributing were the many Colorado Trail users who contribute photographs and those who report to the CTF office about necessary refinements to the book. The CTF needs, and is grateful for, all of our good Friends of The Colorado Trail, the CTF volunteers and donors whose involvement preserves The Colorado Trail.

Support from the U.S. Forest Service, Department of Agriculture, Rocky Mountain Region, is acknowledged and appreciated.

CONTENTS

For ease of navigation, sections of this guidebook are organized by color.

Waterton Canyon Trailhead to Kenosha Pass (Segments 1–5)

Kenosha Pass to Mount Massive Trailhead (Segments 6–10)

Mount Massive Trailhead to Marshall Pass (Segments 11–15)

Marshall Pass to San Luis Pass (Segments 16–20)

San Luis Pass to Junction Creek Trailhead (Segments 21–28)

Collegiate West, Twin Lakes to S. Fooses Ridge (Segments CW01–CW05)

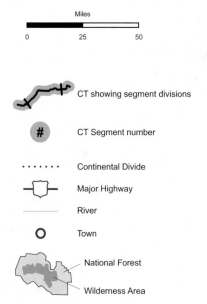

Miles

0   25   50

CT showing segment divisions

CT Segment number

· · · · · · ·   Continental Divide

Major Highway

River

○   Town

National Forest

Wilderness Area

N

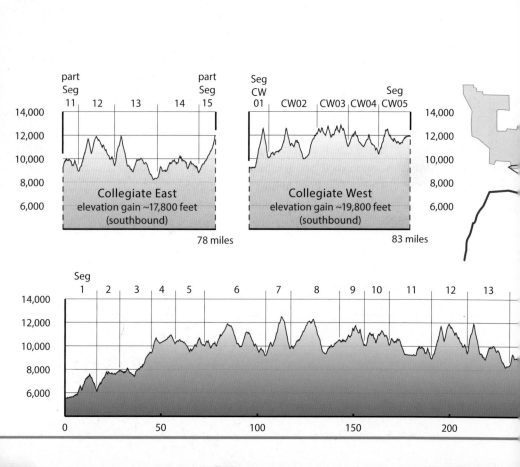

part Seg 11   12   13   14   part Seg 15

14,000
12,000
10,000
8,000
6,000

Collegiate East
elevation gain ~17,800 feet
(southbound)

78 miles

Seg CW 01   CW02   CW03   CW04   Seg CW05

14,000
12,000
10,000
8,000
6,000

Collegiate West
elevation gain ~19,800 feet
(southbound)

83 miles

Seg 1   2   3   4   5   6   7   8   9   10   11   12   13

14,000
12,000
10,000
8,000
6,000

0   50   100   150   200

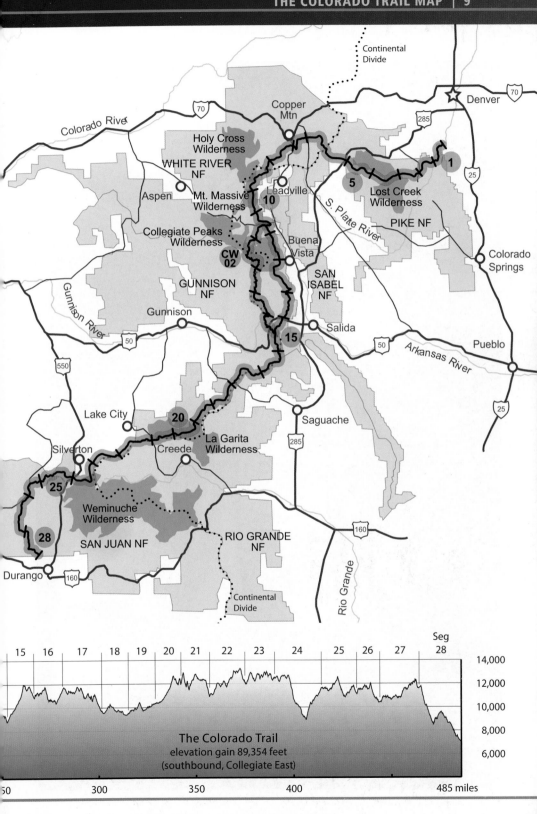

The Colorado Trail
elevation gain 89,354 feet
(southbound, Collegiate East)

FOREWORD BY GUDY GASKILL

COLORADO. The name rolls off the tongue and brings to mind images of red rock walls, cascading waterfalls, lofty peaks, alpine meadows bedecked with wildflowers, and a unique outdoor lifestyle. This lifestyle has created a state of vigorous, healthy, and robust men and women who flock to the mountains to practice and enjoy their climbing, hiking, mountain biking, and horseback skills in the summer and a multitude of snow sports in the winter. It is truly a magnificent state.

I have traveled all over the world, climbed and hiked in many different climates and environments, but each time the plane brings me safely down to terra firma my mind always comes back to the same question: Why did I ever leave Colorado? Colorado is home; a big friendly state with such a variety of scenery. Who could ever forget the azure blue sky, the color deepening as the day draws to an end, the spectacular cumulus clouds that billow up before the afternoon showers, and the show of golds, oranges, and crimsons in the sky on a late summer evening? Who could forget a tunnel of golden aspens, with a treasure of gold coins covering the fragrant earth on a crisp autumn day? Or the brilliance of ice crystals shimmering a million colors in the early morning sun? This is heaven underfoot.

The Colorado Trail, a backcountry path traversing some of the most scenic areas of the Rockies and Continental Divide, is a unique experience for both body and soul. This revised guidebook to the trail describes the wonders and beauty that you will see along the way. It points out the flora and fauna native to the region. It will stir your imagination with its geological observations, creating a desire to know more of the area's ancient history and the powers of nature that formed this landscape. The Colorado Trail also provides a living history lesson as it crosses the paths of the area's earlier inhabitants, from American Indians to nineteenth-century miners and railroad barons.

As early as 1970, the late Merrill Hastings, publisher, ski industry pioneer, and co-conceptualizer of The Colorado Trail, wrote of the increasing need for the conservation of our public lands as the nation looks more and more to the American West in its search for peace and contentment away from the pace of metropolitan life. An idea was born, and in 1987 The Colorado Trail became a reality.

Gudy Gaskill.
PHOTO BY ERIC WUNROW

THE COLORADO TRAIL FOUNDATION

The Colorado Trail

THE "TRAIL TO NOWHERE": That is how the *Empire* magazine section of *The Denver Post* characterized The Colorado Trail in 1984. Bill Lucas of the U.S. Forest Service and Merrill Hastings of *Colorado Magazine* had conceived the idea of a long-distance trail between Denver and Durango in 1973. In 1974, several focus groups were held to develop a plan for building the trail.

Gudy Gaskill, an active member of The Colorado Mountain Club since 1952 and later the first woman president of the CMC, attended the first focus group. Subsequently, in those early years, she never missed a planning meeting. The Colorado Mountain Trails Foundation, predecessor to The Colorado Trail Foundation, was formed to plan, develop, and manage The Colorado Trail, and Gudy Gaskill was asked to chair the committee.

The task ahead was immense: A route had to be scouted through eleven Forest Service districts, linking early trails with existing mining and logging roads. Inquiries had to be

Roundup Riders of the Rockies were early CT advocates and remain involved today.

sent to each district to get permission to build. She emphasized that CTF volunteers were building the trail for about $500 per mile, compared with an estimated Forest Service cost of $25,000 per mile. Gudy made numerous trips to persuade reluctant district rangers to buy into the idea of The Colorado Trail. After a year of intense work, most districts agreed to the plan. At the same time, Gudy was recruiting and training volunteers, leading trail crews, and purchasing supplies.

Despite the massive effort of Gudy and her "dirt-digging volunteers," The Colorado Trail seemed to languish. Hence the "Trail to Nowhere" designation by *Denver Post* writer Ed Quillen. (This article and others are posted at ColoradoTrail.org under Who We Are, Trail History.) That article was just what The Colorado Trail needed. It caught the attention of then Governor Dick Lamm and his wife, Dottie. They joined a trail crew, hosted a fundraiser, and rekindled support and cooperation between the state and Forest Service.

In 1986, Gudy founded The Colorado Trail Foundation, whose nonprofit mission was to complete and maintain the trail. Gudy was a true visionary in realizing that volunteers were the heart, soul, and future of outdoor stewardship. With the Forest Service providing technical assistance, Gudy's volunteers provided the labor. The 468-mile-long trail between Denver and Durango was completed in 1987.

Today, Gudy is still active in The Colorado Trail Foundation and the organization remains volunteer driven. Its board of directors, adopters, crew leaders, crew participants—hundreds of them from all over the world—volunteer their time each year to preserve and improve the trail.

It is Gudy's inspiration and can-do attitude that permeates this effort. For that, the "Mother of The Colorado Trail" has been honored by two U.S. presidents and in 2002 was inducted into the Colorado Women's Hall of Fame.

Volunteers Build and Maintain the Trail

Volunteers led by The Colorado Trail Foundation continue as primary stewards of The Colorado Trail. Work is done in cooperation with the US Forest Service, with such success that, in 2012, the agency requested the CTF add the 80-mile Collegiate West alternative and expand the volunteer stewardship.

Keeping the trail in good shape is a monumental task. Mother Nature has the greatest impact on the trail, toppling trees that block the path and sending runoff that erodes the tread.

A volunteer trail crew, one of many that build and maintain The Colorado Trail.

PHOTO BY DALE ZOETEWEY

The toll is continuous, and without annual maintenance the trail would degrade quickly and become impassable in just a few years. Clearing downed trees and diverting runoff to prevent erosion are just some of the tasks volunteers perform. Where plant growth is prolific, volunteers rework the edges and trim overgrowth. They build bridges and walkways. They clear new tread when needed. It has been a decades-long labor of love by the friends of Colorado's best-known trail, now totaling 567 miles.

CTF volunteers find joy in giving back to the trail.

PHOTO BY CAROLYN BURTARD

CT trekkers hike toward Searle Pass in Segment 8.

PHOTO BY KEITH EVANS

There are many ways volunteers contribute:

Adopters—Colorado Trail Adopters carry out routine trail maintenance. Working through the CTF, they take responsibility for an average of 8 miles of the trail. Each season, just after the snow melts, adopters and their helpers embark on a trail maintenance excursion. Their goal is to clear the trail of fallen trees and debris and dig away the silt and rocks from water diversions. Typical adopters spend several days each year on their section, working and camping until each is clear and in good shape. They also report to the CTF on trail conditions and any additional work needed.

Trail Crews—Volunteer trail crews take on larger trail improvements. For example, when a bridge needs rebuilding, some twenty or so volunteers team up to build a new structure. Crews also build reroutes where needed, construct retaining walls, install signs, build cairns, and establish new and more durable water diversions. About fifteen volunteer trail crews are scheduled each summer, usually from mid-June to mid-August. Crew schedules are usually announced in February, giving volunteers time to integrate one or more outings into their summer plans. Schedules are sent to those on the CTF mailing list and are posted on the CTF website (ColoradoTrail.org) as well. The typical volunteer enjoys traveling The Colorado Trail and finds working on a crew fun, rewarding, and a good way to meet new friends, as well as a great way to give back. Despite the hard work, many return year after year.

Trekking on The Colorado Trail—For three decades, the CTF has offered weeklong supported treks, and many trail volunteers and supporters have first experienced The Colorado Trail on one of these trips. Camping gear is transported ahead of the hikers and guides lead the way. After a day's hike, trekkers arrive at camp to appetizers, cold drinks, comfortable camp chairs, and a backcountry shower. They also enjoy backcountry gourmet meals prepared by the staff. Space is limited to about twelve participants each week, and spots fill quickly. For more information and to register, visit ColoradoTrailHiking.com.

Funding—CTF funding comes primarily from private donations, which are essential to sustaining The Colorado Trail. Funding goes to trail maintenance, including volunteer food and equipment; publications to spread the word about the trail; signs and bridges; insurance for trail volunteers; office expenses; and even thank-you cards for the many volunteers. The foundation is able to accomplish great work with modest resources and is proud of its volunteer tradition and its ability to leverage donations into top-notch trail preservation. The organization is a 501(c)(3) nonprofit and donations are tax deductible.

Help Keep the Trail Clear: The CTF Pocket Chainsaw

People frequently ask the CTF, "How can I get involved?" Beyond donating or becoming an adopter or crew volunteer, here's a great way to contribute, one that you can begin on your next Colorado Trail excursion.

The trail continuously needs to be cleared of fallen trees; they topple with surprising frequency. While CT Adopters do their best and remove most of the fallen trees, they cannot monitor all 567 miles all the time. It is common for trail users to encounter fallen trees and, if carrying a pocket chainsaw, they can eliminate the blockage on the spot.

The pocket chainsaw weighs less than 8 ounces including the carrying case. It is easy to take on every trail outing. Two people team up to make a cut and users find that cutting a log is unexpectedly easy, even one as big as 15 inches in diameter.

The more users who contribute to trail clearing, the clearer The Colorado Trail stays. Pocket chainsaws are available for sale at the CTF website, ColoradoTrail.org (click on CT Store).

A pocket chainsaw is ultra-light, useful, and worth carrying.

HOW TO USE THIS GUIDE

THE COLORADO TRAIL is divided into 28 segments, plus the 5 segments of the Collegiate West alternative, each of which is covered by a chapter in this guide. Segments were established based on convenient access points to the trail. Most can be hiked in a day, although admittedly some require a very long day, even with a light pack. The map of The Colorado Trail on pages 8–9 shows the entire length of the trail, plus major highways, towns, national forests, and wilderness areas along the route. The information presented is from Denver to Durango, in a southbound direction.

Segment Color Coding

This guide is separated into color-coded sections, representing six multi-segment stretches of the trail. Look for the colored tabs to find the section you are interested in.

Segments 1–5

Segments 6–10

Segments 11–15

Segments 16–20

Segments 21–28

Collegiate West Segments CW01–CW05

The Segments

Each segment chapter begins with a short summary of pertinent information for the segment, including the starting and ending points, one-way distance, and approximate elevation gain and loss. The elevation gain (southbound) is the sum of the major ascending portions and, in addition to mileage, is a general indicator of how much effort is required to complete the segment. Elevation loss (southbound) is included as well.

Following that is a list of maps relating to the segment. The first, included in the guidebook, is a vicinity map, which is useful for general orientation purposes. Based on U.S. Forest Service visitor maps, these also provide road information and show trail access points. Listed next are the topographic maps in *The Colorado Trail Map Book*, which is available at ColoradoTrail.org. These full-color maps show The Colorado Trail in detail. Next are the National Geographic Trails Illustrated maps that pertain to that segment. These waterproof, tear-resistant maps cover surrounding areas and trails as well. Pertinent Latitude 40° maps are also listed.

A trekker hops a stream in the San Juan Mountains.

COURTESY OF COLORADO MOUNTAIN EXPEDITIONS

Beneath the map listings is the jurisdiction (the U.S. Forest Service ranger district) for that segment. Contact addresses for the districts are listed on page 322. Because most of The Colorado Trail passes through federally managed public lands, contact the appropriate office if you have questions about regulations.

The symbols for access from Denver (right-facing car) and access from Durango (left-facing car) indicate the normal condition of access roads to the trail from the Denver and the Durango ends of that section. (For thru-hikers going from Denver to Durango, the first is the start of that segment and the latter is the end of that segment.) Please note that a dirt or gravel road listed as easily negotiable by a normal passenger car can become impassible in wet weather. Also, many of these secondary roads are not kept open during winter.

Next are symbols that indicate the likely availability of water in the segment during late summer. More detailed information about the location of water sources is provided in the trail description for each section.

Finally, there is a symbol that pertains to bicycling in that segment. If a mandatory bicycle detour applies, a page number for the detour is listed.

Key to Symbols

Paved or graded-dirt access road

Rough, dirt access road

Four-wheel-drive access road

Plentiful water sources

Scattered water sources

Water is difficult to obtain

Bicycles allowed

Bicycles prohibited

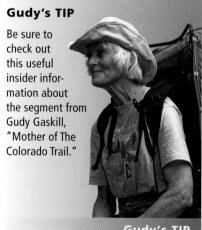

Gudy's TIP

Be sure to check out this useful insider information about the segment from Gudy Gaskill, "Mother of The Colorado Trail."

Gudy's TIP

The Waterton Canyon Trailhead at the Denver end of the Colorado Trail.

PHOTO BY RAVI NAGARAJAN

ABOUT THIS SEGMENT

This section provides general information, interesting facts, and local history about each segment.

TRAILHEAD/ACCESS POINTS

Instructions for reaching the trailheads and trail access points, along with symbols that indicate normal road conditions, are given in this section. All of the beginning and ending points are accessible by vehicle. Many segments have additional trail access points, some of which are accessible by road, some that are not. Generally, a *trailhead* refers to an official access point with a parking area, though these are sometimes primitive and skimpy. *Trail access* refers to a point where the trail crosses or approaches a road, but where no official parking is provided.

SERVICES, SUPPLIES, AND ACCOMMODATIONS

This section describes nearby supply points and services. For major supply points, a town or city map is included, as well as a list of services such as grocery stores, showers, post offices, and laundries. Larger towns offer multiple lodging and dining options. Check with the local chamber of commerce for more information. It should be noted that on some remote segments of The Colorado Trail, no convenient points of resupply are available.

TRAIL DESCRIPTION

Detailed trail descriptions progress from Denver to Durango. They indicate the distance between recognizable features (indicated in bold) from the beginning of the trail segment. Generally, accompanying the mileage is the altitude of that feature in parentheses. The mileages were obtained using professional-grade GPS equipment.

MAPS, ELEVATION PROFILES, AND GPS

Each segment chapter ends with a vicinity map, based on U.S. Forest Service visitor maps. They were chosen for this book, in part, because they show all types of roads and road access reasonably well. The trail in that segment is indicated by a solid line with red highlighting. A dashed line shows adjacent segments. Key features (usually trail intersections, stream crossings, or trail access points) also are shown.

Warning

Be alert for this symbol and box. It highlights a particular caution or warning for that segment.

At the bottom corner of each vicinity map page, a trail elevation profile shows the ups and downs encountered along that segment. Note that the hill steepness is not consistent in each segment due to the variations in the scale of miles. A chart in the other bottom corner lists key features. The distance of these features from both the start of the segment as well as the Denver and Durango ends of The Colorado Trail are indicated, along with GPS coordinates designating the UTM (NAD83) and zone. For more information about using the GPS waypoints, see pages 31–32.

For those who like to have detailed topographical maps, The Colorado Trail Foundation recommends *The Colorado Trail Map Book*. The *Map Book* and other Colorado Trail guides are available at our CT Store, shop.ColoradoTrail.org.

Another valuable publication is *The Colorado Trail Databook*, available at the CT Store and many other retailers. It contains simple maps and many users find that the *Databook* is all they need for their CT excursion.

Map Key

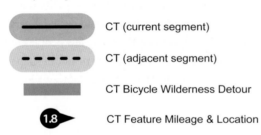

CT (current segment)

CT (adjacent segment)

CT Bicycle Wilderness Detour

CT Feature Mileage & Location

And There's More!

Additional information boxes provide interesting facts or useful information to help you get the most out of your Colorado Trail experience.

 Indicates helpful tips for hikers, and highlights other hikes or climbs in the segment

 Indicates a special viewing opportunity in this segment

 Indicates information for mountain bikers, including other rides in the area that might be of interest

PLANNING FOR THE COLORADO TRAIL

A thru-hiker in Segment 23 above Silverton.
PHOTO BY FELECIA MORAN

WINDING 486 MILES from Denver to Durango, 567 miles in all, through the magnificent heart of the southern Rockies, The Colorado Trail is one of the nation's most beautiful and varied long-distance trails. For recreationalists—hikers, backpackers, mountain bikers, and horseback riders—the CT offers an unparalleled path into the scenic wonders of Colorado's mountains, crossing eight mountain ranges, six national forests, and countless streams and rivers. The topography ranges from the high plains of eastern Colorado to the alpine peaks along the Continental Divide.

The enjoyment of the CT experience is dependent in large part on users' ability to respond to the demands, challenges, and even dangers imposed by this remarkable path through the backcountry. Relatively few people consider thru-hiking the entire trail—it's not an endeavor for the unprepared or out of shape. Most users opt instead for day trips or outings of a few days at a time. However long your excursion is, planning is crucial.

Consider the Season

The Colorado Trail traverses a landscape ranging in altitude from 5,522 feet at its eastern end to over 13,000 feet in the lofty San Juan Mountains in the southwestern corner of the state. Much of the trail is above 9,000 feet, where winters are long and extreme. Snow covers the trail for much of the year, usually persisting through June along high ridges or in shady ravines. For that reason, it is important to carefully consider the time of year for your trek or ride.

Furthermore, while it is possible to travel some segments of the CT in the winter (Segment 9 at Tennessee Pass, for instance, is the start of several classic ski tours), most of the secondary access roads mentioned in this guide are closed to traffic during the winter and well into the spring.

Unlike thru-hikers, day or short-term users can pick and choose among individual segments based on snow cover. Segments 1 through 3 can have scant snow cover (or none at all) between winter storms. By early May, these lower-elevation sections are often snow-free and showing their early wildflowers. Likewise, the first half of Segment 28 at the western end of the trail is low enough in altitude to be hiked in late spring.

An early-season hiker "post-holes" through snow near Georgia Pass in Segment 6.

PHOTO COURTESY COLORADO MOUNTAIN EXPEDITIONS

By early June, portions of the trail up to 9,000 feet are mostly free of snow, sometimes including Segments 4 and 5, as well as that part of the CT traversing the lower flanks of the Sawatch Range in Segments 13 and 14.

The eastern half of the trail holds late-melting snow on Georgia Pass, the Tenmile Range, Searle and Kokomo Passes, as well as the north-facing forested slopes nearby. Melting off even later are the high reaches of the western half of the trail, especially Segments 20 through 28, plus the Collegiate West segments, where snow can linger well into July.

Crossing significant snowpack can turn even a short trip into a monumental, even unsafe, outing. For one thing, The Colorado Trail is not signed for snow travel. Until the snows melt, many CT signs and trail markers are buried in the snow. Also, the signs are too infrequent to guide users traveling atop snow, with trail markers appearing at approximately half-mile intervals. Users can easily get off track.

Another hazard is "post-holing" (sinking deeply into the snowpack while hiking), which quickly becomes exhausting and presents the risk of sprained ankles (and worse) from stepping on branches and rocks hidden beneath the snow. Even if the snow is firm enough to walk atop, hikers can encounter slick, icy surfaces that are hard to negotiate.

Together, rotten spring snowpack, icy slopes, and cornices make travel difficult and dangerous.

Thru-Hiking

So, when should thru-hikers start? The Colorado Trail near the Denver area is gener-ally accessible by the end of the first week of June, sometimes earlier. Based on the average snowpack west of Kenosha Pass, however, thru-hikers hoping to avoid lengthy stretches of deep snowpack should not set out earlier than late June. Eastbound and Collegiate West hikers shouldn't take off from Durango until July because of the lingering snow at the higher elevations of the trail. Winter returns to the high country in October, so hikers should plan to finish their trek before September ends.

The Colorado Trail Foundation recommends that thru-hikers begin their trek from the eastern end, starting at Segment 1 and ending at Segment 28, as described in the pages of this guide. Not only does the trail tend to clear of snow a little earlier on the eastern end, but by starting at the lower-elevation Denver end of the trail, hikers do not encounter tree line until Georgia Pass in Segment 6, some 80 miles into the trek. Hikers starting from Durango, on the other hand, reach tree line much more quickly, barely 20 miles into Segment 28, which doesn't allow much time to acclimatize to higher elevations.

In addition, the average elevation overall for the eastern half of the CT is much lower than the western half, which is dominated by long alpine sections through the San Juan Range, some of the loftiest mountains in the state. The conditioning gained while hiking east to west can help hikers better handle the strenuous, higher-elevation western half.

Foot Care

Experienced hikers report that attention to your feet is most important, both in planning a hike and while on the trail, and that it is particularly important for those on multiday hikes. Why? Because sore feet limit enjoyment, and blisters are common and painful. But, careful attention to your feet can help. Keep in mind that blisters result from a combination of friction, heat, and moisture; plan to minimize these.

Begin focusing on your feet when planning your trip and doing your training hikes. Carefully choose your footwear and socks. Consider lightweight and lower-height shoes that have proven adequate even for a thru-hike and offer advantages including less heat buildup. Cooler feet can mean drier feet and can help avoid blisters. Choose good-quality socks that help wick moisture and dry fast; avoid cotton. Try lighter-weight socks, as some find that they reduce heat buildup. Train in the shoe/sock combination you plan to take on your trip and refine your footwear until you're using what works best for you. Attempt to strengthen and toughen your feet; it will pay off on your CT hike. Some hikers have found that applying a preventative anti-friction/anti-chafing product (stick or cream) during training and even on the trail helps fend off blisters. Study foot care. A highly rated resource is *Fixing Your Feet: Prevention and Treatments for Athletes* by John Vonhof. Secure supplies such as tape, Moleskin, scissors, ointment, and skin-cleaning wipes and know how to use them. Consider carrying extra pairs of socks.

On the trail, from your first steps, employ your knowledge gained in training and planning. Tape your feet in advance if that's what works best. Keep your shoes and socks as dry as you can. If you feel a hot spot, stop right away and care for it to keep from forming blisters or allowing them to grow larger.

Getting to and from the Trail

Both Denver and Durango are served by several national and regional airlines. Express bus and van service is available between Denver International Airport and several resort communities close to The Colorado Trail, including Breckenridge, Frisco, and Copper Mountain. The Regional Transportation District (rtd-denver.com), a bus and light rail system serving the Denver metropolitan area, provides service trail users have found helpful.

Commercial bus lines run between some of the towns and cities listed as resupply points in this guide. Schedules and routes change frequently, however, so inquire about service before setting off on your trip. A few towns have shuttles that CT users can take between the trail and town; notably, the Summit County Stage in Segments 6 and 7. Phone the chambers of commerce mentioned in the Services, Supplies, and Accommodations section of each chapter for information about local shuttle services or taxis.

A unique way to access Segment 24 from either Durango or Silverton is aboard the historic Durango & Silverton Narrow Gauge Railroad. You can book trips and check fares and schedules at durangotrain.com, or call 888-TRAIN07 (888-872-4607).

Resupplying

For those planning an extended or thru-trip on The Colorado Trail, you'll probably want to resupply. While the entire trail has been traversed without resupply, not many will want to carry all the provisions (and weight) for such a trip. Resupply towns are noted in the Services, Supplies, and Accommodations section of each chapter. Many CT thru- and long-distance hikers have reported being able to resupply with relative ease by

Sisters loaded up for their CT thru-hike.
PHOTO BY LINDA JEFFERS

taking side trips to the nearby towns. However, planning is warranted, as some of the small towns have limited supplies and lack the lightweight backpacking meals and gear many long-distance trekkers prefer.

Supplies also can be mailed ahead of time. Address parcels to yourself in care of "General Delivery," and send to the post offices listed in this guide. Or arrange to meet someone at points where the CT crosses a convenient access point. Bring along extras of any small, unique items that are crucial parts of your kit.

Also, please note that there are some long, remote stretches of the CT where convenient resupply is not possible.

Happy trail feet and footwear, nearing completion of the CT.

PHOTO BY JEFF MCGARVIN

Equipment

The Colorado Trail traverses a wide range of life zones from the hot, dry foothills of the Front Range to the harsh alpine tundra of the high mountains, where cold and wind can challenge anyone's gear. Effective, good-quality clothing and other gear can spell the difference between a safe, enjoyable day in the mountains and an unpleasant, or even potentially disastrous, experience.

When preparing for a hike on the CT, always start with the "ten essentials" as your foundation (see Equipment Checklists). Lightweight but sturdy shoes or boots are fine for most trips. Backpackers carrying traditional, heavy-weight loads will want heavier, stiffer boots for good ankle support. Others carrying lighter loads find that trail shoes work best. For clothing, modern synthetics, such as polypropylene and fleece, are lightweight, insulate well, and dry quickly. But traditional wool clothing also is effective, even when damp. Avoid cotton entirely because it loses its insulating ability when wet. Rain gear should be waterproof and breathable.

Study the recommended equipment lists for both day and thru-hikes. For years, long-distance backpackers have been discovering that lighter-weight gear is as effective as older, more traditional gear without sacrificing safety or comfort. With its long segments and strenuous climbs, the CT lends itself well to this "going lighter" approach. An article on pages 26–29 offers tips and suggestions for the weight-conscious packer.

Equipment Checklists

The Ten Essentials

(columns: Have, Packed)

- Food
- Water
- Emergency shelter
- Extra clothing
- First-aid kit

- Flashlight
- Map and compass or GPS
- Matches/fire starter
- Pocketknife
- Sunglasses/sunscreen

For Day Hikes

- **Daypack:** 1,500 to 3,000 cubic inches
- **Insulating layer:** synthetic or wool tops and bottoms
- **Shirt or sweater:** synthetic or wool
- **Pants:** synthetic or wool
- **Parka shell:** waterproof and windproof

- **Pants shell:** waterproof and windproof
- **Hat:** stocking cap or balaclava
- **Gloves:** synthetic or wool
- **Shoes:** broken in
- **Extra socks:** ones that dry quickly

For Backpacking

- **Backpack:** 3,500 cubic inches or more
- **Insulating layer:** synthetic or wool tops and bottoms
- **Shirt or sweater:** synthetic or wool
- **Pants:** synthetic or wool
- **Parka shell:** waterproof and windproof
- **Pants shell:** waterproof and windproof
- **Hat:** stocking cap or balaclava
- **Gloves:** Synthetic, wool, or waterproof
- **Shoes:** sturdy and broken in
- **Extra socks:** ones that dry quickly
- **Waterproof pack cover**
- **Sleeping pad**
- **Stove and fuel**

- **Cooking gear**
- **Eating utensils**
- **Food and food bags**
- **Bear/critter food equip, e.g., Ursack**
- **Tent, tarp, or bivy sack**
- **Waterproof ground cloth**
- **Personal toiletries**
- **Camp shoes**
- **Headlamp**
- **Repair kit and sewing kit**
- **Water filter and/or iodine tablets**
- **Plastic trowel for catholes**
- **Plastic bags for garbage**
- **Rope or cord**

Optional

- Pillow
- Camera gear
- Reading material and/or journal
- Fishing gear

- Binoculars
- Camp chair
- Radio
- Cell phone or satellite messenger
- Walking stick/hiking poles

Why and How to Go Light by Paul Magnanti

One sunny summer day in 1998, I summited Mount Katahdin in Maine. I not only had climbed one of the most majestic mountains in the East, but I had finished a thru-hike of the 2,175-mile Appalachian Trail. It was memorable day, and one I look back on fondly. A week or so later, though, my knees were in pain. I was twenty-four years old, muscular, fit, and in terrific shape, but I was hobbling up and down stairs like an elderly man. It would take almost a month for my body to fully recover.

So, why did I suffer so much discomfort? Blame much of it on my weight—my pack weight.

Why Lighten Up?

Many people say the Appalachian Trail is more physically demanding than any other long-distance hiking trail. Parts of the AT are indeed steeper than anything found on The Colorado Trail, the Pacific Crest Trail, or Continental Divide National Scenic Trail. Nevertheless, when I later thru-hiked the 300-mile Benton MacKaye Trail, which has more difficult grades than on the nearby AT, I was steadily and comfortably hiking about 25 miles per day.

What changed? I was a more experienced hiker, for one. I also was in better shape mentally and physically than I was when I did my AT hike. And, finally, my gear was lighter.

After my AT hike, I vowed never to carry 50 pounds up and down mountains again. Over the next year, I read articles on how to reduce my backpack's weight. I went to a smaller pack. I made my own alcohol stove. I cut the size of my sleeping pad.

I did the physically demanding 273-mile Long Trail in Vermont in 1999 and felt great. The AT thru-hikers I met that year were a little surprised by my small pack. By the time I hiked the 2,650-mile Pacific Crest Trail in 2002, my base pack weight, or BPW (gear weight minus food, water, and fuel), was half that as on my AT hike.

The adventure of hiking the PCT was fantastic—incredible vistas, experiences I will not forget—and I felt great at the end of the journey. With lighter gear, the climbs were easier, I wasn't as tired at the end of the day, and the overall experience was much more enjoyable.

When I hiked The Colorado Trail, with its high elevations, big climbs, and long stretches far from resupply points, my lighter kit really came into its own. I was able to carry more food because of my lighter BPW. Inclement weather or shortened days could be dealt with because of my faster pace. The trail was not something to survive, but an experience to revel in and enjoy.

My gear continues to evolve, but my basic setup has not changed since the PCT: frameless pack, trail runners instead of boots, a good down bag, a simple shelter in lieu of a tent, a cut-down foam pad, and so on. (See complete list at PMags.com.) I would not go on another hike with my Appalachian Trail gear.

Nearing completion of the CT, two hikers are exuberant about their accomplishment and lightweight gear.
PHOTO BY JULIE VIDA AND MARK TABB

The Ultra-light Philosophy

In the process of lightening my load, I've come to look more at why I should take a particular piece of gear rather than what I should take. I do not consider myself an "ultralighter." That term, to me, evokes too technical an image, one where the emphasis is on gear and not on enjoying the trail itself. While gear is important, I think it is the least important part of hiking. I use gear to hike, not hike to use gear.

What I consider before going out are personal safety, comfort, and fun. On three-season solo hikes, my gear list is pretty scant. A simple tarp and thin pad are part of my kit. The stove is left behind. On social backpacks (more camping, less hiking), I'll take the stove, along with a book, and perhaps a small libation to enjoy at night.

Why do I advocate this approach? Because it simplifies things; there is little to come between me and my enjoyment of the outdoors. The simple act of walking can be enjoyed without worrying about how heavy the gear is on my back. A backpacker who isn't exhausted at the end of the day can better appreciate the sunset over the mountains, the sound of the wind in the trees, and the hike just completed.

Over the years my gear has changed and evolved. There has been a gradual decline in my BPW. I am now at a point where I can get lighter only by spending more money to shave ounces rather than pounds. I then have to ask myself how much is it worth to lose that weight in my pack? Or, as one thru-hiker friend said to me, "Losing pounds is cheap; losing ounces is expensive." To me, that can refer to money, time, or comfort. Each hiker has to find that balance for themselves.

Some Simple Changes

There is more than one way to lighten one's load. Most backpackers can easily get to the 15- to 20-pound BPW range without making any radical changes in their hiking or camping styles. Today, there is lighter gear available that is functionally equivalent to more traditional equipment.

A good friend of mine is a prime example of how anyone can benefit from a lighter kit. Backpacking had become for him a trudge rather than a pleasure. He'd be achy, sore, and exhausted at the end of the day. He wanted to enjoy hiking again, but also feel comfortable in camp. He asked me to look over his gear and give him some recommendations. That led to the purchase of a new frame pack, along with a good down sleeping bag and light synthetic jacket. A small pot, canister stove, lightweight two-person tent, and relatively light Therm-a-Rest sleeping pad completed the kit. We chose the gear based on his backpacking style, not mine.

The end result of this makeover? His BPW is now 17 pounds. Most people, if they are in the position to buy new gear, do not have to carry any more than that. His gear is functionally the same as his older, more traditional gear, but without the weight. It is not any less safe, nor does it require any more knowledge regarding its use, nor has he had to sacrifice any comfort. Actually, his comfort level is better now because he is no longer as tired and sore.

Going Even Lower?

As other experienced hikers have noted, it is difficult to go below 15 pounds BPW. The gear becomes more expensive and/or you need to become more of a minimalist. If you are the type of person who hikes all day and spends little time in camp, a minimalist kit may be for you. A cut-down foam pad instead of a Therm-a-Rest, a lined windshirt instead of a heavier jacket, and so on, might work well for you. But if you want more camp comforts and a more traditionalist setup, go for the 15- to 20-pound BPW range.

Remember, there is no such thing as the "best" gear, only what works best for you.

Below 10-pound BPW? You had better be comfortable, knowledgeable, and experienced in a wide range of outdoor situations to go that light. As more than one hiker has found out, it is one thing to read about the joys of going below 10 pounds, but it is something entirely different in real-world situations. What is your experience level? Are you honestly capable of handling whatever Mother Nature may throw at you with only a very minimal kit?

It's best to find that out on a shorter trip before venturing out on a longer trek. Discovering that you do not know how to set up your tarp, that you hate going stoveless, or that you wish you'd brought a thicker sleeping pad is easier to deal with on a weekend outing than in a fall snowstorm deep in the San Juans.

My kit is at about 8 pounds, 12 ounces now. (Lose the camera equipment and it's right at 8 pounds.) I've pretty much reached my limit, and I'm comfortable with it.

Hiking all or part of The Colorado Trail is a wonderful experience. With lighter gear, hiking the CT can be an even more enjoyable experience. You'll have fewer aches and pains and find it less tiring. Buy gear that works for you, go out on some backpacking trips, adjust accordingly, and have fun on your journey!

Other Resources

Lighten Up!, by Don Ladigin: A good "meat and potatoes" guide for traditional backpackers who want to lighten their load. Not as detailed as other guides, but sometimes too many details get in the way of the overall goal. It's a good guide for the why of going lightweight rather than the specific what. Start with this book if you want to go from a 30-pound BPW to 15 pounds.

Lightweight Backpacking and Camping, edited by Ryan Jordan: A detailed, gear-oriented workshop in book form. This book is aimed more toward high-end gear for lightening your load. But if you want diverse opinions from many different sources and wish to fine-tune your techniques, this book is a great guide. The editor is the publisher of backpackinglight.com.

Pmags.com: My website offers my take on the basics of backpacking and going light. Articles include: "Beginners Backpacking Primer," "Lightweight Backpacking 101," and "My Evolving Gear List."

It took many miles, many years, and much tweaking to get to my current level of gear. What I've learned may be instructive as you put together your own kit.

An old-style CT marker shows the way.

PHOTO BY AARON LOCANDER

Signs, Publications, and Navigating

The Colorado Trail is reasonably well marked. Alert trail users can generally navigate using the CT signs alone, including the double-peaked triangular logo markers on posts and trees. Nevertheless, things happen. Signs fall down, markers sometimes become souvenirs, and bad weather can cause travelers to lose their way. Also, trail confidence markers are not allowed in Wilderness Areas. It is not uncommon for a CT user to veer off the trail unintentionally.

Whether out for just the day or committed to completing the entire route in a single trip, all CT users should carry at least one of the official guides to help them stay on the trail. These include *The*

Colorado Trail Guidebook, The Colorado Trail Databook, and *The Colorado Trail Map Book.*

Many users have reported that the *Guidebook,* or portions of it, and a compass were adequate to navigate the trail. Others prefer carrying the *Databook,* partly because it is lighter and fits in a pocket. It includes mileages, plus simple maps that indicate where water and campsites can be found. Still others appreciate the detail provided on topographic maps and choose the *Map Book* instead. A waypoint-programmed GPS unit or smartphone with app can be invaluable, especially when the trail is covered by snow.

Over the years since The Colorado Trail was developed, a variety of signage has been used to mark the trail, from simple creosote posts to triangular plastic markers, from expensive redwood signs to reflective metal markers, and even to blazes on tree trunks. All have one thing in common: They display the instantly recognizable, mountain-shaped Colorado Trail logo.

In some segments, the CT's path coincides with another developed trail and shares signage with that trail. For instance, the CT is co-located with the Continental Divide National Scenic Trail for 314 or so miles, where markers for both are placed. In other sections, routes marked with blue diamonds denote cross-country ski trails that join the CT for short distances before veering off.

A trail intersection sign at the south end of the Collegiate Loop atop the Continental Divide.

PHOTO BY DAVID DOLTON

Unfortunately, both the tread itself and the signs marking it are susceptible to the elements, encroaching vegetation, downed trees, avalanches, and vandals. With the CT's many confusing intersections, indistinct or spotty tread in places, and the sporadic placing of trail signs, it is important to use the navigational aids available to the CT hiker.

Using GPS

A small, lightweight GPS receiver is a great tool for navigating The Colorado Trail. It can be loaded with waypoints, either manually or by electronic data transfer. Waypoints organized sequentially serve as a series of invisible cairns along the trail. Since a GPS receiver always knows exactly (to within a few meters) where it is, it can automatically calculate the bearing and distance to any waypoint stored in its memory. As a result, you can easily determine how far it is to a campsite, which fork you should follow, or what the bearing and distance are to a reliable water source. A GPS receiver can be particularly helpful early in the season when snow can obscure the trail and trail signage.

Volunteer trail surveyor Jerry Brown embarks on his fifth CT thru-trip.
PHOTO BY CARL BROWN

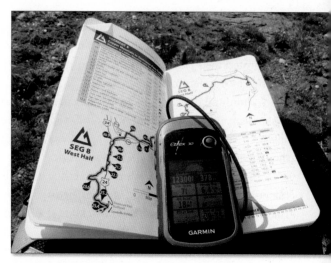
The Databook and a GPS are well-used CT navigation tools.
PHOTO BY ED HYATT

Data for the trail was obtained using professional survey-grade GPS equipment. This guidebook lists the waypoints for some 500 features along the CT, including trail and road intersections, stream crossings, and other important features. You can load these manually into your GPS unit. Mileage entries include a descriptive phrase, approximate elevation, plus waypoint data in UTM, a rectangular, straight-line system of X-Y coordi-nates, not unlike a checkerboard. GPS users can manually enter a UTM coordinate to verify where they are.

The waypoint database for The Colorado Trail is around 1,430 points. You can download these CT waypoints from bearcreeksurvey.com. On this site you'll also find tips for setting your GPS to the correct units and coordinate system before you load any waypoint data.

Be sure to follow the instructions for your particular GPS manufacturer. Before entering UTM data into the GPS unit, set the GPS position format to UTM/UPS and set the datum (may be called spheroid) to either NAD83 or WGS84. Once the UTM waypoint has been entered, GPS users can easily convert to latitude-longitude, if desired, by switching the coordinate format. Waypoint users need to be aware that the UTM zone switches in Segment 27 from UTM Zone 13 to Zone 12 at the 108-degree longitude line. It returns to Zone 13 early in Segment 28. Most GPS receivers will make this transition automatically. If for some reason your GPS doesn't, turning it off, then on again, will usually do the trick.

Using Cell Phones

Smart cellular phones are becoming increasingly popular on the trail, not only for voice and text communication, but for photography and navigation as well. Careful users protect their phone in a waterproof/shockproof bag or container to avoid calamities reported by travelers in previous seasons.

More and more trail users are using phone apps, such as The Colorado Trail Hiker, to supplement their hard-copy guides and maps. They're available for download at reason-able cost. The Colorado Trail Hiker app offers a free demo for Segment 1 of the CT for those interested in seeing how such apps work.

There are drawbacks, however, to relying on a cell phone on the CT. Connectivity can be spotty all along the trail. Signal strength varies widely, sometimes allowing only voice or text communication, and often none at all. Signals tend to be stronger near urban areas and high points.

Another concern is battery life. Searching for a signal can quickly drain battery strength. Turning off the phone or putting it in airplane mode (in which the satellite and GPS functions still work) can alleviate this somewhat, but users should bring chargers and cords to use where outlets are available (primarily in stopover towns) and portable battery chargers (power sticks) where they are not.

Users have reported limited success with portable solar chargers, but as those devices become lighter and more efficient, they are sure to grow in popularity. Be aware, however, that shaded areas and cloudy days can curtail their effectiveness.

Water Along the Trail

A hiker relaxes, refreshes, and replenishes his water supply at a creek along the trail.

PHOTO BY AARON LOCANDER

Drinking water is readily available along most segments of The Colorado Trail, and the text and features tables in this guide point out many potential sources. On the first page of each segment, a symbol indicates whether water sources are scarce, abundant, or scattered in a typical year. There are some segments where careful water planning is strongly advised. In these cases, reliable sources may be up to 20 miles apart, especially during drought years or in late summer when many seasonal streams have dried up.

Except for water available at campgrounds, picnic areas, and the like that is clearly marked as potable, water from all sources should be purified before drinking. In addition to the abundance of wild critters in the backcountry, grazing livestock, mostly sheep and cattle, are very common, even at higher elevations. All can introduce protozoa and bacterial organisms to water sources. You should treat all drinking water by one of four recommended methods: boiling, filtration, chemical disinfectant, or ultraviolet water purifier.

In addition, always practice Leave No Trace principles to safeguard the water supply for other users. That includes camping at least 100 feet from any stream, lake, or spring.

Chemically treating water obtained along the trail is one way to make it safe for drinking.

PHOTO BY ROGER FORMAN

Safe Drinking Water

In times past, one of the great outdoor pleasures for a hiker was to dip a Sierra cup into a fast-flowing stream for a long drink of ice-cold water. Today, hikers know that this can be an invitation for a nasty pathogen to invade your system.

While day-hikers on the CT typically carry adequate water for their needs, it is a constant daily chore for thru-hikers to meet their need for safe drinking water. Most likely possibilities for contamination in the Colorado backcountry include —*Giardia lamblia, Cryptosporidium,* and occasionally, some strains of bacteria and viruses in areas closer to towns.

While agricultural runoff is seldom a backcountry problem, chemical discharge from old mines is common in Colorado. The rule of thumb is to look in the stream for plants, insects, and other ample signs of life.

There are four proven methods for treating water to make it safe, and trail users will want to learn before deciding which method they choose:

▲ Boiling is the simplest, if you have adequate fuel, and kills most pathogens. While there is debate about boil times, a minimum of 5 minutes at a rolling boil is recommended.

▲ Chemical disinfection (including iodine, chlorine-based halazone tablets, and silver ion/chlorine dioxide tablets) is not as reliable as boiling, but provides some protection against *Giardia* and most bacteria, but not *Crypto*. Tablets are light and easy to carry, but don't reduce sediment from sources that are murky. Very cold water should be left to treat overnight.

▲ Filters are popular for backcountry water purification because they're relatively quick/easy and they remove sediments. Check the specifications for individual devices before buying one, and choose a filter with small enough pores to eliminate *Giardia* and *Crypto*. Many filters won't eliminate viruses, but some systems will. An advantage of filters is you can drink immediately after filtering and fill your containers again, which can reduce carried weight.

▲ Ultraviolet water purifiers are relatively new on the scene and they treat water quickly. These battery-powered devices use UV light rays instead of chemicals or filters. They are effective when used in relatively clear water and can work well to eliminate *Giardia* and *Crypto* but don't always kill viruses. Pre-filtering can be required to reduce turbidity.

Hygiene is also worth mentioning. Backcountry experts agree, "Besides proper treatment of water, basic sanitation will help prevent gastro-intestinal illnesses hikers sometimes experience. After any bowel movements and before eating, be sure to wash your hands. Alcohol gel sanitizer is lightweight, effective, inexpensive and requires no water."

Biking

Mountain biking is popular in Colorado, including along the stretches of The Colorado Trail where it's allowed. Particularly popular are the Buffalo Creek bicycle trails in the Pike National Forest around Segment 3; the CT west of Kenosha Pass in Segment 6; the dramatic ride over Searle and Kokomo Passes in Segment 8; the nationally known Monarch Crest ride along the Continental Divide in Segments CW05, 15 and 16; the flower-filled meadows west of Molas Pass in Segment 25; and Segment 28 near Durango. In addition to cyclists enjoying day trips, there are some intrepid cyclists who "bikepack" the trail, carrying gear for multiday trips.

Cyclists need to be aware that portions of the trail that pass through federally designated wilderness areas, as well as other bike-regulated sections, are off-limits to cyclists and their bicycles. These include the Lost Creek Wilderness in Segments 4 and 5, the Holy Cross and Mount Massive areas in Segments 9 and 10, the Collegiate Peaks in Segments 12, 13 and CW02, La Garita in Segments 19 through 21, the Weminuche Wilderness in Segment 24, and the entire Segment CW03 between Cottonwood Pass and Tincup Pass Road. Riders are strongly urged not to violate these prohibitions; it is illegal and a real hot-button issue among trail users.

Cyclists roll atop Elk Ridge between Searle and Kokomo Passes in Segment 8.
PHOTO BY DAN MILNER

Mountain bikers face many technical challenges.

PHOTO BY JESSE SWIFT AND BILL TURNER

This guide notes the mandatory bicycle detours and describes carefully chosen detour routes around sections where bicycles are prohibited. While small portions of the detours involve riding on busy highways, the majority of the miles are spent on little-used back roads and jeep trails through country every bit as scenic as the main CT route.

Most mountain bicyclists are responsible trail users and their thoughtfulness is appreciated. Also appreciated are the efforts by cyclists to be courteous to other trail users and to slow down when encountering hikers and riders and to pass responsibly. It is especially important that cyclists converse with horse riders well in advance of passing to keep from spooking their animals. Cyclists who avoid skidding are also appreciated. Skidding tires gouge the tread, which fosters erosion and can create significant repair work for volunteer trail crews.

Those cycling on the CT, as on other trails, are cautioned to be properly prepared. Make sure your bike is in good working order before leaving and that you are capable of making basic repairs on the trail.

Horseback Riding

Riders enjoy the scenery while their horses focus on the trail.

PHOTO BY BILL MANNING

The Colorado Trail is open to horses for the entire 567 miles, with a few restrictions in wilderness areas, usually regarding group size and the need to use certified, weed-free feed. Check with the appropriate ranger district for specific regulations for each wilderness area.

While many riders have completed the CT without problems and have thoroughly enjoyed their trip, others have reported some difficulties to The Colorado Trail Foundation. The CTF's maintenance guidelines call for the trail corridor to be cleared of vegetation 4 feet on either side of the centerline of the tread and to a height of 10 feet. While we strive to meet these guidelines, 8 feet wide and 10 feet high has not been achieved everywhere.

Low branches can usually be avoided without

too much trouble and downed trees bypassed. However, riders may need to remove obstructions and should carry some sort of saw, such as one of the handy pocket chainsaws available from the CT store at shop.ColoradoTrail.org. There may be some places, however, where the trail corridor is too narrow for a heavily loaded packhorse to pass. Tight spots can typically be passed by off-loading the pack animal, proceeding through the narrow section, and reloading.

Off-loading pack stock might be necessary at the Gudy Gaskill Bridge across the South Platte River at the beginning of Segment 2. Although the CTF expended considerable effort building a well-designed crossover to thwart prohibited motorized use, the heavy steel guardrail at the east end of the bridge can prove challenging for a pack animal to pass. Some horses become panicky when encountering barriers. Be aware of this potential problem and familiarize your horse with such obstacles.

Similarly, some horses become upset when encountering hikers and backpackers. Most hikers, if asked, are happy to move well clear of the trail while the horse passes.

Most of the streams that cross the CT have a suitable ford around the foot-bridges. A few of the larger streams have sturdy wooden bridges suitable for horses. Some horses become agitated, though, at the sound of their steel shoes on a wooden bridge. Familiarization, again, with these types of obstacles can reduce problems on the trail.

Roundup Riders on one of their group's Colorado Trail rides.
PHOTO BY ROY BERKELEY

The Colorado Trail has proved to be much harder on horseshoes than one might suspect. In a group of twenty horses on a weeklong ride on the CT, at least one horse required shoe repair every evening for loose or lost shoes. Carrying repair tools is essential.

Photography on the Trail

Cell phones are the most popular cameras on The Colorado Trail. A growing number of optically excellent point-and-shoots are next. Some hikers carry DSLR's with interchangeable lenses. What camera you carry depends on your photographic intent, how light you pack, and the trip length. A day or section hiker can think differently about camera gear than a thru-hiker counting ounces.

Take spare batteries and cards. Consider carrying a portable charger. Trail towns have places where you can recharge, just be sure to pack your charging cord and USB adapter. To prolong battery life, turn cameras off when not in use and put cell phones in airplane mode. Keep batteries warm.

The Colorado Trail is rough on cameras. Protect them with suitable cases and plastic bags. Keep cameras accessible, around your neck, strapped to your chest, or in a pocket.

It's easy to forget where you took a picture. Taking notes helps, as does taking pictures of trail markers, road signs, trail-heads, and distinctive landmarks.

Please share your photos with the entire Colorado Trail Foundation family by way of our website, Facebook, Instagram,

Indian Trail Ridge with La Plata Mountains in the distance, Segment 27.
PHOTO BY DEAN KRAKEL

and Twitter. We welcome high- and full-resolution contributions to our photo library for use in newsletters, publications, and this guidebook.

Safety

Along the more isolated portions of The Colorado Trail, assistance may be many hours, even days, away. Travelers should keep the following things in mind:

- ▲ *Be aware of weather conditions:* Watch the sky and be alert. Hypothermia, dehydration, and lightning are all potential hazards.
- ▲ *Start early:* Summer afternoon thunderstorms are common in the high country. Start early and plan to be off exposed ridges before storms brew.
- ▲ *Don't travel alone:* It's safest to hike with companions; at the very least, make sure you leave a detailed itinerary with others.
- ▲ *Be in shape:* Get in condition and acclimatize to altitude before beginning your trek.
- ▲ *Use sun protection:* The UV radiation in Colorado can be very intense. Wear sunscreen and/or a long-sleeve shirt and pants and wide-brimmed hat. Sunglasses are strongly recommended.
- ▲ *Carry and use your map/guide/GPS:* Although the CT is generally well marked, travelers should always carry a guide or map, compass or GPS, and know how to use these tools.
- ▲ *Satellite messenger:* Consider buying/taking one of these, in part for its function to alert search and rescue. It can also keep loved ones informed and help with any rendezvous. Increasingly, cell phones are offering similar functionality and are worthy of consideration.

To activate a rescue group, contact the nearest county sheriff. See page 322 for a list of contact numbers. Counties and other jurisdictions may pass along the costs of a search and rescue, which can often reach thousands of dollars, to the people involved. To keep search-and-rescue efforts at a high standard, The Colorado Trail Foundation recommends purchasing a Colorado Outdoor Recreation Search and Rescue "CORSAR" card. Proceeds go to the state's Search and Rescue Fund, which reimburses teams for some costs incurred in searches and rescues. Funds remaining at the end of the year are used to help pay for training and equipment. Anyone with a current hunting or fishing license is already covered by the fund. The CORSAR card costs $3 for one year or $12 for five years. Cards are available at some Colorado retailers or online at https://www.colorado.gov/pacific/dola/colorado-outdoor-recreation-search-and-rescue-corsar-card.

Be aware that cell phone connectivity is spotty in the Colorado backcountry, and, at many locations, users will find there is no signal. CT travelers sometimes find cell phone signals when they're near towns and at high points. Signal strength varies and at times is

A hiker assesses the weather to determine whether to proceed or stay put for a while.
PHOTO BY CHRIS SZCZECH

only sufficient to send a text. Where stronger connectivity exists, voice transmission will be possible.

Backcountry Ethics

The Colorado Trail runs almost entirely through national forest lands. In some areas, the trail crosses or is adjacent to private property or patented mining claims. Keep in mind that if problems arise, private landowners could withdraw rights. Please respect private property and no trespassing signs.

Remember also that federal law protects cultural and historic sites on public lands, such as old cabins, mines, and American Indian sites. These assets are important to us all and should not be scavenged for personal gain or enjoyment.

Practicing the Leave No Trace principles listed on pages 323–325 will ensure that our public lands remain pristine well into the future. It is your responsibility to be aware of rules and regulations on public lands crossed by the CT. Contact the agencies listed on page 322 for more information.

Additional Resources

In addition to *The Colorado Trail Guidebook, Map Book,* and other available maps, the following resources may be helpful to those wishing to hike all or part of The Colorado Trail:

▲ *The Colorado Trail Databook* is a concise, inexpensive, pocket-sized guide that contains essential information such as mileage, water sources, and road crossings. After planning their trip using the *Guidebook,* many users choose to carry the lighter *Databook* on the trail. The *Databook* is available via the online CT Store, shop. ColoradoTrail.org.

▲ The Colorado Trail Foundation's website, ColoradoTrail.org, is the first place anyone interested in the CT should go. It answers many common questions and offers trail updates, including recent reroutes.

For on-the-trail use, the Databook is a great resource.

▲ The Colorado Trail Foundation's Facebook page, facebook.com/ ColoradoTrailFoundation, is a hub for CT info, tips, and photos.

▲ The Facebook group page for each new year's class of trail travelers has become a very active gathering place for Q&A and advice that's often trail tested. Search Facebook for group page titles such as "Colorado Trail Thru-Hike 2016."

▲ Pmags.com is the website of Paul Magnanti, a veteran long-distance hiker and friend of the CTF. The site features a Colorado Trail "End to End" Guide, kept up to date and concisely summarizing resupply options, transportation, resources, and other useful information.

Cascade Creek in Segment 25.

PHOTO BY AARON LOCANDER

Wilderness Area Regulations

Colorado has forty-three designated wilderness areas, encompassing more than 3.7 million acres. The Colorado Trail passes through six of them. From north to south they are the Lost Creek, Holy Cross, Mount Massive, Collegiate Peaks, La Garita, and Weminuche wilderness areas. Colorado Trail users may find a register at wilderness boundaries and may be asked to fill out a simple form and display their copy while passing through.

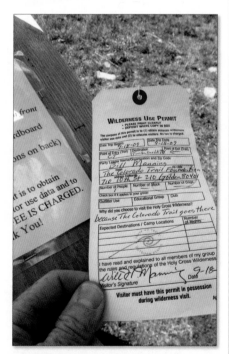

On entering wilderness areas, users encounter a register where they are asked to fill out a permit that helps the Forest Service gather usage information.

PHOTO BY BILL MANNING

Trail enthusiasts can minimize their impact by adhering to the Leave No Trace principles outlined on pages 323–325, and by following these general rules governing wilderness areas:

▲ Camp at least 100 feet from lakes, streams, and trails
▲ Use a stove rather than building a fire
▲ Bury human waste 6 inches deep and 200 feet from water sources
▲ Pack out toilet paper and trash
▲ Keep dogs leashed or under voice control
▲ Detour around the area if you are on a bike. It is prohibited to ride or even carry (possess) a bicycle in a wilderness area

Each wilderness area may have additional rules specific to that area including group size limits, dog laws, equestrian feed parameters, dispersed camping specifications, and other regulations.

THE HERITAGE OF THE COLORADO TRAIL

Sawatch Range. PHOTO BY ROGER O'DOHERTY

FOR THOUSANDS OF YEARS, this land was their land—the towering peaks, the expansive intermountain parks full of game, the cool mountain streams. The southern Rockies were home to a succession of cultures that left little impact upon the land other than the paths through the mountains that defined their seasonal wanderings, some of which we still travel on today as part of The Colorado Trail.

By the 1600s, the Ute Indians, whose forebears probably arrived from the Great Basin a few centuries earlier, had established themselves in the mountains of west-central Colorado. Perhaps the first tribe to acquire horses, they pursued a nomadic existence following the movement of game, seeking spiritual guidance on mountaintop vision quests, and engaging in sporadic warfare with other tribes—the Arapahos, Navajos, and Comanches—who encroached on their mountain territory.

By the time white settlers arrived in the nineteenth century, two tribes of the several bands of Utes dominated western Colorado, the Tabegauche and the Uncompahgre. A succession of mostly failed treaties were signed that eventually would exile these bands to a small corner in the southwest part of the state and a reservation in Utah.

One of those treaties, negotiated in 1858, prohibited the Utes from entering areas where valuable minerals had been discovered, in effect limiting them to western and southern Colorado. Soon after, as miners continued to push west, conflicts erupted, resulting in the so-called Kit Carson Treaty of 1868. It was negotiated by a delegation of Utes, including Chief Ouray, who were led to Washington, D.C., by Carson, the famed scout and American Indian fighter. This treaty pushed the Utes farther into an area corresponding with the San Juan Mountains, west of the Continental Divide.

Two agencies were set up to distribute goods to the Indians: the White River Agency to the north and the Los Pinos Agency west of Cochetopa Pass. But blatant trespassing continued as prospectors probed the mineral-rich lands of the San Juans. The infamous Brunot Treaty of 1873, once again facilitated by Chief Ouray, assisted by his friend Otto Mears, tried to settle the matter. The precious San Juans were ceded to the eager miners and the Utes were settled on reservations, where they were expected to shift from their traditional nomadic lifestyle to an agrarian one.

Many resisted the change, however, continuing with their age-old ways. Coupled with continued pressure from white settlers who coveted land north of the San Juans, the Brunot Treaty began to unravel. The conflict boiled over, culminating in the Meeker Massacre of 1879 at the White River Agency that left eleven white men dead. A final treaty forced on the Utes by an enraged white populace banished the Uncompahgre band to a new reservation in Utah, and the long occupation of Colorado's mountain region by the Utes ceased.

Chief Ouray, who had attempted to walk a fine line between two clashing cultures, never saw the heartbreaking removal of Utes from Colorado. He died while traveling to confer with other tribal leaders and is commemorated by a mountain peak bearing his name along the Continental Divide near Marshall Pass.

The First Explorers

The Spanish, whose knowledge of the vast region north of their empire was limited, were the first whites to explore the area that became Colorado. In 1765, Juan Maria de Rivera explored the San Juan country on his way to Utah, describing to his backers the mineral wealth of the region. Two friars, Fathers Dominquez and Escalante, followed in 1776. Charged with finding a route to California, their journeys throughout the Southwest, including the present-day Durango area, and the detailed maps they produced had a great influence on subsequent travelers.

A few years later, an expeditionary force led by Juan Bautista de Anza entered the region in pursuit of raiding Comanche bands. They traveled through the San

View from Indian Trail Ridge in Segment 27.
PHOTO BY JEFF ALVAREZ

Luis Valley, noting the topography of the eastern flank of the San Juan Mountains and the Cochetopa Hills, and crossed over Poncha Pass, viewing the skyscraping Sawatch Range.

Others came after, and by the early 1800s the Spanish Trail wound through southwest Colorado as caravans carried goods from Santa Fe to California.

With the completion of the Louisiana Purchase in 1802 and the Treaty of Guadalupe Hidalgo following the war with Mexico in 1848, exploration of the region shifted to American interests. Trappers and mountain men penetrated the southern Rockies, following the ancient American Indian trails and using the same low passes over the Continental Divide that would later see wagon roads, railways, highways, and The Colorado Trail.

Government-sponsored expeditions set out to discover the character of this new land—destined, many believed, to become part of the country—and what lay beyond the seemingly impenetrable barrier known then as the "Shining Mountains." An 1820 expedition led by Major Stephen Long crossed the plains and tentatively explored along the Rocky Mountain front, including present-day Waterton Canyon (the start of today's Colorado Trail), as it investigated the source of the South Platte River.

Scouting the Way

Soon after the conclusion of the Mexican War, Congress planned five expeditions to study proposed routes for a transcontinental railroad. Thomas Hart Benton, an influential senator and strong proponent of Manifest Destiny, provided financial backing for several subsequent expeditions led by his son-in-law, Captain John C. Fremont, already known for his trailblazing in California. His ill-fated fourth expedition in the winter of 1848 attempted to cross the Continental Divide at the Cochetopa Hills and ended in disaster in the snowy mountains.

Despite that setback, Benton and others pushed to find a feasible rail route through the southern Rockies. In 1852, Captain John W. Gunnison, an officer with considerable experience in exploring and surveying the West, was dispatched to explore a mid-latitude rail route that would cross the Sangre de Cristo Mountains, pass through the San Luis Valley, cross the Continental Divide via one of the low passes in the Cochetopa Hills, and continue on to Utah and the Great Basin.

After great difficulty hacking a wagon road over Cochetopa Pass from a scant Indian trail—felling trees, moving huge rocks, and lowering wagons on ropes down the steep, western side—Gunnison's party emerged only to find the way blocked by an impassable gorge, now known as the Black Canyon of the Gunnison. Convinced that a rail route through the area was not practical, Gunnison nevertheless pushed on into Utah, only to be killed with several of his companions by a band of Paiutes. His second-in-command, Lieutenant E. G. Beckwith, continued westward, completing the survey the following year.

While the Gunnison Expedition met with tragedy, it was to have an important impact, providing information about the country that would influence future settlement. Eventually, rails would cross the Divide at Marshall Pass, just a few miles east of Gunnison's crossing.

Following the Civil War, the government turned its attention to the settlement of the West. It sent out surveys to explore the country's resources and produce maps that would be useful to the miners, farmers, ranchers, and town builders who were clamoring for information. The two most important of these in Colorado were the War Department–led Wheeler and civilian-based Hayden Surveys.

Both surveys ranged widely over the Colorado mountains, scaling summits to set up triangulations stations, naming topographic features, analyzing the geology and mineral deposits, and studying the agricultural potential. Many of the prominent features encountered today by Colorado Trail users, including scores of peaks, rivers and streams, and mountain passes, bear names recorded by the men of these surveys.

Land of Riches

Most of The Colorado Trail through the southern Rockies winds along the so-called "Mineral Belt," a geologic band trending from the northeast to southwest that contains the riches that attracted early prospectors and miners. After gold was discovered in Colorado in 1858, boom towns sprang up overnight and many, just as quickly, faded as the next big strike occurred.

By the early 1870s, when big silver finds began to stabilize the mining industry

An old miner's cabin in Elk Creek in Segment 24.
PHOTO BY PETE KARTSOUNES

in the state, more permanent towns and cities began to thrive. And although the eventual collapse of silver prices in the late 1890s threatened the economy of these young settlements, many live on to this day—places like Breckenridge, Leadville, Creede, Lake City, and Silverton—offering resupply points to The Colorado Trail user. Others left their rusting and fallen relics behind for the CT hiker to explore and ponder. What was fortuitous in the eventual creation of The Colorado Trail was the network of footpaths, wagon roads, and rail lines linking remote communities.

Railroads Come and Go

Railroads quickly became the key to the development of the state's mining towns and cities, and entrepreneurs vied to be the first to penetrate the mountain barriers and reach the new diggings.

The competition was fierce in the early 1880s between two narrow-gauge lines, John Evans' Denver South Park & Pacific and General William J. Palmer's Denver & Rio Grande Western, to reach the quickly growing Gunnison and San Juan mining districts. Today's CT user follows the original path of the DSP&P as it once chugged into Waterton Canyon, then catches up with it again at Kenosha Pass. CT users also encounter the old roadbed left

behind at Chalk Creek, where the line once snaked up the valley to bore under the Continental Divide through the Alpine Tunnel. Likewise, users cross the old roadbed of the D&RGW at Tennessee and Marshall Passes.

While these lines are long gone, a remnant of the D&RGW, rechristened the Durango & Silverton Narrow Gauge Railroad, still crosses the CT in the scenic Animas Canyon as a tourist train. The Colorado Midland Railroad was another short-lived line whose remains the CT visits near Mount Massive, where the

A rusting steam boiler and windlass sit next to an abandoned mine near Carson Saddle in Segment 22.
PHOTO BY ANDREW SKURKA

Hagerman Tunnel once took the rails under the Continental Divide at 11,500 feet.

With the waning of mining in the first half of the twentieth century, the rails were torn up and a colorful time in the state's history vanished forever. Many of those abandoned railbeds and old wagon roads have become the roads and highways that today serve as CT access routes.

In the 1930s, workers from the Civilian Conservation Corps and other Depression-era programs began a wave of trail building in the state that lasted into the 1950s, providing the tread for many miles of the current CT. These trails were built primarily for fire management, often paralleling mountain ranges and sending off numerous side trails. The Main Range Trail, which coincides with large sections of The Colorado Trail on the eastern slope of the Sawatch Range, is one example. Other trails were built to facilitate fish stocking of high country lakes and streams.

With the spectacular growth in backpacking, hiking, and other recreational pursuits, starting in the 1960s, these forgotten Indian trails, wagon roads, logging tracks, abandoned railbeds, and fire trails became the new highways into Colorado's spectacular backcountry. Linked by miles of new tread built by thousands of dedicated volunteers, The Colorado Trail has become part of this rich heritage.

Here is a sampling of historical highlights found along each of the six sections of The Colorado Trail.

WATERTON CANYON TH TO KENOSHA PASS (SEGMENTS 1–5)

In the first few miles of Waterton Canyon, The Colorado Trail follows the roadbed of the Denver South Park & Pacific Railroad. Just downstream of the Gudy Gaskill Bridge sits the shuttered South Platte Hotel, once a busy stopover for travelers on their way to the mines of Leadville and Gunnison. The DSP&P is encountered again at Kenosha Pass, where an interpretive display notes where the switchyard and maintenance shops once stood in the meadows atop the pass. The tracks over the pass were torn up in the 1930s. The DSP&P lost its famous race to reach Gunnison to the Denver & Rio Grande Western, and achieved its loftier goal of reaching the Pacific only after it was sold in foreclosure to the Union Pacific Railroad.

KENOSHA PASS TO MOUNT MASSIVE TH (SEGMENTS 6–10)

In 1942, a new city sprang up practically overnight in the mountain wilderness of Colorado. Camp Hale was established in the East Fork Valley as a winter and mountain training site for soldiers during World War II. The large flat valley, surrounded by steep hillsides, proved ideal for teaching skiing, rock climbing, and cold weather survival skills. The famed 10th Mountain Division trained here. Little known is that from 1959 to 1965, when the camp was deactivated, the site was used by the CIA to secretly train Tibetan rebels. Though there's little remaining of the camp to see today, its legacy is commemorated by a monument and display atop Tennessee Pass and at nearby Ski Cooper, as well as with the 10th Mountain Division hut system.

MOUNT MASSIVE TH TO MARSHALL PASS (SEGMENTS 11–15)

Three distinct peaks frame the view on the route to Marshall Pass: Mount Ouray, named for Chief Ouray; Chipeta Mountain, named for Ouray's wife; and Pahlone Peak, named after their son. From this point west, The Colorado Trail largely travels through the ancestral lands of the Utes, whose story is one of great freedom and loss, as whites ignored treaties and eventually pushed them out and onto reservations. Ouray attempted to straddle a middle path between the conflicting cultures, but in the end mostly gave in to white demands. Today he is considered one of Colorado's pioneers, remembered with a portrait at the State Capitol and the lofty peak that bears his name.

MARSHALL PASS TO SAN LUIS PASS (SEGMENTS 16–20)

Winding along the long section of the Continental Divide known as the Cochetopa Hills, The Colorado Trail crosses several historic passes. For centuries, these low points on the continent's backbone were used by both American Indians and animals. "Cochetopa" means buffalo, presumably because the beasts migrated to and from the San Luis Valley through here. Whites also were attracted to these easier crossings, sometimes with bad results. Explorer John C. Fremont's expedition to cross the Divide in the winter of 1848 led to disaster, with rumors of cannibalism—not the last time that charge was heard in these mountains. In 1874, a party of miners disappeared in nearly the same area. Months later, only Alfred G. Packer emerged. Packer was later convicted of murdering and dining on his companions.

SAN LUIS PASS TO JUNCTION CREEK TRAILHEAD (SEGMENTS 21–28)

You'll hear it long before you reach the bottom of Elk Creek and the Animas River Canyon in Segment 24—the long, mournful whistle of the Durango & Silverton Narrow Gauge Railroad. Completed in 1881, only nine months after construction began out of Durango, the railroad, then known as the Denver & Rio Grande Western, carried passengers and freight to the booming silver mines at Silverton. Through the years, slides, floods, snow, war, and financial instability threatened the line. Tourism saved it, and it continues to operate today, carrying passengers in vintage railcars pulled by historic steam locomotives.

COLLEGIATE WEST, TWIN LAKES TO S. FOOSES RIDGE (SEGS CW01–CW05)

The five Collegiate West segments, like those in the Collegiate East, are rich in mining, railroad, and cultural history dating back thousands of years to the land's early occupants. Starting on the south shore of Twin Lakes, trail users can wander through the remains of the nineteenth century Interlaken Resort, where tourists once arrived by train and stagecoach. Across Hope Pass stands the ghost town of Winfield, one of many reminders in the area, including the scattered remnants of played-out mines, of the state's rich mining heritage. Follow a former roadbed for the narrow-gauge Denver South Park & Pacific Railroad to the now rock-covered entrance to the 1,800-foot Alpine Tunnel—the first tunnel built under the Continental Divide in Colorado. On approaching Monarch Pass from the south, the CT passes by the low boulder walls of a "game drive" built by prehistoric hunters as early at 3000 B.C. and used until as late as A.D. 1800.

THE NATURAL HISTORY OF THE COLORADO TRAIL

BY HUGO A. FERCHAU, Past Thornton Professor of Botany, Western State College

Moose in pond along Elk Creek, Segment 24 near Silverton.

PHOTO BY FELECIA MORAN

Marmot on rock, common at high elevations along the CT.

PHOTO BY TOM HODGE

THIS BRIEF LOOK AT ROCKY MOUNTAIN ECOLOGY is intended for both those new to Colorado Trail country and those locals who have rarely ventured into its vastness. Veterans of these wilds could probably write an equally good account. Regardless, there is no question that the natural history of this region is the prize, the reward for making the effort to hike the CT, and I would underscore the value of walking, not running, as you pass through it.

Over many years of leading groups of students through the Rockies, it has been my experience that those who reach camp well ahead of the rest can rarely relate any interesting observations. They might as well have worked out in a gym.

To get the most out of your Colorado Trail experience, take the time to look, to sit, to let nature present itself to you, and to soak up all that it has to offer. You may pass this way but once.

Observing Wildlife

For some reason, we commonly use the term "wildlife" to refer only to animals. Plants, evidently, are considered to be somewhat trapped or tamed, or at least subdued. There is less drama associated with plants because we can prepare for our encounters with them, whereas animals tend to take us by surprise—there all of a sudden, gone just as quickly. As a botanist, I recognize that most people would rather talk about a bear than about the bearberry.

Having been over most of The Colorado Trail, I cannot think of a single day that did not reveal much about the Rocky Mountain fauna. By the same token, I have seen students hike for days without seeing a single animal. This apparent contradiction can be explained by the fact that native animals are not in a zoo. They have instinctual and learned behaviors that enable them to avoid potential or perceived threats, such as hikers.

To see these animals, you must meet them on their own terms. Several general rules apply:

▲ Dawn and dusk are when animals tend to be most active, so rise early and get on the trail ahead of other hikers.

▲ Animals require water regularly, so look to their sources.

▲ Many animals will ignore you if you become part of the scenery, which means being quiet and still.

▲ Familiarizing yourself with the behavior of the animal, or animals, you wish to observe will increase your chances for success. Nocturnal rodents, for example, can be spotted at night by a patient observer with a flashlight.

Early-season trail users should note that deer and elk give birth in June. Try to avoid being disruptive if traveling at this time of year. Though some may be fearful of wildlife encounters, there is little need for concern. In years of student trips, we have experienced no attacks. I have seen mountain lion and bear from reasonable distances, and I am sure they have observed me from distances that would have excited me had I known about them. I have seen bear droppings on the trail on a cold morning that were so fresh that steam was still rising from them. My wife woke up from a nap one afternoon and found fresh bear claw marks on a tree above her head. Good judgment will help you avoid being molested. An animal seeks food, not your company. If you have no food in your presence, you will generally not be bothered. If you choose to keep food, even nuts or a candy bar, in your tent, you may wake up to find a hole chewed in the floor and the steely eyes of a mouse or pack rat staring back. After arriving in camp, hang your food away from your sleeping area—75 to 100 yards is a good distance.

Lush flowering bluebells in Segment 24 sparkling with morning dew.

PHOTO BY ROGER FORMAN

Plants

The highly variable topography of the central Rocky Mountains hosts a kaleidoscopic variety of vegetation. The accompanying diagrams indicate the types of vegetation encountered on The Colorado Trail, as well as their relationship to each other. Note that the zones are not defined by elevation alone, but also depend on local climatic factors.

In the field, of course, things can be more complicated. In areas that have been disturbed by fire or logging, for instance, different types of vegetation will exist in different relationships. Diagram 1 shows the relationship between various plant communities in a climax situation, that is, in an ecologically stable, undisturbed environment. When the land has been disturbed, the plants proceed through a succession phase before eventually evolving back into a climax state.

Diagram 2 shows the relationship between various types of vegetation during succession. Because of the severe climate and short growing season in the Rockies, successional vegetation patterns may persist for more than a hundred years. In addition, a single hillside may be covered with successional vegetation in one place and climax vegetation in another.

Riparian Vegetation: This is the vegetation found along stream banks, and it plays a variety of important roles, such as controlling erosion and providing cover and feed for wildlife. On the Western Slope, the area of Colorado on the western side of the Continental Divide, lower-elevation stream banks are dominated by a variety of trees, primarily cottonwood, alder, maple, and red osier dogwood. With increasing elevation, the cottonwoods become less evident, while the shrubs persist, eventually becoming dominated by willows.

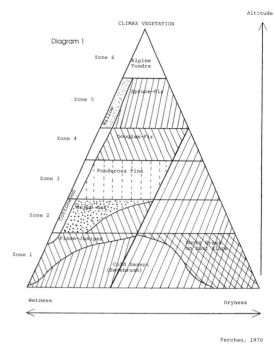

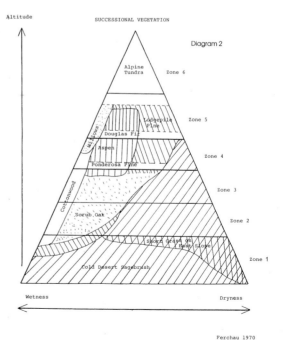

East of the Divide, cottonwoods are not as evident, but, as on the Western Slope, a mixture of shrubs prevails, becoming increasingly dominated by willows at higher elevations.

The diversity of plant life is spectacular at high elevations in the Colorado mountains. PHOTO BY FELECIA MORAN

Despite what appears to be very aggressive growth by riparian species, they are among the most sensitive to human activity. And because of their proximity to water, they are typically among the most threatened and endangered.

Sagebrush: Sagebrush, common to the cold, dry desert scrubland of the Rockies, is found from low to surprisingly high elevations. Interspersed with grasses, it predominates the primary grazing land of central and western Colorado.

Scrub Oak and Piñon-Juniper Woodland: This dryland plant community is most evident on The Colorado Trail where it climbs through the foothills above Denver. It also is seen occasionally at higher elevations, on the driest and most stressed sites, as the trail approaches Kenosha Pass. Junipers tend to be widely spaced, interspersed by grasses, while scrub oak tends to clump together so closely as to be almost impenetrable.

This vegetation makes for good game habitat, and hikers should be prepared for deer to pop up almost anywhere, particularly in early June. In late summer, this woodland is prone to wildfire, which can move rapidly through dry terrain. Such fires are often started by lightning strikes, and occasionally by hikers, who are reminded to pay attention to their campfires.

Ponderosa Pine: This is the lowest-elevation timber tree. Because of its good lumber quality and proximity to civilization, it has been the most extensively cut. Thus you may see large old ponderosa stumps among woodland vegetation, indicating a logged ponderosa forest where the tall pines have not yet returned. These long-needled pines tend to grow well spaced, with grasses flourishing in between. As a result, ranchers like to graze their stock among ponderosa, particularly in early spring. On the East Slope, ponderosa pine is found on less-stressed south-facing hillsides. On the Western Slope, it is encountered above the open, arid countryside of the sagebrush community.

Douglas Fir: Though related, this predominant tree is not to be confused with the giant firs of the Pacific Northwest. In the Rockies, these are the runts of the litter. The Douglas fir occupies moist, cool sites. East of the Divide, these trees are found on the slopes opposite of ponderosa pine, and on the Western Slope they grow above the level of the ponderosa. In both regions, Douglas fir tend to grow closer together, with little ground cover underneath. Because Douglas fir is the tree type most likely to burn, much of its habitat is occupied by successional vegetation.

Spruce-Fir Forest: This, the highest-elevation forest, is composed of Engelmann spruce and subalpine fir. Because of the late snowmelt, moist summertime conditions, and early snowfall, this vegetation has been the least altered by fire. Many of the spruce-fir forests in the Rockies are 400 years old. These dense forests tend to contain many fallen logs, which can be a real deterrent to hiking. The logs are typically moist, and hikers walking over them may be surprised when the bark slips off and they lose their footing. Ground cover may be lacking and a thick humus layer may be present.

Approaching timberline, the spruce-fir stands tend to be more open. The trees are clustered, with grasses and beautiful wildflowers interspersed between. These clusters provide refuge for elk at night. At timberline, the trees are bushlike, weather-beaten, and windshorn. They often grow in very dense clumps, which can provide ideal refuge for hikers. Animals are aware of this, too, and thus, while waiting out a storm, you may have the pleasure of observing a great deal of small mammal activity.

Forest in Segment 12, CT Collegiate East.
PHOTO BY DAVID DOLTON

Lodgepole Pine and Aspen: These are ordinarily successional species that can occupy a given site for up to 200 years. The lodgepole pine often succeeds disturbed Douglas fir and spruce-fir communities and grows on the driest sites. Its seeds are opened by fire. A wildfire will cause the deposition of thousands of seeds, and, a few years later, dense stands of seedlings and saplings appear. There is virtually no ground cover in the deep shade beneath the saplings and competition is fierce between the closely spaced trees. The dryness of such sites encourages repeated fires.

Aspens occupy moister sites. A clump of aspen among lodgepole pines suggests a potential source of water. Aspens reproduce from root suckers, and any ground disturbance such as a fire causes a multitude of saplings to appear. On drier sites aspens are typically interspersed with Thurber fescue, a large bunchgrass. In moderately moist sites, the ground cover will consist of a multitude of grasses, forbs, and shrubs. In wet aspen sites, ground cover is often dominated by bracken fern.

Alpine Tundra: Though it strikes many people as odd, the tundra can be likened to a desert because it sees only minimal precipitation. During winters, fierce winds prevent snow from accumulating in depth anywhere except in depressions. During summers, the snowmelt drains quickly off the steeper slopes, leaving the vegetation to depend on regular afternoon showers for survival.

Despite the harsh conditions, alpine tundra is quite diverse, and includes such different environments as meadows, boulder fields, fell fields, talus, and both temporary and permanent ponds. The cushionlike meadows are a favorite site for

Elk herd above tree line on Cataract Ridge in Segment 23.
PHOTO BY PETE TURNER

elk herds. Boulder fields are home to pikas, marmots, and other animals, and the protected spaces between the boulders can produce some of the most beautiful wildflowers. Fell fields are windswept sites from which virtually all mineral soil has been blown away, leaving behind a "pavement" that, despite its austerity, can produce some interesting plants. Talus fields consist of loose rock, and also host some interesting plants and animals. Tundra ponds often teem with invertebrates and are good sites for observing the fascinating bird known as the ptarmigan.

Wildflowers

Who can resist the elegant grace of Colorado's state flower, the blue columbine, or not be moved by nature's showy display blanketing the slopes astride The Colorado Trail in mid-summer? There are hundreds of species of flowering plants of conspicuous varieties (actually thousands, including inconspicuous plants such as grasses and sedges) along the CT as it winds its way through all five of the major Colorado lifezones.

Lifezones are delineated by elevation and are defined by their unique ecosystems and plant communities. Beginning on the margin of the high plains at 5,800 feet at Waterton Canyon (Segment 1), The Colorado Trail climbs to a lofty 13,271 feet on the slopes of Coney Summit (Segment 22). In the process, it ascends through these lifezones: plains (3,500–6,000 feet), foothills (6,000–8,000 feet), montane (8,000–10,000 feet), subalpine (10,000–11,500 feet), and alpine (11,500–14,400 feet). An alert hiker will notice the progression of plant communities along the way, which is driven by changes in climate, soil chemistry, snow accumulation, and other factors.

A trekker identifies wildflowers in Segment 20.
PHOTO BY DON WALLACE

As the season unfolds, the colorful pageantry climbs up the slopes along with The Colorado Trail hiker. A Durango-bound thru-hiker starting among late-May blooming cactus and the bright, spring-green slopes in Waterton Canyon will reach tree line at Georgia Pass still blanketed by snow. But by the time hikers climb atop Indian Trail Ridge near the end of their trek in mid-July, they will stroll through the tundra carpeted with an incredibly colorful display of alpine flowers.

The next two pages offer a sampling of some of the more common wildflowers prevalent in each of the six sections of The Colorado Trail delineated in this guide. In general, each section has characteristics that dictate the types of flowering plants a trail user may encounter. However, most of these plants are not unique to any one portion of the CT and may be found in any suitable habitat along the trail. (For instance, the many species and subspecies of Indian paintbrush exist throughout the state in a variety of habitats.)

Each plant listed here is identified by one of its common names, along with its scientific name. A plant can have several different common names, often varying by region, and the existence of a myriad of subspecies can frustrate precise identification for the amateur. You'll need to get a good hand lens for close examination of biological features as well as an excellent flower guide for Colorado plants. *Rocky Mountain Flora* by James Ells (Colorado Mountain Club Press) is an excellent field guide with more than 1,200 color photos.

WATERTON CANYON TRAILHEAD TO KENOSHA PASS (SEGMENTS 1–5)

Most of this section is at lower elevations. Plants from the plains zone merge in Platte Canyon with foothills zone residents. Blooms begin as early as late April and extend well into June. Look for prickly pear cactus (*Opuntia macrorhiza*), yucca (*Yucca glauca*), tiny filaree (*Erodium caepitosa*), and showy prickly poppy (*Argemone polyanthemos*). The dry, gravelly soils beyond the canyon support sand lily (*Leucocrinum montanum*), while you may

PHOTO BY JOE BRUMMER

PHOTO BY LORI BRUMMER

PHOTO BY LORI BRUMMER

find **pasqueflower** (*Anemone patens*) in the damp ravines. Close to Kenosha Pass, wild iris (*Iris missouriensis*) bursts forth in the meadows of South Park.

KENOSHA PASS TO MOUNT MASSIVE TRAILHEAD (SEGMENTS 6–10)

Most thru-hikers cross the high passes of the Continental Divide and Tenmile Range too early for most flowers to appear. Look, however, for sweet-smelling alpine forget-me-not (*Eritrichium elongatum*) and alpine springbeauty (*Claytonia megarhiza*) in the fell fields and rock crevices. As the snow melts along the trail, snow buttercup (*Ranunculus adoneus*) and **globeflower** (***Trollius albiflorus***) spring out of retreating snowbanks. Once in the shadow of Mount Massive, alpine wallflower (*Erysimum capitatum*) and Ryberg penstemon (*Penstemon rydbergii*) are common.

MOUNT MASSIVE TRAILHEAD TO MARSHALL PASS (SEGMENTS 11–15)

In this section, The Colorado Trail runs largely through thick montane forests, alternating between rather barren lodgepole stands and some lovely aspen forests. In aspen glens and forest clearings, tall heart-leaved arnica (*Arnica cordifolia*), larkspur (*Delphinium nuttallianum*), **red columbine** (***Aquilegia elegantula***), and monkshood (*Aconitum columbianum*) rise above the undergrowth. Sharing the sunny benches above reservoirs with the ubiquitous sage are shrubby cinquefoil (*Pentaphylloides floribunda*) and rabbitbrush (*Chrysothamnus nauseosus*). The latter is a late bloomer and harbinger of fall.

MARSHALL PASS TO SAN LUIS PASS (SEGMENTS 16–20)

On this high, lonely section along the Divide, the midsummer wildflowers are a cheerful

PHOTO BY JOE BRUMMER

PHOTO BY LORI BRUMMER

PHOTO BY BILL MANNING

companion to the CT hiker. Grasses and sedges dominate the sweeping ridgetop panoramas, punctuated by **alpine sunflower (*Rydbergia grandiflora*)**, with its huge heads turned to the rising sun, and the more understated American bistort (*Bistorta bistortoides*). Farther west, the Divide rises to true alpine tundra near San Luis Peak, and the slopes are carpeted with dwarf plants like alpine avens (*Acomastylis rossii turbinata*), alpine phlox (*Phlox condensata*), and moss campion (*Silene acaulis subacaulescens*).

SAN LUIS PASS TO JUNCTION CREEK TRAILHEAD (SEGMENTS 21–28)

For the thru-hiker, the best is saved for last. West of Molas Pass, The Colorado Trail enters a verdant landscape of rolling mountains, rising above lush subalpine meadows and culminating in mid-July in spectacular displays on Indian Trail Ridge. Blue columbine (*Aquilegia coerulea*), wild geranium (*Geranium caespitosum*), and silky phalecia (*Phaecelia sericea*) nod in the breeze. Along the rushing streams, monkeyflower (*Mimulus guttatus*), Parry primrose (*Primula parryi*), and **kingscrown (*Rhodiola integriflia*)** dip roots in cold melt water.

COLLEGIATE WEST, TWIN LAKES TO S. FOOSES RIDGE (SEGS CW01–CW05)

Look for these wildflower varieties as you pass through this newest addition to the CT: the purple-hued **elephant heads (*Pedicularis groenlandica*)** (you may be lucky enough to spot the less common white variety as well); rose paintbrush (*Castilleja rexiifolia*), which are quite common and come in several varieties and colors; glacial daisy (*Erigeron glacialis*), with its lavender petals with yellow centers; and the purple hall's penstemon (*Penstemon hallii*).

GEOLOGY ALONG THE COLORADO TRAIL

BY JACK REED

A Geologic Chronicle

The diverse collage of landscapes traversed by The Colorado Trail is the result of the complex geologic history of western Colorado. At first the ages and types of rocks along the trail seem almost random, but if we study them carefully and try to decipher their stories we find that they record a fascinating chronicle of geologic events that began 1.8 billion years ago and continue today. They tell of the slow shift of continents, the rise and destruction of mountain ranges, the ebb and flow of ancient seas, and the tireless work of wind, water, and glacial ice in shaping the ever-changing landscape. The geologic story of the rocks along the trail can be condensed into eight major chapters.

Typical outcropping of Pikes Peak granite in Segment 3.
PHOTO BY JULIE VIDA AND MARK TABB

CHAPTER 1
THE BASEMENT ROCKS

The oldest rocks in the Colorado mountains are metamorphic and igneous rocks, the oldest of which formed between 1.8 and 1.6 billion years ago during the consolidation of the part of the continental plate that ultimately would include Colorado. Those rocks are collectively called "basement rocks" because they formed first and underlie all of the other rocks of the region.

The metamorphic rocks are chiefly gneiss and schist derived from volcanic and sedimentary rocks that were subjected to high temperatures and enormous pressure during

Eroded formations of volcanic air-fall ash near Snow Mesa in Segment 21.

PHOTO BY AARON LOCANDER

Sloping beds of sedimentary rocks at Section Point along Segment 26.

PHOTO BY NATE HEBENSTREIT

burial to depths as great as eight miles below the surface. The metamorphic rocks were intruded by extensive bodies of granite several times: once when they were being metamorphosed, once about 1.4 billion years ago, and once again about 1.1 billion years ago. Basement rocks are exposed along the CT, particularly in the Front Range, the Sawatch Range, and the Needle Mountains.

CHAPTER 2
ROCKS OF THE WESTERN SEAS

Following their formation, the basement rocks were uplifted and eroded to a nearly flat land surface. Then, about 515 million years ago during the early part of the Paleozoic Era, the western edge of North America began to subside and shallow seas flooded eastward onto the continent.

As those seas ebbed and flowed across the Colorado region for the next 150 million years or so, extensive, relatively thin layers of sandstone, shale, and limestone were deposited within them. The CT crosses those beds in only a few places, once in Segment 9 just before Tennessee Pass and again in Segments 24 and 25 near Molas Pass, but they are spectacularly exposed in Glenwood Canyon.

CHAPTER 3
THE ANCESTRAL ROCKY MOUNTAINS, THE MOUNTAINS NO ONE KNEW

About 320 million years ago in the late Paleozoic Era, plate tectonic movement brought North America together with South America and Africa. One of the results of that collision was the uplift of great mountain ranges in the Colorado region. Those ancestral ranges were probably just as rugged as our modern Rocky Mountains, but their bases lay at or near sea level.

As those ancient mountains rose, the early Paleozoic sedimentary rocks that once blanketed the basement were stripped by erosion, and debris from the rising mountains was swept into basins between the ranges where it accumulated to thicknesses of thousands of feet. The peaks that formed those Ancestral Rocky Mountains are now completely gone, but the thick layers of red conglomerate, sandstone, and shale that were deposited in the basins that flanked them are now widely exposed and make up some of the most spectacular modern ranges. You can see them near the start of the CT on the eastern flank of the Front Range, in Segment 8 between Copper Mountain and Tennessee Pass, and in Segments 25–28 between Molas Pass and Junction Creek.

CHAPTER 4
THE GREAT CRETACEOUS SEAWAY

Following the leveling of the Ancestral Rockies, extensive layers of sandstone and shale were deposited across their eroded stumps. Those rocks were originally laid down as windblown desert sands, and as sand and mud along sluggish streams and in shallow lakes. Then, about 100 million years ago in the Cretaceous Period of the Mesozoic Era, waters of a great seaway that covered much of central North America began to spread westward across the future site of Colorado. Sand from the beaches that flanked the advancing seaway formed what is now called the Dakota Sandstone. As the water deepened, thick deposits of black mud accumulated and are now preserved as thousands of feet of black shale that overlie the Dakota

Chalk Cliffs at the south end of Segment 13. The cliffs are not actually chalk, but 34 million year-old granite altered by hot springs waters.

PHOTO BY CARL BROWN

Sandstone. Seaway deposits are exposed along the CT only on the ridges north of Swan River in the western part of Segment 6. Some of the deposits that immediately predated the seaway cap the high ridge that the CT follows in Segments 27 and 28.

Conglomerate boulder in CT Segment 25.
PHOTO BY LINDA JEFFERS

CHAPTER 5
THE LARAMIDE OROGENY

As the Cretaceous seaway was beginning to withdraw about 75 million years ago, the first stirrings of the Laramide Orogeny began. This was the episode of mountain building that laid the foundations for most of the present mountain ranges. Plate movements along the western edge of the continent began to buckle the Earth's crust, raising domes and elongate welts, most of which were bounded by folds or faults along which slabs of rock were moved several miles relative to the rocks beneath them.

During the orogeny, extensive bodies of granite and porphyry (a light-colored, fine-grained rock studded with large rectangular crystals of feldspar) intruded both the basement rocks and the overlying sedimentary strata. Many of those intrusions took place along the Colorado Mineral Belt, a northeast-to-southwest trending belt that extends from the western San Juan Mountains to the Front Range near Boulder and contains most of the important gold and silver mining camps in Colorado.

Erosion began to attack the uplifts as soon as they began to rise, carving mountain ranges from the more resistant rocks and depositing debris in the intervening basins. Uplift continued for as long as 30 million years, but as it waned erosion largely reduced the Laramide mountains to low rounded hills and a few low mountains separated by flat, sediment-filled basins. Parts of this post-Laramide landscape are preserved today, particularly in the area where the CT where crosses the Front Range.

CHAPTER 6
THE GREAT VOLCANIC FLARE-UP

Igneous activity dwindled after the Laramide Orogeny, but about 36 million years ago, during development of the subdued post-Laramide landscape, it resumed with a vengeance. Volcanoes spewed huge volumes of lava, volcanic ash, and related deposits over large parts of the post-Laramide landscape, and many bodies of granite and porphyry were emplaced at depth beneath them. Those eruptions continued for about 10 million years, from the Eocene into the Oligocene Epoch of the Tertiary Period. Most of the San Juan Mountains are carved from a remnant of the extensive volcanic field that was built during that time.

CHAPTER 7
UPLIFT AND EROSION

The penultimate episode in the shaping of the present mountain landscape began about 26 million years ago during the late Oligocene Epoch, when the tectonic forces that had compressed and shortened the Earth's crust during the Laramide changed direction and began to pull the crust apart. As the crust extended, a number of faults developed. The most significant are the faults bounding the Rio Grande Rift, which is a series of fault-bounded basins that extends southward from Leadville through the Upper Arkansas and San Luis valleys, and through New Mexico all the way to El Paso, Texas. Some of those faults are still active today.

Development of the faults was accompanied by regional uplift of the post-Laramide landscape, which originally stood only a few thousand feet above sea level, to its present elevation of 8,000 to more than 10,000 feet. During this uplift, which may still be continuing, all of the major canyons were incised into the post-Laramide surface, and the present mountain ranges were carved from the uplifted roots of the Laramide mountains and from the volcanic rocks of the San Juan volcanic field. During erosion, the more resistant rocks, such as the basement rocks, some of the sedimentary rocks from the Ancestral Rockies, the younger granite and porphyry, and some of the volcanic rocks, tended to form mountains, whereas softer, less-resistant rocks formed valleys and basins.

Redbeds along Indian Trail Ridge in Segment 27.
PHOTO BY JESSE SWIFT AND BILL TURNER

Red Mountain and neighboring peaks in the Lake City caldera near Segment 22.

PHOTO BY ROGER FORMAN

CHAPTER 8
THE ICE AGES

Most of the erosion of the uplifted roots of the Laramide mountains was the work of the weathering of the rocks and the removal of material by streams and rivers. In the last 2 million years, however, since the advent of the Quaternary Epoch, glaciers have played a major role in the developing mountain landscape. Although there were several earlier periods of glaciation in the Colorado mountains, the principal glacial advances that shaped the present landscape were the Bull Lake glaciation, between about 170,000 and 120,000 years ago, and the Pinedale glaciation, between about 30,000 and 12,000 years ago. They carved the spectacular glacial amphitheaters, gouged out the U-shaped glacial valleys, deposited the conspicuous moraines, and shaped the basins that hold many of the jewel-like mountain lakes.

Sources and Additional Reading

Blair, Rob, Origins of landscapes. In: Blair, Rob, Casey, T.A., Romme, W.H. and Ellis, R.N., eds., *The Western San Juan Mountains, Their Geology, Ecology, and Human History*. University of Colorado Press, Boulder CO, 1996.

Chronic, Halka, and Williams, Felicie, *Roadside Geology of Colorado* (2nd Edition). Mountain Press, Missoula MT, 2002.

Hopkins, Ralph L., and Hopkins, Lindy B., *Hiking Colorado's Geology*. The Mountaineers, Seattle WA, 2000.

Mathews, Vincent, ed., *Messages in Stone* (2nd Edition). Colorado Geological Survey, Denver CO, 2009.

Raup, Omer B., *Colorado Geologic Highway Map*, 1:1,000,000 scale. Colorado Geological Survey, Denver CO, 1991.

Reed, Jack, and Ellis, Gene, *Rocks Above the Clouds: A Hiker's and Climber's Guide to Colorado Mountain Geology*. Golden: Colorado Mountain Club Press, 2009.

Tweto, Ogden, *Geologic Map of Colorado*, 1:500,000 scale. U.S. Geological Survey, 1979

View of Lake San Cristobal and Slumgullion Slide showing the curved river valley that follows the outer wall of the Lake City caldera. At left, Red Mountain is in a lava dome within the caldera.

COURTESY OF COLORADO MOUNTAIN EXPEDITIONS

Waterton Canyon Trailhead to Kenosha Pass (Segments 1–5)

Segment 1: Waterton Canyon Trailhead to South Platte River Trailhead

Waterton Canyon and the South Platte River.

Distance: 16.8 miles

Elevation gain: Approx. 2,830 feet

The Elevation loss: Approx. 2,239 feet

USFS maps: Pike National Forest, pages 72–73

The Colorado Trail Databook 6: pages 10–11

The CT Map Book: pages 9–10

National Geographic Trails Illustrated map: No. 135

Latitude 40° map: Summit County Trails

Jurisdiction: South Platte Ranger District, Pike National Forest

Access from Denver end:

Access from Durango end:

Availability of water: ☕

Bicycling: 🚲

"A broken toggle or cotter pin may be difficult to replace along the trail, as sporting good stores are far apart. Make sure your backpack is in excellent condition before setting off."

If you are a thru-hiker, you need to make sure your gear is in top shape. Although this guide points out towns along the way for resupply, they are few and far between. Carry spares of small, critical items.

Gudy's TIP

ABOUT THIS SEGMENT

The first segment of The Colorado Trail begins at the Waterton Canyon Trailhead on the South Platte River. The trail follows a well-maintained dirt road for the first 6.7 miles, climbing an average of 40 feet per mile. There are mileage signs every half-mile. Enjoy the moderate walking and biking—it won't last for long! The canyon was carved in 1.7 billion-year-old metamorphic rocks from the Front Range uplift during the Laramide Orogeny.

Bighorn sheep are often seen in Waterton Canyon, where their habitat is protected.

PHOTO BY SEAN RILEY

Because of its proximity to the Denver metro area, this is by far the busiest section of The Colorado Trail. In spite of its popularity, this portion of the trail is very enjoyable, offering the potential for spotting deer and bighorn sheep that scramble along the canyon walls. Since this road is used by the Denver Water Board to access Strontia Springs Dam, there are several restrictions: Motor vehicle access is limited to official vehicles, no dogs are allowed on this stretch of trail, and there is no camping until after the single-track trail begins at 6.7 miles. The road is open from a half-hour before sunrise to a half-hour after sunset.

Lenny's Rest at mile 7.9 is a great place to stop for lunch or a snack after the first challenging climb on the CT. There are nice displays of wildflowers, including Colorado's state flower, the blue columbine, along the small creeks and in the drainages the trail passes.

The best camping in Segment 1 is found along Bear Creek (mile 8.7). There are several good spots available there. Once past the creek, however, there are few good sites. Plan your day with this in mind. If you do plan to continue beyond this point, be aware that the next reliable water source is more than 8 miles away when you reach the South Platte River again.

Camping is NOT permitted within sight of the river along the first 7 miles of Segment 1. Dogs are also prohibited on the Denver Water Board Road, which serves as the first 6.7 miles of The Colorado Trail.

Trail users who want to travel with their dogs will be happy to know that the first 6.4 miles of Segment 1 is the only stretch of the CT where dogs are prohibited. You can maximize your CT "dog miles" by choosing an alternate starting point at the east end of Segment 1. Begin instead at the Indian Creek Trailhead and Campground, which is accessible via CO Hwy 67, approximately 10 miles west of Sedalia. From the parking lot, proceed through the equestrian campground to the west for a quarter-mile and join the Indian Creek Trail. Proceed 4.1 miles until the trail intersects the CT at mile 7.9.

There is additional information on The Colorado Trail Foundation website, ColoradoTrail.org, including a map titled "Singletrack & Dogs Route" (click on Trip Planning, then Dogs). Another option is to arrange for someone to bring your dog to the start of Segment 2 at the South Platte River Trailhead.

TRAILHEAD/ACCESS POINTS

Waterton Canyon Trailhead: Take I-25 south out of Denver to the C-470 exit. Go west on C-470 for 12.5 miles and take the Wadsworth Boulevard (CO Hwy 121) exit. Go left (south) on Wadsworth for 4.5 miles, then turn left onto Waterton Canyon Road. Continue 0.3 mile to the large trailhead parking area on the left. If this parking area is full, there is another parking area a quarter-mile north up the road. It is connected to the lower parking lot by a trail.

South Platte River Trailhead: See Segment 2 on page 74.

SERVICES, SUPPLIES, AND ACCOMMODATIONS

Denver and its suburbs have a full array of services.

TRAIL DESCRIPTION

The Colorado Trail begins across the road from the parking lot on Waterton Canyon Road at **mile 0.0** (5,522 feet) Continue past the interpretive display and through another parking area that is closed to the public. Bear right at a fork in the road at **mile 0.4** (5,522), staying on the main dirt road for the next 6.2 miles. There is no camping permitted along this stretch of trail and dogs are not allowed.

At **mile 6.2** (5,786), there is a turnoff on the right for Strontia Springs Dam, worthy of a photo, plus vault toilet and water. The CT bears to the left. Go straight at the intersection with a side road on the left that is also Roxborough Trail at **mile 6.4** (5,889). Dogs can join the CT at this point. At **mile 6.6** (5,931), where the main road curves sharply to the right, leave the main road and go left onto a smaller road. At **mile 6.7** (6,024), there is an intersection. Bear to the left and follow the single-track trail. The

trail begins to climb more steeply from here.

The first campsite is at **mile 7.0** (6,180), but it is small and does not have a nearby water source. The trail continues climbing, following a series of switchbacks until reaching a bench known as Lenny's Rest in honor of Eagle Scout Leonard Southwell, at **mile 7.9** (6,543). There is an intersection here with Indian Creek Trail #800, a single-track sometimes used as an alternate to Waterton Canyon. The trail then descends, crossing Bear Creek at **mile 8.7** (6,177). This is the last reliable water source until the end of Segment 1 at the South Platte River. There are several good campsites in this area.

At **mile 9.8** (6,689) the CT begins to parallel and then occasionally cross West Bear Creek. There is a good, dry campsite at **mile 11.8** (7,309) near leaning rocks.

The trail continues climbing to a ridge at **mile 12.6**

A volunteer improves a water diversion to stem trail erosion.
PHOTO BY BILL MANNING

(7,517), the segment's highest point. From here, the CT descends 4 miles before reaching a gentle, grassy slope on a hillside with possible campsites at **mile 16.6** (6,240) offering the convenience of river water a short distance below. Travel another 0.2 mile before reaching Douglas County Rd 97 and the South Platte River Trailhead, the end of Segment 1, at **mile 16.8** (6,117). From here, the trail continues over the river on the Gudy Gaskill Bridge, the last water for over 10 miles. Due to private property, there is no camping along the river.

Waterton Canyon

A favorite with day-hikers, bike riders, anglers, birders, and others, Waterton Canyon can be a sometimes crowd-filled beginning to a 486-mile trek through the heart of the Colorado Rockies. The Colorado Trail follows a Denver Water Board service road for the first 6.7 miles, itself once a roadbed for the Denver, South Park & Pacific Railroad, built in 1877.

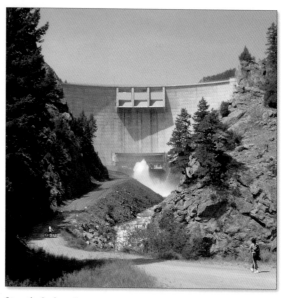

Strontia Springs Dam.
PHOTO BY LAWTON "DISCO" GRINTER

Water was the driving force in the development of the canyon. Explorer Stephen Long, an Army major charged with finding the headwaters of the Platte River, camped here in 1820. Years later, the town of Waterton sprang up, serving as headquarters for the Denver Water Board's decades-long effort to harness the resource for the thirsty city that was developing on the plains nearby. Near the mouth of the canyon is the Kassler Treatment Plant, a national landmark noted for its technologically advanced (for 1912) slow-sand filtration system. Farther up the road, you can see the original diversion dam for the 130-year-old High Line Canal, a 65-mile irrigation canal that snakes its way through the Denver metro area. Other diversion dams also take water from the Platte to Marston Reservoir, a few miles to the north.

At mile 6.4 on the trail, the 243-foot-high Strontia Springs Dam soars above the river. Finished in 1983, its 1.7-mile-long lake and extensive tunnel system tie together elements of the huge metro-area water delivery network.

If water developers had had their way, an even more immense reservoir, Twin Forks, would have been built upstream, threatening the canyon and inundating a portion of the CT. The proposal was beaten back in 1990, and for now, once past the dam, civilization is left behind and the canyon remains much as Stephen Long must have found it, with fir and pine sheltering the slopes and elusive bighorn sheep frolicking on the crags.

Viewing Bighorn Sheep

The Rocky Mountain bighorn sheep, the state mammal, is a fitting symbol of Colorado. With their massive curving horns, rams present a majestic silhouette that matches the grandeur of their rugged surroundings. Waterton Canyon is home to a band of bighorn that has been increasingly threatened by encroaching human activities.

The Waterton band is unusual because of its existence at such a low elevation and so close to a major city. Before human settlement, however, bighorns often wintered in the foothills and even ventured out onto the plains. Today, they are found mostly at higher elevations, often near or above tree line, usually avoiding forested country and civilization.

Bighorn are susceptible to lungworm and pneumonia, the spread of which appears to be tied to the stress of human pressure. Also, traditional routes to salt licks, important to the animals' mineral requirements, are being cut off. The construction of the Strontia Springs Dam in the 1980s severely impacted the Waterton band, which has recovered somewhat since then.

Visitors frequently spot the sheep, sometimes right along the service road. CT users should not harry, startle, or attempt to feed the animals. Thru-hikers have several chances to view this magnificent animal along the CT, usually near or at tree line in open, rolling terrain, such as along the Continental Divide in Segments 15 and 16, and then again in the high fastness of the La Garita and Weminuche wilderness areas.

Bighorns in Waterton Canyon present an opportunity for photographers.
PHOTO BY MIKE BOLLINGER

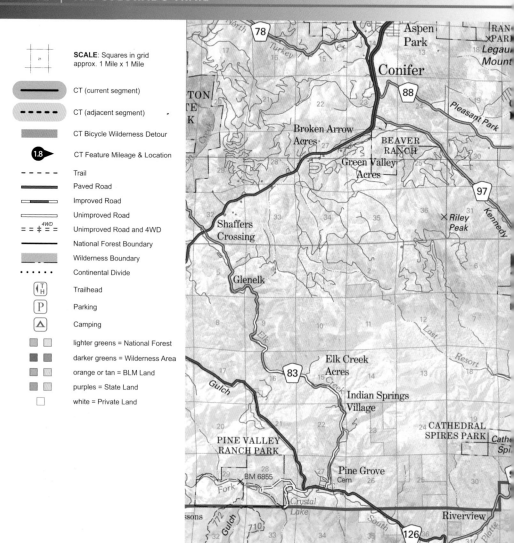

SCALE: Squares in grid approx. 1 Mile x 1 Mile

CT (current segment)

CT (adjacent segment)

CT Bicycle Wilderness Detour

1.8 CT Feature Mileage & Location

Trail

Paved Road

Improved Road

Unimproved Road

Unimproved Road and 4WD

National Forest Boundary

Wilderness Boundary

Continental Divide

Trailhead

Parking

Camping

lighter greens = National Forest

darker greens = Wilderness Area

orange or tan = BLM Land

purples = State Land

white = Private Land

SEGMENT 1 FEATURES TABLE   Pike National Forest

Mileage	Features & Comments	Elevation (feet)	Mileage from Denver	Mileage to Durango	UTM-E	UTM-N (NAD83)	Zone
0.0	Begin Segment 1	5,522	0.0	484.6	491,827	4,371,302	13
6.2	Pass Strontia Springs Dam	5,786	6.2	478.4	489,428	4,365,023	13
6.6	Turn left onto smaller road	5,931	6.6	478.0	489,774	4,364,575	13
6.7	Road ends, begin single-track	6,024	6.7	477.9	489,711	4,364,357	13
7.9	Lenny's Rest bench	6,543	7.9	476.7	489,598	4,363,840	13
8.7	Cross Bear Creek	6,177	8.7	475.9	489,297	4,363,337	13
9.8	Cross West Bear Creek	6,689	9.8	474.8	489,063	4,362,460	13
12.6	High point on ridge	7,517	12.6	472.0	486,841	4,361,820	13
16.8	End Segment 1	6,117	16.8	467.8	485,565	4,361,212	13

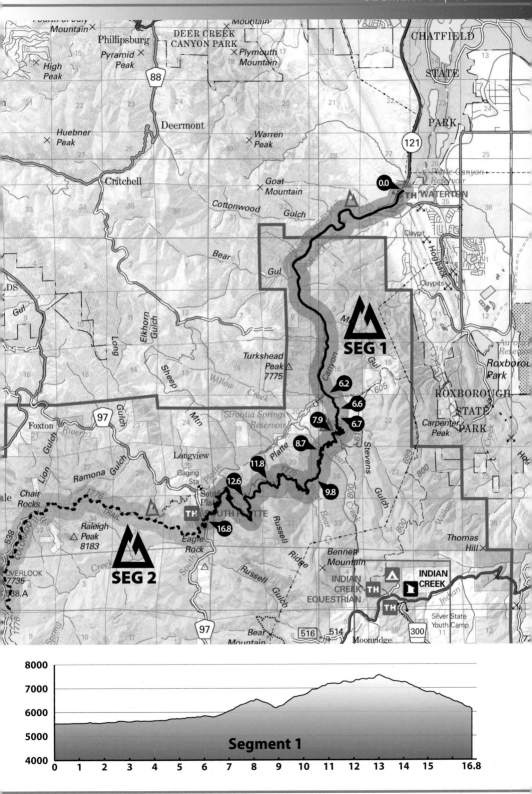

Segment 2: South Platte River Trailhead to Little Scraggy Trailhead

The evening sun illuminates Raleigh Peak as viewed from a recent CT reroute near Top of the World.

PHOTO BY BILL BLOOMQUIST

Distance: 11.5 miles

Elevation gain: Approx. 2,482 feet

Elevation loss: Approx. 753 feet

USFS map: Pike National Forest, pages 78–79

The Colorado Trail Databook 6: pages 12–13

The CT Map Book: pages 10–11

National Geographic Trails Illustrated map: No. 135

Jurisdiction: South Platte Ranger District, Pike National Forest

Access from Denver end: 🚗

Access from Durango end: 🚗

Availability of water: ☕

Bicycling: 🚲

"When you reach the South Platte River (at the end of Segment 1), fill up on water because it is a long, dry climb to Top of the World ridge."

This segment is relatively low in elevation and shade is scarce due to a wildfire in 1996. As a result, it can be brutally hot. Use your water carefully and hike early in the day when it is cooler.

Gudy's TIP

ABOUT THIS SEGMENT

As it crosses the South Platte River the trail passes from metamorphic basement rocks into coarse-grained 1.1 billion-year-old Pikes Peak granite. This granite erodes to form spectacular spires, rounded domes, and smooth rocky faces. It decomposes into coarse porous mineral soil that holds little water. Forests that grow on this dry loose soil are especially prone to wildfires.

The effects of the 1996 Buffalo Creek Fire are the dominating feature of Segment 2 and provide a great learning opportunity. The fire burned more than 12,000 acres and the impacts are still obvious. There are long stretches of the segment that have no shade because all of the trees were burned. The landscape is revegetating nicely, however, and many plants that love disturbances such as fire have taken hold. Keep your eyes open for paintbrush, buckwheat, yucca, and sunflowers, which bloom extensively in the summer.

There is EMERGENCY drinking water available at an unmanned fire station a short walk north of where the CT first approaches Jefferson County Rd 126. There is a water faucet at the rear of the building. Fill your water bottle, TURN OFF THE WATER, and leave the area immediately.

ONE OTHER CAUTION: Property owners along this segment tend to zealously guard their privacy. Don't trespass or park your vehicle on private land.

It is imperative to be well prepared when heading into Segment 2. Users won't find water after the South Platte River until the faucet at the fire station building visible from the trail near **mile 10.0** and County Rd 126. The lack of trees exposes trail users to the direct sun, making the temperature feel much warmer than in a shaded forest. In addition, there is no camping allowed along the South Platte River and any campsite in Segment 2 will be dry. Keep this in mind when beginning the section. Carry plenty of water and hike early or late to avoid the heat of the day.

TRAILHEAD/ACCESS POINTS

South Platte River Trailhead: From Denver, drive southwest on US Hwy 285 for about 20 miles to the mountain town of Conifer. One-quarter mile past the end of town, exit the highway to your right. At the stop sign turn left, proceed under the highway, turn right, proceed a few feet to the stop sign, and turn left. This is Jefferson County Rd 97, better known as Foxton Road. Proceed about 8 miles on Foxton Road to a stop sign at an intersection with Jefferson County Rd 96. Turn left on 96 and go 5.5 miles to the boarded-up South Platte Hotel. Cross the bridge and the road becomes Douglas County Rd 97. Seven-tenths of a mile on, you will see the 141-foot-long Gudy Gaskill Bridge on the right. This is the South Platte River Trailhead, the start of Segment 2 of The Colorado Trail.

This trailhead also can be reached from the south via Woodland Park and north on CO Hwy 67 to Deckers (a one-store town). Follow the river via Douglas County Rds 67/97 to the trailhead.

Little Scraggy Trailhead on FS Rd 550: 🚗 See Segment 3 on page 80.

TRAIL DESCRIPTION

Segment 2 begins by crossing the South Platte River on the Gudy Gaskill Bridge, **mile 0.0** (6,117 feet), the last water source for over 10 miles. Due to private property, there is no camping along the river. At the end of the bridge, the trail makes right turns and goes under the bridge along the river. Soon after, the trail veers right, leaving the river, and begins climbing steadily up several switchbacks. At **mile 1.1** (6,592), pass an abandoned quartz mine and enter the Buffalo Creek Fire area. Note how the forest is beginning to regenerate.

At **mile 2.5** (6,841), the trail passes a distinct outcrop of pink granite and continues through rolling terrain. There are several good campsites along this stretch of the trail, including a site between boulders at the top of a ridge at **mile 5.2** (7,745). From this spot, the Chair Rocks are visible to the west. Raleigh Peak (8,183) is about a mile to the southeast and Long Scraggy Peak (8,812) is about 4 miles to the south.

After a slight downhill, The Colorado Trail crosses Raleigh Peak Road at **mile 6.0** (7,691). A dry campsite can be found to the left of the trail at **mile 6.6** (7,684). At **mile 7.3** (7,613), cross an old jeep road and continue through the burned area. Approaching mile 10.1 is a metal building on the right, the unmanned fire station with emergency water spigot on the northeast corner. Turn left at **mile 10.1** (7,622), where the trail parallels Jefferson County Rd 126 for 0.3 mile. Cross Jefferson County Rd 126 at **mile 10.4** (7,675) and follow the Forest Service dirt road as it bends to the south. Here at **mile 10.7** (7,712) a dry campsite can be found.

Segment 2 ends when the trail reaches a large parking area at the Little Scraggy Trailhead on FS Rd 550 at **mile 11.5** (7,834). There is a toilet and an information display here. This trailhead is a Forest Service fee area. Camping is not allowed in the parking area, but is permissible outside this area in the vicinity of The Colorado Trail.

SERVICES, SUPPLIES, AND ACCOMMODATIONS – BUFFALO CREEK

The town of **Buffalo Creek**, on Jefferson County Rd 126, is 3.2 miles north of the trail at mile 10.1. Once a whistle stop on the Denver, South Park & Pacific Railroad, the town survives with a few cabins, a small general store (unique!), a pay phone, and a Forest Service work center.

Distance from CT: 3.2 miles
Elevation: 6,750 feet
Zip code: 80425
Area code: 303

Snacks/Post Office (limited hours)
J. W. Green Mercantile Co.
17706 Jefferson County Rd 96
(303) 838-5587

Fire!

On May 18, 1996, the human-induced Buffalo Creek Fire burned nearly 12,000 acres of the Pike National Forest, including most of the western half of Segment 2, and nearly destroyed the small mountain community of Buffalo Creek. Following the wildfire, several torrential rainstorms swept the area, including one on July 12 that dumped almost 5 inches of rain on the denuded slopes, causing severe flash flooding. Two people died and millions of dollars in property damage occurred. Downstream, some 300,000 cubic yards of sediment were swept into Strontia Springs Reservoir and miles of habitat were lost along area creeks and rivers.

The fire torched the Top of the World Campground and other features along the CT, dramatically changing the character of the landscape. Once a walk through pleasant pine forests, the CT in Segment 2 now has expansive views. Today, grasses and small plants are well established, but few trees survived the inferno, and it will be centuries before the area recovers to become a mature forest again.

It's little consolation to the victims, but a wildfire can be a good thing. Before human settlement, such fires occurred on a frequent basis, clearing out debris, rejuvenating the soil with nutrients, and keeping the amount of fuel low, which meant that rarely would a fire burn large or hot enough to destroy mature trees. Decades of fire suppression, and perhaps a decrease in logging, contributed to a disaster in the making.

A hiker passes through landscape recovering from fire. PHOTO BY ANDREW SKURKA

The Buffalo Creek area, in fact, is part of an almost continuous 2,500-square-mile swath of ponderosa pine forest that is primed for catastrophic fires, as was borne out only a few years later by the even more apocalyptic 138,000-acre Hayman Fire, which struck only a few miles to the south.

If there is an unintended boon for the CT hiker or rider, it is the vistas that have opened up in the area. The weathered domes of rough Pikes Peak granite—including the Cathedral Spires, Raleigh Peak, and Long Scraggy Peak—are striking sights from the trail. Early-season CT users are rewarded with acres of wildflowers in the opened-up slopes, including sand lily and paintbrush in the dry, gravelly areas and pasqueflower and spring beauty in the damper ravines.

Pincushion cactus in bloom. PHOTO BY BILL BLOOMQUIST

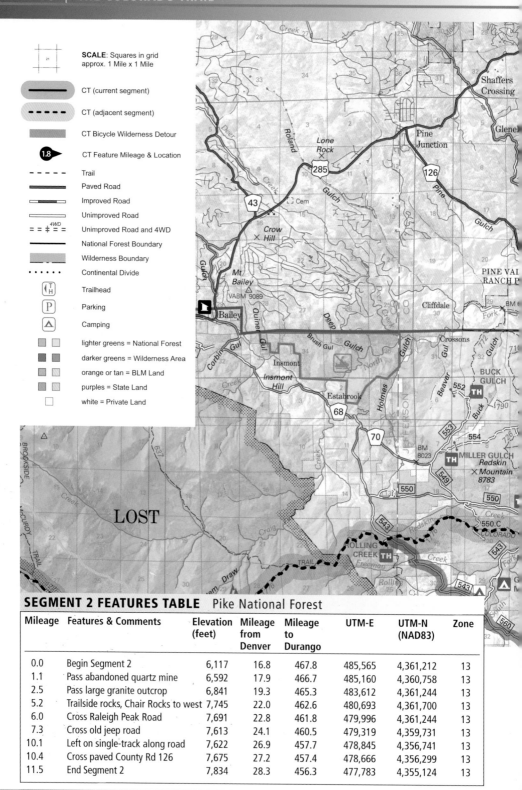

SCALE: Squares in grid approx. 1 Mile x 1 Mile

CT (current segment)

CT (adjacent segment)

CT Bicycle Wilderness Detour

CT Feature Mileage & Location

Trail

Paved Road

Improved Road

Unimproved Road

Unimproved Road and 4WD

National Forest Boundary

Wilderness Boundary

Continental Divide

Trailhead

Parking

Camping

lighter greens = National Forest

darker greens = Wilderness Area

orange or tan = BLM Land

purples = State Land

white = Private Land

SEGMENT 2 FEATURES TABLE Pike National Forest

Mileage	Features & Comments	Elevation (feet)	Mileage from Denver	Mileage to Durango	UTM-E	UTM-N (NAD83)	Zone
0.0	Begin Segment 2	6,117	16.8	467.8	485,565	4,361,212	13
1.1	Pass abandoned quartz mine	6,592	17.9	466.7	485,160	4,360,758	13
2.5	Pass large granite outcrop	6,841	19.3	465.3	483,612	4,361,244	13
5.2	Trailside rocks, Chair Rocks to west	7,745	22.0	462.6	480,693	4,361,700	13
6.0	Cross Raleigh Peak Road	7,691	22.8	461.8	479,996	4,361,244	13
7.3	Cross old jeep road	7,613	24.1	460.5	479,319	4,359,731	13
10.1	Left on single-track along road	7,622	26.9	457.7	478,845	4,356,741	13
10.4	Cross paved County Rd 126	7,675	27.2	457.4	478,666	4,356,299	13
11.5	End Segment 2	7,834	28.3	456.3	477,783	4,355,124	13

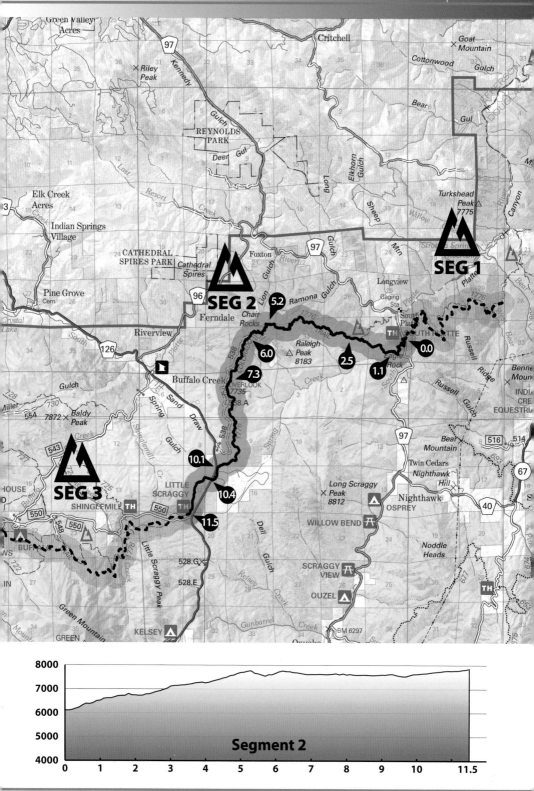

Segment 2

Segment 3: Little Scraggy Trailhead to Rolling Creek Trailhead

Granite outcrops good for camping and photo ops.

PHOTO BY BILL MANNING

Distance: 12.2 miles

Elevation gain: Approx. 1,975 feet

Elevation loss: Approx. 1,549 feet

USFS map: Pike National Forest, pages 84–85

The Colorado Trail Databook 6: pages 14–15

The CT Map Book: pages 11–13

National Geographic Trails Illustrated maps: Nos. 105, 135

Jurisdiction: South Platte Ranger District, Pike National Forest

Access from Denver end:

Access from Durango end: 🚗

Availability of water: ☕

Bicycling: 🚲

"The trailhead on FS Rd 550 now charges a parking fee, so plan for that."

This has become a popular trailhead, especially on weekends and with mountain bikers. For the $5 daily use fee, a toilet and picnic tables are provided, but there is no water available.

Gudy's TIP

ABOUT THIS SEGMENT

Segment 3 is very popular with mountain bikers and day-hikers due to its proximity to Denver. The pine and fir forests, along with many small creeks, make this segment quite inviting. In addition, winter snow usually melts by early spring, allowing for this segment to be accessible earlier than many of the higher portions of the CT. Thru-hikers will appreciate the plentiful water sources and shaded portions of the trail after making it through the previous segment, which is very dry and often brutally hot. While most of this section is relatively flat, the climbs should not be taken for granted, especially considering the trail eclipses the 8,000-foot mark at the end of the segment.

The beginning of Segment 3 has a parking lot and bathroom. There is a parking fee.

PHOTO BY JULIE VIDA AND MARK TABB

TRAILHEAD/ACCESS POINTS

Little Scraggy Trailhead on FS Rd 550:
Drive southwest from Denver on US Hwy 285 for approximately 32 miles to Pine Junction (it has a traffic light). Turn left (southeast) on Jefferson County Rd 126 (Pine Valley Road) and proceed through the hamlets of Pine and Buffalo Creek. Continue 4 miles past the bridge over the South Platte River in Buffalo Creek to the intersection with FS Rd 550. This intersection is also 1 mile past Spring Creek Road. Turn right (west) on FS Rd 550 and drive 0.1 mile to the parking area. The Colorado Trail trailhead is at the northwest end of the parking area. To park you must pay a fee.

Rolling Creek Trailhead: See Segment 4 on page 86.

SERVICES, SUPPLIES, AND ACCOMMODATIONS

These amenities are available in Buffalo Creek, see Segment 2 on page 74, and in Bailey, see Segment 4 on page 86.

TRAIL DESCRIPTION

Segment 3 begins at the Little Scraggy Trailhead next to the interpretive display at the northwest end of the parking area, **mile 0.0** (7,834 feet). Head west on the trail. The CT and side trails in Segment 3 are part of the Buffalo Creek trails network popular with mountain bicyclists. At **mile 0.6** (7,855), the trail crosses FS Rd 550, then rolls before dropping slightly to a small intermittent stream at **mile 1.3** (7,813) and, beyond, a small campsite on the left side of the trail.

The trail crosses the Shingle Mill Trail at **mile 1.9** (7,795), then crosses another small intermittent stream with marginal camping at **mile 2.1** (7,746). At **mile 2.8** (7,709), where there's an abandoned jeep trail, cross a stream, then cross another stream at **mile 3.4** (7,760). Cross Tramway Creek at **mile 5.1** (7,797), where there are some good campsites, and take a left at the Tramway Trail at **mile 5.6** (7,681). Intersect the Green Mountain Trail and take a right at **mile 6.3** (7,645). Cross a small stream at **mile 6.4** (7,592). From here, the trail descends slightly to an intersection at **mile 7.0** (7,516) with a trail that leads to Buffalo Creek Campground, a fee area about a quarter-mile north. Go straight through this intersection and continue on to another intersection at **mile 7.5** (7,441), this time following the CT to the right.

At **mile 7.6** (7,405), cross Meadows Group Campground Road, then go through a gate and veer left at **mile 7.7** (7,364). (For Buffalo Creek Trailhead go right 0.2 mile.) After a nice walk along Buffalo Creek to a bridge, cross it and FS Rd 543 at **mile 8.0** (7,391). Turn left at an intersection with Redskin Creek Trail at **mile 8.3** (7,448). At **mile 9.1** (7,900) there

Aspen alight in the early morning.
PHOTO BY MORGAN AND ROBYN WILKINSON

is a dry campsite. Ahead is a rifle range south of the trail and it's common to hear shots; stay on the trail. The trail climbs to **mile 9.6** (7,930), where it crosses the road to Buffalo Creek Gun Club. At **mile 11.9** (8,127), cross a small stream where there's good camping. After a short but steep climb, arrive at FS Rd 560 (Wellington Lake Road) and Rolling Creek Trailhead, the end of Segment 3 at **mile 12.2** (8,279).

Mountain Biking

Bicyclists, the trail user group that travels the fastest, have sometimes been singled out, especially for their potentially startling interaction with other users. IMBA, the International Mountain Bicycling Association, has been a leader in making recommendations for responsible riding, including these useful tips:

▲ **Yield to Others and Pass with Courtesy:** Mountain bikers should yield to hikers and equestrians. Slow down when approaching other trail users and respectfully make others aware you are approaching. Pass with care and be prepared to stop if necessary.

▲ **Equestrians:** Because horses can spook easily and the chance for injury is high, use extra caution around equestrians. If you want to pass a horse, establish voice contact with the rider. Begin speaking with something like, "cyclists here, may we pass?" Your voice can calm both horse and rider, helping prevent horses from being spooked. Be prepared to stop until asked to proceed.

▲ **Ride Slowly on Crowded Trails:** Just like a busy highway, when trails are crowded you must move slowly to ensure safety for all trail users.

▲ **Say No to Mud:** Riding a muddy trail can cause unnecessary trail widening and erosion that may lead to long-lasting damage.

▲ **Respect the Trail, Wildlife, and Environment:** Be sensitive to the trail and its surroundings by riding softly and never skidding. Skidding through turns or while braking loosens trail soil and fosters trail erosion.

Trail users and the Forest Service have collaborated to establish a network of trails popular with cyclists on and around Segment 3 of the CT. The trail system is called the Buffalo Creek Recreation Area. For information and trail map, see the website for the Front Range Mountain Bike Patrol, frmbp.org. For information on IMBA, visit its website at imba.com or phone (303) 545-9011.

Cyclists enjoy an extensive network of side trails in Segment 3.

PHOTO BY PETER MORALES

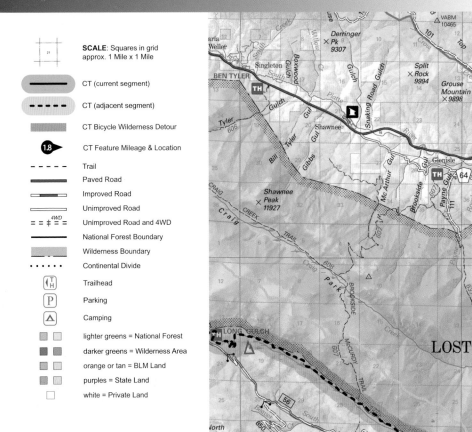

SCALE: Squares in grid approx. 1 Mile x 1 Mile

CT (current segment)

CT (adjacent segment)

CT Bicycle Wilderness Detour

1.8 CT Feature Mileage & Location

Trail

Paved Road

Improved Road

Unimproved Road

Unimproved Road and 4WD

National Forest Boundary

Wilderness Boundary

Continental Divide

Trailhead

Parking

Camping

lighter greens = National Forest

darker greens = Wilderness Area

orange or tan = BLM Land

purples = State Land

white = Private Land

SEGMENT 3 FEATURES TABLE Pike National Forest

Mileage	Features & Comments	Elevation (feet)	Mileage from Denver	Mileage to Durango	UTM-E	UTM-N (NAD83)	Zone
0.0	Begin Segment 3	7,834	28.3	456.3	477,783	4,355,124	13
0.6	Cross FS Rd 550	7,855	28.9	455.7	477,117	4,354,829	13
1.9	Cross Shingle Mill Trail	7,795	30.2	454.4	475,591	4,354,778	13
2.8	Cross stream	7,709	31.1	453.5	475,402	4,353,638	13
5.1	Cross Tramway Creek	7,797	33.4	451.2	473,709	4,353,530	13
5.6	Take sharp left at Tramway Trail	7,681	33.9	450.7	473,322	4,353,875	13
6.3	Go right at Green Mountain Trail	7,645	34.6	450.0	472,598	4,353,856	13
7.0	Pass trail to Buffalo Creek Campground on right	7,516	35.3	449.3	471,694	4,354,181	13
7.5	Stay right	7,441	35.8	448.8	471,187	4,354,505	13
7.6	Cross Meadows Group Campground Rd	7,405	35.9	448.7	470,946	4,354,572	13
8.0	Cross creek on bridge then FS Rd 543	7,391	36.3	448.3	470,682	4,354,577	13
8.3	Go left at intersection	7,448	36.6	448.0	470,526	4,354,688	13
9.6	Cross gun club road, stay on trail	7,930	37.9	446.7	468,473	4,354,753	13
11.9	Cross small stream	8,127	40.2	444.4	465,855	4,354,444	13
12.2	End Segment 3	8,279	40.5	444.1	465,429	4,354,406	13

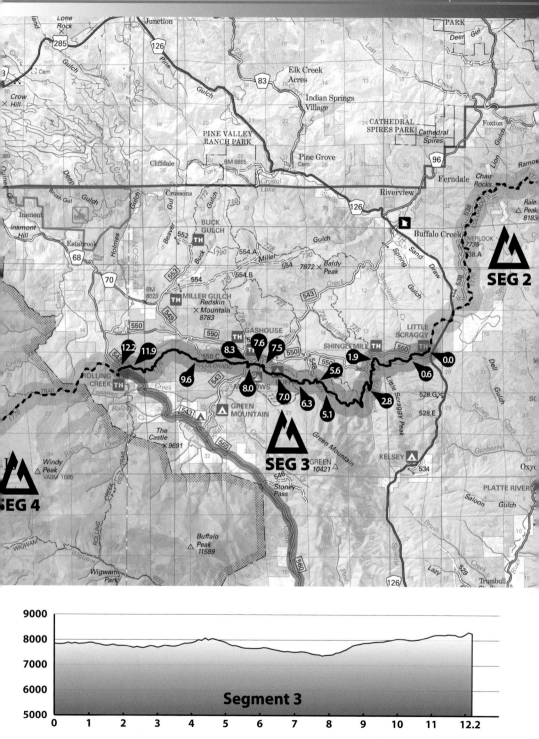

Segment 4: Rolling Creek Trailhead to Long Gulch

Looking east down Long Gulch.
PHOTO BY JULIE VIDA AND MARK TABB

Distance: 16.6 miles

Elevation gain: Approx. 3,271 feet

Elevation loss: Approx. 1,373 feet

USFS map: Pike National Forest, pages 92–93

The Colorado Trail Databook 6: pages 16–17

The CT Map Book: pages 13–15

National Geographic Trails Illustrated map: No. 105

Jurisdiction: South Park and South Platte Ranger Districts, Pike National Forest

Access from Denver end:

Access from Durango end: 🚗

Availability of water: ☕

Bicycling: 🚲 See pages 90–91

"Segments 1 through 3 and Segment 5 see heavy use by day-hikers and cyclists. You'll find peace and solitude in the Lost Creek Wilderness Area."

This is the first of six designated wilderness areas the CT passes through on its 486-mile route. Review the wilderness regulations on page 42; especially note that bicycles are prohibited and dogs should be leashed.

Gudy's TIP

ABOUT THIS SEGMENT

Segment 4 enters the Lost Creek Wilderness Area shortly after the trail leaves the main parking area and trailhead. Because of that, mountain bikers have to begin the long, mandatory detour to Rock Creek. At mile 1.5 the trail passes out of Pikes Peak granite and back into metamorphic rocks. There are abundant water sources and a lot of potential campsites along this section. The meadows along the North Fork of Lost Creek are great places to spot wildlife, including deer and bears. Be sure to keep your eyes and ears open! Many volunteers have helped build bridges and fill in boggy sections of the trail near the head of the meadow system. If you see a trail crew in the area, please thank them for their efforts.

TRAILHEAD/ACCESS POINTS

FS Rd 560/Rolling Creek Trailhead: 🚗 Drive west from Denver on US Hwy 285 for about 39 miles to Bailey. Turn left and head southeast on Park County Rd 68 (the main intersection in town) that eventually turns into FS Rd 560 (Wellington Lake Road). After about 5 miles, you come to a Y in the road. Take the right branch, which continues as FS Rd 560. Two miles farther on, take the right fork again (still FS Rd 560). Continue another mile to Rolling Creek Trailhead, a small parking area on the right. Drive slowly; it is easy to miss. A small road goes a short distance southwest to another small parking area.

North Fork Trailhead: 🚙 This trailhead is remote and the last 4 miles of the road are seldom used (except during hunting season). It is suitable only for four-wheel-drive vehicles with high clearance. Drive southwest from Denver on US Hwy 285 for 58 miles to Kenosha Pass. Continue another 3.2 miles to a gravel side road on the left marked Lost Park Road (Jefferson County Rd 56 and later FS Rd 56). Proceed a little more than 16 miles to a side road (FS Rd 134) that branches to the left and starts to climb. Follow it about 4 miles to its end. The CT is just a short walk across the valley on the other side of the stream. The

Hiking west in Long Gulch, an open meadow that extends for nearly seven miles.
PHOTO BY BERNIE KRAUSSE

Brookside-McCurdy Trail comes into the trailhead from the southeast and joins the CT, going northwest along it for a couple of miles, then exiting to the north.

Lost Park Campground Access: An alternate way to the North Fork Trailhead in a two-wheel-drive vehicle is to pass by the left turn to FS Road 134 and continue on FS Rd 56 four more miles to its end at Lost Park Campground. Walk north on the Brookside-McCurdy Trail 1.7 miles, joining the CT at the North Fork Trailhead.

Long Gulch Trailhead: See Segment 5 on page 94.

SERVICES, SUPPLIES, AND ACCOMMODATIONS – BAILEY

Bailey, west of Denver on busy US Hwy 285 (approximately 8 miles northwest of the Rolling Creek Trailhead using FS Rd 560 and Park County Rd 68, has a small business center.

Distance from CT: 8 miles
Elevation: 7,750 feet
Zip code: 80421
Area code: 303

Dining,
several places including:
RiverBend Taproom
Eatery & Market
60006 US Hwy 285
(303) 816-9406

Coney Island
10 Old Stage Coach Rd.
(303) 838-4210

Hog Heaven Bar-B-Que
63658 US Hwy 285
(303) 838-8814

Rustic Station
1 Co Rd 68
(303) 838-1246

Gear
(possibly including fuel canisters)
Knotty Pine
60641 US Hwy 285
(303) 838-5679

Groceries
(convenience-store type)
Conoco Bailey Self-Service
US Hwy 285
(303) 838-5170

Info
Chamber of Commerce
PO Box 477
(303) 838-9080

Laundry
Sudz Laundromat
Near US Hwy 285
(303) 838-4809

Lodging
Lynwood Park B&B and Hostel
59786 S US Hwy 285
(303) 838-4243

Bailey Lodge & Cutthroat Cafe
US Hwy 285
(303) 838-2450

Post Office
Bailey Post Office
24 River Dr.
(800) 275-8777

TRAIL DESCRIPTION

Segment 4 begins along FS Rd 560, Rolling Creek Trailhead, **mile 0.0** (8,279 feet), where there's a small parking area and sign. Go west on the jeep road to another small parking area at **mile 0.3** (8,354), where there is an information display and trail register. The Colorado Trail is on the right side of the parking area and heads in a northwesterly direction. At **mile 1.0** (8,527), take a left when the trail joins an old logging road. After passing a fence, where there is a possible dry campsite, continue uphill to **mile 1.9** (9,016),

Volunteers improve one of many boggy sections in Long Gulch.

PHOTO BY CHUCK LAWSON

where the trail enters the Lost Creek Wilderness Area. As with all wilderness areas, bikes and motorized vehicles are not permitted. Expect none of the triangular CT confidence markers you're used to seeing, as reassurance markers are not allowed in Wilderness.

There are small seasonal streams, including one at **mile 2.4** (9,146), and potential campsites in the next two miles. Intersect the Payne Creek Trail on the right at **mile 3.3** (9,307) and continue straight ahead. Cross the headwaters of Craig Creek at **mile 4.5** (9,375). There are good campsites nearby. At **mile 5.6** (9,897), reach an intersection where the trail leaves the old road. Take a left onto the single-track trail and begin a steep climb. Reaching a saddle at **mile 7.4** (10,483), the trail rejoins the old road, begins descending, and crosses a small spring at **mile 8.0** (10,343), then leaves the wilderness area at **mile 8.2** (10,314). After entering a large, grassy valley, follow the North Fork of Lost Creek upstream. There are many potential campsites along the way.

The Brookside-McCurdy Trail joins The Colorado Trail at **mile 8.9** (10,199) by a trail register. Then at **mile 9.2** (10,249) cross a seasonal stream. At **mile 11.3** (10,428), the Brookside-McCurdy Trail goes to the right, while the CT bears to the left. Leave the valley

at **mile 14.5** (10,929) and enter the forest at the head of the North Fork of Lost Creek. The trail descends steeply from here. After crossing a small stream at **mile 16.5** (10,200), hike a short distance to an intersection with Long Gulch Trail above FS Rd 56 at **mile 16.6** (10,176) and the end of Segment 4. For trailhead parking, take Long Gulch Trail 0.2 mile downhill (south).

Mules are loaded with heavy culverts that volunteers will install to help keep the trail dry.

PHOTO BY CHUCK LAWSON

The Hayman Fire

Beginning in a campfire circle on the morning of June 8, 2002, the Hayman Fire quickly escaped to become the largest wildfire in Colorado's recorded history. Drought conditions, high winds, and record hot weather spurred the blaze, which burned nearly 138,000 acres over three weeks. The fire destroyed 133 homes and cost nearly $40 million. The fire leapt highways, clear-cuts, and prescribed burn areas, pushing into the heavy underbrush and timber in the southern portion of the Lost Creek Wilderness Area, stopping just a few miles short of the CT. Thus, CT hikers will see little evidence of this catastrophe. But mountain bikers, who have to bypass to the south of the wilderness on Forest Service roads, will see firsthand nature's fury. Campers in the wilderness are reminded to use a stove and forgo building fires.

Lost Creek Wilderness Bicycle Detour

This long, mandatory bike detour in Segments 4 and 5 bypasses the Lost Creek Wilderness Area to the south. A shorter detour north of the wilderness exists, following US Highway 285, but cyclists have reported the uphill and curvy ride as dangerous due to the almost nonexistent shoulder and fast speeds of sometimes-inattentive automobilists.

Riders begin this detour at the end of Segment 3, mile 12.2, next to the Rolling Creek Trailhead. At **mile 0.0** (8,279), turn southeast and follow Wellington Lake Rd, County Rd 68 (sometimes known as FS Rd 560, gravel). Alongside Wellington Lake at an intersection at **mile 2.8** (8,038), continue straight toward Stoney Pass onto FS Rd 560 (Stoney Pass Road, gravel). At **mile 3.8** (8,079), cross a stream. At **mile 5.2** (8,575), reach the top of Stoney Pass.

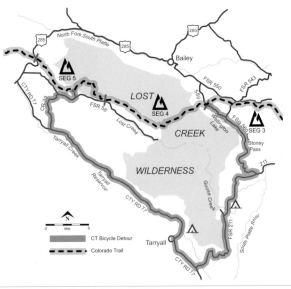

At **mile 8.1** (7,919), cross a stream, and another at **mile 8.6** (7,919). At **mile 9.7** (8,224), continue straight ahead, ignoring FS Rd 545 fork on the right. At an intersection with FS Rd 541 at **mile 12.0** (7,495), go left (east), staying on FS Rd 560.

At **mile 13.6** (7,475), leave FS Rd 560, take sharp right (west) onto FS Rd 211 (Matukat Rd, gravel). At **mile 18.8** (7,556), cross a stream. At **mile 19.0** (7,621), turn right continuing on FS Rd 211, ignoring the left fork to Lost Valley Ranch. At **mile 21.8** (7,716), cross Goose Creek. After about 0.1 mile, pass the road to Goose Creek Campground on the right (fee, potable water, toilet). At **mile 35.6** (8,291), pass a private campground.

Riders in Segment 3 prior to the Lost Creek detour.
PHOTO BY JESSE SWIFT AND BILL TURNER

At **mile 35.9** (8,226), from FS Rd 211, turn right (northwest) onto County Rd 77 (Tarryall Rd, paved). At **mile 41.0** (8,701), cycle through the nearly abandoned town of Tarryall. At **mile 49.4** (8,751) is a junction to Outpost Wilderness Adventure Camp (owa.com, potential for bunkhouse lodging). At **mile 54.1** (8,884), cycle past Tarryall Reservoir. At **mile 63.0** (9,223), turn right onto Park County Rd 39 (gravel). At **mile 68.7** (9,560), turn right (east) onto Lost Park Rd (FS Rd 56, gravel). At **mile 70.8** (9,520), at a sign for

Approaching FS 560 and the Lost Creek detour.
PHOTO BY BILL MANNING

the CT and Rock Creek Trailhead, turn left (northwest) onto FS Rd 133 (dirt). At **mile 71.6** (9,726), cyclists rejoin CT Segment 5 at mile 8.0 near Rock Creek Trailhead. The trailhead parking is north of the CT less than 0.1 mile.

SCALE: Squares in grid approx. 1 Mile x 1 Mile

CT (current segment)

CT (adjacent segment)

CT Bicycle Wilderness Detour

CT Feature Mileage & Location

Trail

Paved Road

Improved Road

Unimproved Road

Unimproved Road and 4WD

National Forest Boundary

Wilderness Boundary

Continental Divide

Trailhead

Parking

Camping

lighter greens = National Forest

darker greens = Wilderness Area

orange or tan = BLM Land

purples = State Land

white = Private Land

SEGMENT 4 FEATURES TABLE Pike National Forest

Mileage	Features & Comments	Elevation (feet)	Mileage from Denver	Mileage to Durango	UTM-E	UTM-N (NAD83)	Zone
0.0	Begin Segment 4	8,279	40.5	444.1	465,429	4,354,406	13
0.3	Road ends, go right onto trail	8,354	40.8	443.8	465,294	4,354,122	13
1.0	Go left on old logging road	8,527	41.5	443.1	464,474	4,354,588	13
1.9	Enter Lost Creek Wilderness	9,016	42.4	442.2	463,618	4,353,766	13
3.3	Pass Payne Creek Trail on right	9,307	43.8	440.8	461,803	4,353,395	13
5.6	Turn left onto single-track trail	9,897	46.1	438.5	459,175	4,351,669	13
7.4	Top of saddle, rejoin old road	10,483	47.9	436.7	457,542	4,350,771	13
8.2	Exit Lost Creek Wilderness	10,314	48.7	435.9	456,422	4,351,041	13
8.9	Brookside-McCurdy Trail joins CT for the next 2 miles	10,199	49.4	435.2	455,590	4,350,933	13
11.3	Brookside-McCurdy Trail exits CT to the right	10,428	51.8	432.8	452,524	4,352,903	13
14.5	Head of North Fork of Lost Creek	10,929	55.0	429.6	448,413	4,355,450	13
16.6	End Segment 4	10,176	57.1	427.5	446,882	4,355,620	13

Segment 5: Long Gulch to Kenosha Pass

South Park near the west end of Segment 5 offers expansive views and fall color.

COURTESY OF THE COLORADO TRAIL FOUNDATION

Distance: 14.6 miles

Elevation gain: Approx. 1,858 feet

Elevation loss: Approx. 2,055 feet

USFS map: Pike National Forest, pages 98–99

The Colorado Trail Databook 6: pages 18–19

The CT Map Book: pages 15–17

National Geographic Trails Illustrated map: No. 105

Jurisdiction: South Platte and South Park Ranger Districts, Pike National Forest

Access from Denver end:

Access from Durango end:

Availability of water:

Bicycling: See page 90–91

"Between Black Canyon and Kenosha Pass, stop to take in the incredible vistas of South Park and the mountainous backdrop."

South Park is a fault-bounded basin filled with sedimentary rocks that date from the time of the Ancestral Rocky Mountains and Cretaceous seaway. These rocks are overlain with younger sediments deposited during erosion of the mountains formed during the Laramide Orogeny. In this segment, you get your first look at the Continental Divide, dominated by a lofty pyramid, Mount Guyot (pronounced gee-oh). Note Georgia Pass, the low point to the right of Mount Guyot, where the CT first enters the alpine ecosystem before crossing the Great Divide in Segment 6.

Gudy's TIP

ABOUT THIS SEGMENT

The trees are one of the highlights of Segment 5. The trail passes through several spectacular stands of aspen, a species that shares extensive root systems that produce colonies that can live thousands of years. The CT also passes by bristlecone pines. This five-needled pine lives at high elevations, and despite the poor soil and long winters, hearty individual bristlecones can live up to 5,000 years. If you are not familiar with the trees along the CT, be sure to bring a guidebook specifically for this section. Toward the end of the segment, views of the Continental Divide open up, giving thru-hikers a good idea of the change in terrain to come.

TRAILHEAD/ACCESS POINTS

Long Gulch Trail Access: 🚗 Drive west from Denver on US Hwy 285 for about 60 miles to Kenosha Pass. Continue another 3.2 miles to a turnoff on the left side of the road marked Lost Park Road. Follow this road for 11 miles. Look for a gully on the left side and a road marked FS Rd 817. Drive or walk up this road for 0.1 mile to its end at the very small Long Gulch Trailhead. Walk a short distance up the gully to the Forest Service register. Angle slightly to the right and follow the access trail to its intersection with the CT.

Rock Creek Trailhead (FS Rd 133): 🚗 Follow the aforementioned Long Gulch Trail instructions to Lost Park Road. Drive 7.5 miles on Lost Park Road to a primitive road that branches off to the left, FS Rd 133. Follow this uphill 1.2 miles to the intersection with the CT where there's a small parking area just beyond on the right.

Kenosha Pass Trailhead: 🚗 See Segment 6 on page 100.

Mid-June snowpack lies ahead at Georgia Pass.
PHOTO BY BERNARD WOLF

SERVICES, SUPPLIES, AND ACCOMMODATIONS

The town of Jefferson is approximately 4.5 miles southwest of Kenosha Pass on US Hwy 285. See Segment 6 on pages 100–109.

TRAIL DESCRIPTION

A hiker in Segment 5 has a broad view of the Continental Divide to the west.

PHOTO BY ANDREW SKURKA

NOTE: This description begins at the trailhead parking area and sign just off Lost Park Road. A side trail, marked as the Long Gulch Trail, goes 0.2 mile up the hillside to intersect The Colorado Trail. Thru-hikers will not encounter this trailhead unless they make a specific detour to it.

From the trailhead, cross the creek on a small bridge and go uphill for 0.2 mile to the CT, **mile 0.0** (10,176 feet). Westbound hikers will turn left at this well-marked intersection. There is a good campsite near here, with water available from the fast-moving creek. Cross the creek about 300 feet past the intersection. The trail enters the Lost Creek Wilderness Area at **mile 0.3** (10,263). Then at **mile 1.6** (10,380) it heads through a mixed aspen-fir forest with some bristlecone pines. Cross a seasonal stream at **mile 2.9** (10,366). There is a good campsite nearby. Cross a marshy area at **mile 3.1** (10,387) and streams at **mile 3.9** (10,347) and **mile 4.5** (10,258). There is another creek at **mile 5.3** (10,174) with several good campsites.

The CT leaves the Lost Creek Wilderness Area at **mile 6.6** (9,816) and crosses Rock Creek at **mile 7.3** (9,534) where users should refill their bottles. Turn left when intersecting the Ben Tyler Trail at **mile 7.4** (9,519). Ranch buildings are visible ahead. Pass through a Forest Service gate at **mile 7.6** (9,555), continue to the Rock Creek Trailhead at **mile 8.0** (9,726), and cross the road. Cross Johnson Gulch and a small, seasonal stream at **mile 8.4** (9,521). This possible water source is the last until Kenosha Pass and there's room to camp.

Just past the stream, the CT crosses a jeep road and eventually passes through a stand of large aspen trees. At **mile 10.6** (9,956) continue straight on the CT at a T road intersection. There are great views of the mountains to the south and west and toward the town of Jefferson. The trail eventually reaches a parking area at **mile 14.4** (10,010). It continues to the left, and after crossing US Hwy 285, reaches the end of Segment 5 at **mile 14.6** (9,969).

Lost Creek Wilderness Area

The name Lost Creek conjures up an image of an enigmatic place. And indeed, this 119,790-acre wilderness area has a fascinating history of lost gold, vanished dreams, and hidden places.

Lost Creek begins in the open meadows of Lost Park, sandwiched between the granite knobs of the Kenosha and Tarryall mountains. The last native bison killed in Colorado fell in Lost Park in 1897. From here the creek descends into a deeply etched canyon, vanishing among tumbled boulders and underground tunnels, and reappearing nine times. The "lost" stream eventually re-emerges as Goose Creek at the southeast end of the wilderness area.

More than a century ago, the notorious Reynolds Gang terrorized nearby South Park, holding up stagecoaches and lone riders for their gold. The stories vary, but some say the gang stashed their lost cache in Handcart Gulch, north of Kenosha Pass, while others claim it is hidden among the strange granite outcrops that dot the hills above Lost Park, a frequent hideout for the gang.

Dreamers often vanished into the recesses of Lost Creek looking for riches. Both the Lost Jackman Mine and the Indian Mine were supposed to be fabulously rich in gold; but if they ever existed at all, they are lost forever to time.

Perhaps the most ambitious scheme was an early twentieth-century attempt to build an unusual subterranean dam on Goose Creek, which would have flooded a major valley, to

The entrance to the Lost Creek Wilderness Area near the beginning of Segment 5.
PHOTO BY LAWTON "DISCO" GRINTER

meet the water needs of Denver.

Fortunately, this effort failed, and Denver citizens have benefited more by having this magnificent wilderness preserved at their doorstep.

The Lost Creek Wilderness Area was established in 1980. Despite heavy use by recreationalists, there are still some unexplored corners and hidden places in the Lost Creek. In the early 1990s, prolific peak-bagger Bob Martin frequently visited the area in his quest to climb every peak in Colorado over 11,000 feet. He discovered a half-dozen remote "eleveners" tucked away in the wilderness area without signs of previous ascent. He reports that most were difficult scrambles, some requiring the assistance of a rope.

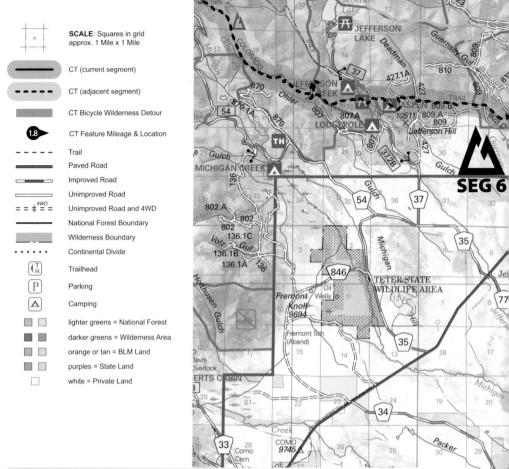

SCALE: Squares in grid approx. 1 Mile x 1 Mile

— CT (current segment)

- - - - CT (adjacent segment)

CT Bicycle Wilderness Detour

1.8 CT Feature Mileage & Location

- - - - Trail

Paved Road

Improved Road

Unimproved Road

Unimproved Road and 4WD

National Forest Boundary

Wilderness Boundary

· · · · · Continental Divide

Trailhead

Parking

Camping

lighter greens = National Forest

darker greens = Wilderness Area

orange or tan = BLM Land

purples = State Land

white = Private Land

SEG 6

SEGMENT 5 FEATURES TABLE   Pike National Forest

Mileage	Features & Comments	Elevation (feet)	Mileage from Denver	Mileage to Durango	UTM-E	UTM-N (NAD83)	Zone
0.0	Begin Segment 5	10,176	57.1	427.5	446,882	4,355,620	13
0.3	Enter Lost Creek Wilderness	10,263	57.4	427.2	446,494	4,355,578	13
2.9	Cross seasonal stream	10,366	60.0	424.6	445,292	4,357,257	13
3.1	Cross marshy area	10,387	60.2	424.4	445,247	4,357,475	13
3.9	Cross seasonal stream	10,347	61.0	423.6	444,712	4,358,504	13
4.5	Cross seasonal stream	10,258	61.6	423.0	444,333	4,358,566	13
5.3	Cross creek	10,174	62.4	422.2	443,443	4,359,029	13
6.6	Exit Lost Creek Wilderness	9,816	63.7	420.9	441,738	4,357,965	13
7.3	Cross Rock Creek	9,534	64.4	420.2	441,104	4,357,452	13
7.4	Left at junction with Ben Tyler Trail	9,519	64.5	420.1	441,079	4,357,404	13
7.6	Pass through gate, turn right	9,555	64.7	419.9	441,333	4,357,157	13
8.0	Cross road at Rock Creek Trailhead	9,726	65.1	419.5	440,776	4,357,207	13
8.4	Cross Johnson Gulch	9,521	65.5	419.1	440261	4,357,095	13
14.4	Go left at parking area	10,010	71.5	413.1	435,018	4,362,945	13
14.6	End Segment 5	9,969	71.7	412.9	434,724	4,362,829	13

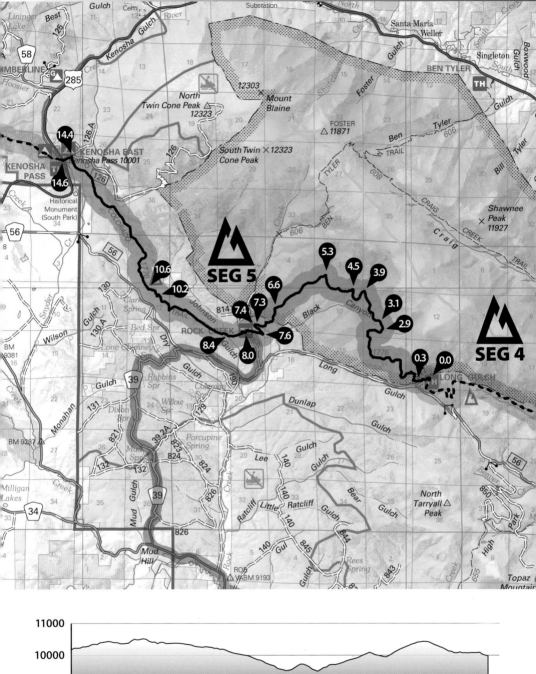

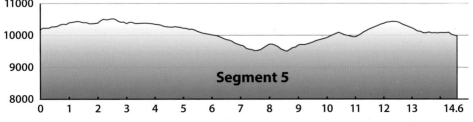

Segment 5

Kenosha Pass to Mount Massive Trailhead (Segments 6–10)

Segment 6: Kenosha Pass to Gold Hill Trailhead

Distance: 32.7 miles

Elevation gain: Approx. 5,196 feet

Elevation loss: Approx. 5,968 feet

USFS maps: Pike and White River National Forests, see pages 108–109

The Colorado Trail Databook 6: pages 20–23

The CT Map Book: pages 17–20

National Geographic Trails Illustrated maps: Nos. 104, 105, 108, 109

Latitude 40° map: Summit County Trails

Jurisdiction: South Park and Dillon Ranger Districts, Pike and White River National Forests

Access from Denver end:

Access from Durango end:

Availability of water: 🥤

Bicycling: 🚲

A cyclist pedals through golden aspen west of Kenosha Pass.

PHOTO BY NICK WILDE

"If you decide to take the old, shorter CT route down the Swan River Road, be forewarned that it is very dusty and unpleasant for hiking. The new official CT route is a much more enjoyable experience."

Unless you're in a big hurry, stay on the new CT route, which offers water, campsites, and a secluded walk through the woods.

Gudy's TIP

ABOUT THIS SEGMENT

Segment 6 is the longest segment on The Colorado Trail. Along its 32.7 miles, it reaches the Continental Divide, passes through several distinct watersheds, runs along a ridge near Keystone Ski Resort, and ends in the resort town of Breckenridge. There are lots of good places to camp near the major streams and many other potential campsites between water sources and near small streams.

There are great views to the south and north when crossing Georgia Pass atop the Divide, and southbound users first encounter the sometimes co-located Continental Divide National Scenic Trail (CDNST), with which the CT shares a total of 234.8 miles in two lengthy sections.

It is not uncommon to encounter snowdrifts above tree line well into July, so be prepared. In addition to snow, summer thunderstorms can move in quickly and catch people off guard. Keep track of the time and weather conditions when heading into alpine areas. At mile 25.3 the CT crosses from metamorphic basement rocks into black shale deposited in the Cretaceous seaway. The two types of rock are separated by the Elkhorn Mountain thrust, a Laramide fault along which the basement rocks have been carried westward more than 5 miles across the younger shale. The same fault forms the eastern margin of South Park.

The Middle and North forks of the Swan River have several great campsites, but this part of the trail is accessible to motor vehicles via the roads near the rivers. Keep this in

The view toward Georgia Pass and the Continental Divide at the beginning of Segment 6.
PHOTO BY MORGAN AND ROBYN WILKINSON

mind when choosing campsites because there may be other folks there as well.

The last few miles of Segment 6 go through large areas where trees have been killed by mountain pine beetles and the character has changed dramatically. Fire suppression and relatively warm winters have aided the beetles in proliferating and wreaking havoc. To reduce the risk of dead trees falling on trail users, authorities have cut down many of the trees along the trail corridor. Cut trees remain on the ground in many of the open areas, but these landscapes have begun to revegetate nicely.

Evening light over South Park after a rainy day.
PHOTO BY MICK GIGONE

TRAILHEAD/ACCESS POINTS

Kenosha Pass Trailhead: From Denver, drive southwest on US Hwy 285 for about 58 miles to Kenosha Pass. Kenosha Pass Campground is on the right and the Kenosha Pass Picnic Area can be seen on the left side of the highway, back in the trees. Both are fee areas. You may park alongside the highway, however, without paying the fee. The beginning of Segment 6 is on the righthand (northwest) side of the highway, just past the turn-in to the campground. The CT is visible from the highway, proceeding into the forest in a northwesterly direction. Water is available in the campground from a hand pump, after payment of the fee.

Jefferson Lake Road Access: This access requires a fee payment. From Kenosha Pass, continue southwest on US Hwy 285 for 4.5 miles to the town of Jefferson.

Turn right on Jefferson Lake Road. Drive 2.1 miles to an intersection. Turn right and proceed about a mile to the fee collection point. Continue 2.1 miles to where the CT crosses the road. A small parking area is 0.1 mile farther on the left. Another larger parking area is 0.6 mile down the road, near the Jefferson Lake Campground.

Georgia Pass Trail Access: Using the driving instructions for the afore-mentioned Jefferson Lake Road access, turn right on Jefferson Lake Road, which is also known as the Michigan Creek Road. After 2.1 miles, where Jefferson Lake Road turns right, continue straight on Michigan Creek Road for 10 miles to Georgia Pass where

there's a parking area. The last 2 miles are a little rough, but most vehicles with reasonable ground clearance can make it. From the pass and parking area, find the CT to the northeast and up a very rough jeep road 0.4 mile.

North Fork of the Swan River Access: From Denver, travel west on I-70 for about 75 miles to exit 203 (Frisco/Breckenridge). Proceed south on CO Hwy 9 for 7 miles to a traffic light at Tiger Road. Turn left on Tiger Road and drive 7 miles to an intersection with the drainage of the North Fork of the Swan River. Turn left on a single-lane road for 0.5 mile to a nice open area, suitable for camping, just before the road enters the forest. The CT comes out of the forest about 100 yards up a drainage on the left side of the road and proceeds north out of the valley up a closed logging road.

One of many small, refreshing creeks in the segment.
PHOTO BY BERNARD WOLF

Middle Fork of the Swan River Access: Follow the aforementioned instruc-tions for the North Fork access until the point where one turns left onto the single-lane road. Instead of turning left, continue straight for a little over a mile, then turn left up the Middle Fork of the Swan. Continue up the Middle Fork for 1.5 miles to the CT crossing. Stay alert because the CT crossing is not obvious.

Gold Hill Trailhead: See Segment 7 on page 110.

TRAIL DESCRIPTION

Segment 6 begins on the west side of Kenosha Pass. There are large parking areas on both sides of the highway. After signing in at the trail register at **mile 0.0** (9,969 feet), continue into the forest where the trail passes under a power line and reaches a ridge shortly afterward with great views to the west. At **mile 1.5** (10,273), cross an old, unused

---

SERVICES, SUPPLIES, AND ACCOMMODATIONS – JEFFERSON

The town of **Jefferson** is approximately 4.5 miles southwest of Kenosha Pass on US Hwy 285. Historically it was a train stop and now has a population of 18 with a tiny market in a 100-year-old building that doubles as the post office.

Distance from CT: 4.5 miles to Jefferson
Elevation: 9,499 feet
Zip code: 80456
Area code: 719

Basic Supplies
The Jefferson Market
38600 US Highway 285
(719) 836-2389

Post Office (limited hours)
51 Crozier St
(719) 836-2238

---

jeep road. After passing through a stand of aspen trees and open meadows, the trail crosses an irrigation ditch at **mile 2.8** (9,920) and FS Rd 809 at **mile 3.0** (9,852). Just past the road, cross Guernsey Creek, a small stream at **mile 3.1** (9,828). There are several good campsites in this area.

The trail continues west toward the Continental Divide. Cross FS Rd 427 at **mile 4.4** (10,161) and Deadman Creek on a bridge at **mile 4.5** (10,164). At **mile 5.0** (10,180) cross a small stream and continue on the trail as it turns left. Gain a saddle and pass through a Forest Service gate at **mile 5.2** (10,262). Cross Jefferson Lake Road

White globeflower near Georgia Pass.
PHOTO BY DAVE JONES

at **mile 5.9** (10,014) and Jefferson Creek at **mile 6.0** (9,975). At **mile 6.1** (9,986) there is an intersection. Take a right on the West Jefferson Trail for 0.1 mile, then go left at the fork at **mile 6.2** (9,983). From here, the climb to Georgia Pass begins.

At **mile 7.8** (10,699), the CT intersects the Michigan Creek Trail. Stay to the right. After the trail leaves a subalpine fir forest and emerges above tree line, pass the Jefferson Creek Trail on the right at **mile 11.7** (11,667) and cross a jeep road at **mile 12.1** (11,838). Be aware of changing weather patterns when above tree line. Reach the top of Georgia Pass and the Continental Divide at **mile 12.3** (11,874).

Descend in a northerly direction. Reach Glacier Creek Road at **mile 12.5** (11,798). This is the point where users first encounter the Continental Divide National Scenic Trail, which comes in from the north. The CT and CDNST are co-located for the next 314 miles (including along the CT Collegiate West) and into Segment 24 where the two trails diverge. Cross the road and descend on single-track as it turns right. After entering the trees, cross an ATV trail at **mile 15.4** (11,135). Keep descending, passing a pond, then a small stream just above the bottom of the canyon. There are good campsites in this area. Cross the bridge over the Middle Fork of the Swan River and go right for 50 feet on Middle Fork Road at **mile 17.1** (10,203). The Colorado Trail diverges left into the woods onto a single-track trail.

The trail crosses a small stream and curves right in the next 2 miles. Reach the North Fork of the Swan River and marshy bottom at about **mile 19.4**, crossing on a raised walkway and bridge, beyond which there is good camping. The trail turns right (east) and then curves left as it follows the perimeter of the camping area. Cross a road at **mile 19.7** (9,981). Go right at an intersection at **mile 20.1** (10,067). From here, the trail begins to climb out of the drainage. Keystone Ski Resort eventually comes into view along the high point of the ridge to the northeast. Where the trail twice intersects the West Ridge Loop Trail (from Keystone Gulch), first at **mile 22.6** (11,114) and then at **mile 23.8** (11,022), stay left. After a long descent on a series of switchbacks, the trail intersects Red Trail at **mile 26.1** (10,035) and goes to the left again.

After dropping into a small valley and passing a power line, take a right at the fork at **mile 27.5** (9,973). Cross Horseshoe Gulch at **mile 28.8** (9,458) and follow the trail as it heads north with camping 0.2 mile ahead. Intersect and go left at Blair Witch Trail at **mile 29.4** (9,458). Intersect and go left at Hippo Trail at **mile 29.7** (9,700). Descending with Breckenridge coming in view, at a switchback intersect Campion Trail at **mile 31.8** (9,240), and go left. Reach neighborhood and pond at **mile 31.9** (9,200). Cross Swan River on a bridge, then cross Revette Drive where one could park for a few hours. At **mile 32.5** (9,203), cross CO Hwy 9 adjacent to where the free Summit Stage bus stops. Go right (north) on bike path, cross Blue River on a bridge, and reach Gold Hill Trailhead at **mile 32.7** (9,197). Follow the bike path for 0.2 mile until reaching the Gold Hill Trailhead on the left and the end of Segment 6 at **mile 32.9** (9,197).

Snow remains through June on the high peaks.   PHOTO BY BERNARD WOLF

Mountain Pine Beetles

On approaching the town of Breckenridge, it becomes apparent there is something amiss with the local forests. The needles of many of the pine trees are red, indicating the trees have died or are dying. Other pines have large popcorn-shaped masses of resin called "pitch tubes." On still others you can see wood dust from boring insects in the crevices of the bark or on the ground at the base of the tree. Some of the trees have foliage that is turning yellow, and eventually will turn red. These all are signs of infestation by the mountain pine beetle (*Dendroctonus ponderosae*), an insect native to Colorado's pine forests.

The beetle is only about the size of a grain of rice and has a one-year life cycle, but it has been able to kill 3.3 million acres of Colorado forest as of 2011. The mountain pine beetle normally attacks trees that are under stress from injury, poor soil conditions, root damage, or old age. In addition to these problems, forests in Colorado and Wyoming have become overcrowded due to fire suppression, enabling the beetles to proliferate and move easily from tree to tree.

The beetle population is normally held in check by cold winter temperatures, but relatively warm winters in recent years have not killed off sufficient amounts of beetles to stop the outbreak, which has been building over the past decade. Now, nearly all of the pine trees in the area are dead or dying. The risk of fire in these tracts of forests is incredibly high and potentially devastating to local communities. Eventually, the dead trees will burn or be blown over in windstorms, thinning out the forests and beginning a new cycle of life in the region.

The Legacy of Two Passes

Sign points to Georgia Pass.
PHOTO BY ANTHONY SLOAN

📷 The Colorado Trail crosses two historic mountain passes in Segment 6. Kenosha Pass, which isn't especially high by Colorado standards, never reaching tree line, has been an important crossing for centuries. It was used by bands of Ute Indians, then white trappers, to reach hunting grounds in South Park. Explorer John C. Fremont crossed the pass in the 1840s. During the Colorado gold rush in the mid-1800s, prospectors used the pass to reach placer diggings around Fairplay.

When a toll road was built to the new diggings, it was stagecoach driver Clark Herbert who named Kenosha Pass after his Wisconsin hometown. The silver boom of the 1870s brought the narrow-gauge tracks of the Denver, South Park & Pacific Railroad through Kenosha Pass. A switchyard was built on its flat meadows. When the tracks were removed in 1937, a modern highway, essentially following the old rail route, was built and continues to bring visitors and commerce over Kenosha Pass into South Park.

With the discovery of gold in 1860 near present-day Breckenridge, miners poured over the Continental Divide at another relatively low point, christening it Georgia Pass. With the coming of the railroad, the wagon road over Georgia Pass fell into disuse, becoming the obscure jeep track that it is today.

Atop Georgia Pass with Mount Guyot behind.
PHOTO BY PETE TURNER

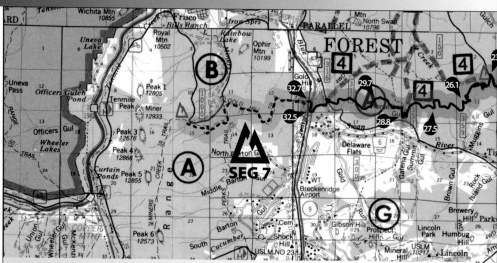

SEGMENT 6 FEATURES TABLE   White River and Pike National Forests

Mileage	Features & Comments	Elevation (feet)	Mileage from Denver	Mileage to Durango	UTM-E	UTM-N (NAD83)	Zone
0.0	Begin Segment 6	9,969	71.7	412.9	434,724	4,362,829	13
1.5	Cross jeep road	10,273	73.2	411.4	432,603	4,363,668	13
3.0	Cross FS Rd 809	9,852	74.7	409.9	431,008	4,364,547	13
3.1	Cross Guernsey Creek	9,828	74.8	409.8	430,950	4,364,524	13
4.4	Cross FS Rd 427	10,161	76.1	408.5	428,883	4,364,683	13
4.5	Cross Deadman Creek	10,164	76.2	408.4	428,671	4,364,711	13
4.9	Go right on jeep road	10,228	76.6	408.0	428,069	4,364,828	13
5.0	Cross small stream, trail turns left	10,180	76.7	407.9	428,095	4,364,805	13
5.9	Cross Jefferson Lake Road	10,014	77.6	407.0	427,277	4,364,791	13
6.0	Cross Jefferson Creek	9,975	77.7	406.9	427,198	4,364,680	13
6.1	Go right on West Jefferson Trail	9,986	77.8	406.8	427,051	4,364,626	13
6.2	Go left at fork	9,983	77.9	406.7	426,967	4,364,744	13
7.8	Stay right at Michigan Creek Trail	10,699	79.5	405.1	425,237	4,364,884	13
11.7	Pass Jefferson Creek Trail on right	11,667	83.4	401.2	422,370	4,367,556	13
12.1	Cross jeep road	11,838	83.8	400.8	421,847	4,367,858	13
12.3	Georgia Pass high point	11,874	84.0	400.6	421,619	4,367,998	13
12.5	Cross Glacier Road, trail curves right	11,798	84.2	400.4	421,696	4,368,342	13
15.4	Cross ATV trail	11,135	87.1	397.5	420,857	4,370,885	13
17.1	Right 50 feet on Middle Fork Road	10,203	88.8	395.8	420,411	4,372,426	13
19.7	Cross North Fk Swan River then road	9,981	91.4	393.2	419,661	4,374,519	13
20.1	Go right at intersection	10,067	91.8	392.8	419,339	4,374,809	13
22.6	Go left at intersection	11,114	94.3	390.3	418,778	4,377,279	13
23.8	Go left at intersection	11,022	95.5	389.1	417,675	4,378,355	13
26.1	Go left at junction with Red Trail	10,035	97.8	386.8	416,521	4,377,391	13
27.5	Go right at fork	9,973	99.2	385.4	415,356	4,377,124	13
28.8	Horseshoe Gulch, left at Blair & Hippo	9,458	100.5	384.1	414,089	4,376,884	13
32.5	Cross CO Hwy 9 then right on path	9,203	104.2	380.4	410,431	4,377,005	13
32.7	End Segment 6	9,197	104.4	380.2	410,455	4,377,354	13

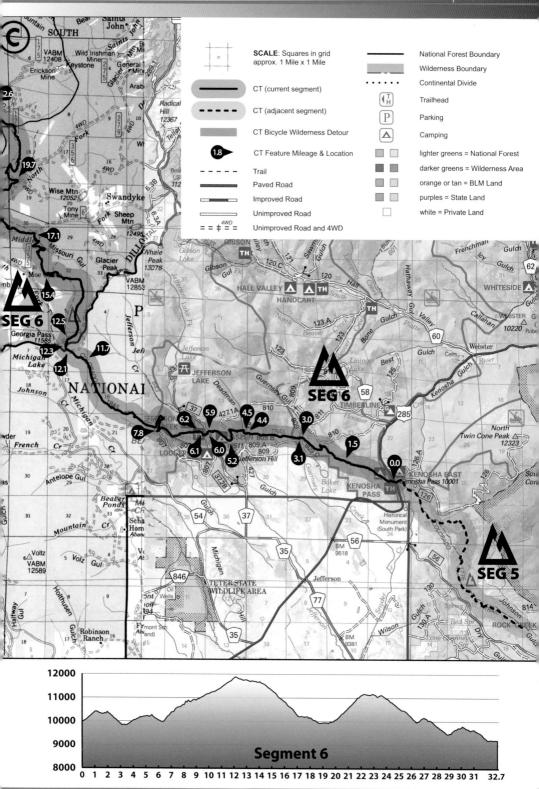

SCALE: Squares in grid approx. 1 Mile x 1 Mile

CT (current segment)

CT (adjacent segment)

CT Bicycle Wilderness Detour

1.8 CT Feature Mileage & Location

Trail

Paved Road

Improved Road

Unimproved Road

Unimproved Road and 4WD

National Forest Boundary

Wilderness Boundary

Continental Divide

Trailhead

Parking

Camping

lighter greens = National Forest

darker greens = Wilderness Area

orange or tan = BLM Land

purples = State Land

white = Private Land

Segment 6

Segment 7: Gold Hill Trailhead to Copper Mountain

An exhilarating view of the Tenmile Range.

PHOTO BY BERNARD WOLF

Distance: 12.8 miles

Elevation gain: Approx. 3,674 feet

Elevation loss: Approx. 3,053 feet

USFS map: White River National Forest, pages 116–117

The Colorado Trail Databook 6: pages 24–25

The CT Map Book: pages 20–21

National Geographic Trails Illustrated maps: Nos. 108, 109

Latitude 40° map: Summit County Trails

Jurisdiction: Dillon Ranger District, White River National Forest

Access from Denver end:

Access from Durango end:

Availability of water:

Bicycling: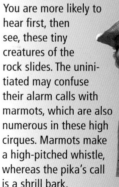

"The hanging glacial valley at 11,000 feet in the Tenmile Range supports a huge colony of pikas."

You are more likely to hear first, then see, these tiny creatures of the rock slides. The uninitiated may confuse their alarm calls with marmots, which are also numerous in these high cirques. Marmots make a high-pitched whistle, whereas the pika's call is a shrill bark.

Gudy's TIP

ABOUT THIS SEGMENT

This segment of The Colorado Trail climbs 3,600 feet in 6 miles across 1.7 billion-year-old basement rocks to gain the crest of the Tenmile Range, then descends 3,000 feet in another 6 miles through similar rocks to the narrow valley below. This is the first time the trail is above tree line for several miles, rewarding those who reach the tundra with great views of the surrounding mountains and communities below.

A well-deserved rest at the top.
PHOTO BY PETE AND LISA TURNER

Take note of the alpine wildflowers in the summer—the blooms can be magnificent. There can be snow along the high parts of this segment until mid-July and summer thunderstorms can move in quickly. There are good water sources throughout, but camping is limited due to the thick forests and steep watersheds. The best camping is near Miners Creek. Plan ahead to avoid potential problems.

TRAILHEAD/ACCESS POINTS

Gold Hill Trailhead: 🚗 Drive west from Denver on I-70 for about 75 miles to exit 203 (Frisco/Breckenridge). Proceed south on CO Hwy 9 for about 6 miles. The trailhead is on the right side of the highway at the intersection with Gateway Drive. (If you cross the bridge over the Blue River, you have gone 0.25 mile too far.)

Ross Avens are wonderfully colorful at high altitude.
PHOTO BY BILL MANNING

Miners Creek Access Point: 🚙 The CT can be accessed via the Miners Creek four-wheel-drive road at about mile 4.8. Miners Creek Road departs south of Peak One Boulevard at the south edge of Frisco (just west of the Summit County government offices).

Copper Far East Lot: 🚗 See Segment 8 on page 118.

SERVICES, SUPPLIES, AND ACCOMMODATIONS – BRECKENRIDGE/FRISCO

Breckenridge is approximately 4 miles south of the Gold Hill Trailhead on CO Hwy 9. Frisco has comparable services and is located approximately 5 miles northwest of the trailhead. The Summit Stage provides free bus service between the towns. There is a bus stop on Hwy 9 about 0.2 mile south of the trailhead. Both towns are restored mining/railroad towns serving the popular Summit County resorts.

Distance from CT:
4 miles to Breckenridge
(5 miles to Frisco)
Elevation: 9,605 feet
Zip code: 80424 (Frisco 80443)
Area code: 970

Bus
Summit Stage
(970) 668-0999

Gear (including fuel canisters)
Mountain Outfitters
112 S. Ridge St.
(970) 453-2201

Groceries
City Market
400 N. Park Ave.
(970) 453-0818

Info
Chamber of Commerce
311 S. Ridge St.
(970) 453-2913

Laundry
Norge Laundry
105 S. French St.
Breckenridge
(970) 547-4614

Frisco's Washtub Coin Laundry
406 Main
Frisco
(970) 668-3552

Lodging
Fireside Inn B&B and Hostel
114 N French St.
(970) 453-6456

Medical
Breckenridge Medical Clinic
555 S. Park Ave.
(970) 453-1010

Post Office
Breckenridge Post Office
311 S. Ridge St.
(970) 453-5467

Frisco Post Office
35 W. Main St.
(970) 668-0610

Showers
Breckenridge Recreation Center
880 Airport Rd.
(970) 453-1734

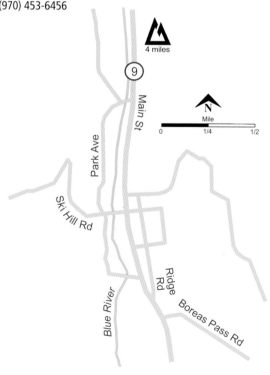

Atop the Tenmile Range at the end of June, when the snow has melted enough to pass over.
PHOTO BY BERNARD WOLF

TRAIL DESCRIPTION

Segment 7 begins at the Gold Hill Trailhead on the west side of CO Hwy 9, **mile 0.0** (9,197 feet). Leave the parking lot on single-track to the west and begin climbing where trees killed by pine beetles have been cut down. The trail ascends moderate slopes on the fall line here, though authorities have contemplated minor reroutes (traverses and switchbacks) to mitigate tread erosion and be more sustainable. The trail climbs to **mile 1.0** (9,659), where there is a well-marked, three-way logging road intersection. Bear to the left. At **mile 1.2** (9,748) continue straight ignoring trail on the left. Cross a logging road at **mile 1.6** (9,990), passing an old clear-cut area that recently has been replanted. At **mile 2.0** (10,158) the CT turns to the right through a colonnade of young trees at another well-marked intersection. At **mile 3.2** (9,952) the trail turns left at the intersection with the Peaks Trail near some beaver ponds. There is water here and good camping.

At **mile 3.4** (10,018), turn right on the Miners Creek Trail. The trail sign here does not identify The Colorado Trail, but there are confidence markers on trees on both sides of the intersection. Over the next mile, cross and recross a small tributary to Miners Creek several times. There are good campsites in the vicinity of the crossings. At **mile 4.8** (10,555), the Miners Creek Trail reaches a parking area for jeep access to the trail. Continue on the Miners Creek Trail by bearing to the left after passing most of the parking area.

Hikers on the ridge of the Tenmile Range.

PHOTO BY JEFF SELLENRICK

There are campsites on both sides of the parking area. Cross Miners Creek at **mile 4.9** (10,583) and several more times in the next mile, most with potential campsites. The last crossing of Miners Creek before entering the tundra is at **mile 6.1** (11,120).

The trail continues in a southerly direction, climbing below Peak 3, Peak 4, and Peak 5 before reaching a seasonal stream at **mile 7.6** (12,320). Continue climbing until you reach the crest of the Tenmile Range at **mile 8.0** (12,495). The views on a clear day are magnificent. Along the way up, Lake Dillon and the town of Dillon are visible to the north, Breckenridge sits stately to the east, and Copper Mountain lies 2,500 feet below to the west. After topping out, follow the ridge, passing just west of Peak 6.

Descending south, reach a seasonal spring at **mile 9.0** (12,176). Continue on a steep descent to reach tree line at **mile 9.9** (11,720). The trail then makes a sharp right turn where the Wheeler Trail diverges south at **mile 10.4** (11,249). Traverse downhill to the northwest, crossing several small seasonal streams before reaching the valley floor and joining a paved rec path. Continue straight, crossing a bridge over Tenmile Creek at **mile 12.4** (9,767). Continue 50 yards more alongside the Copper Far East Parking Lot and trailhead where the trail diverges left onto dirt single-track. There is good access to water and possible campsites before reaching CO Hwy 91, where parking is prohibited, and the end of Segment 7 at **mile 12.8** (9,820). Ahead, there is no camping within the first 4 miles of Segment 8 while on Copper Mountain Resort property.

Tundra Plants

 In portions of Segments 6 and 7, the CT passes into the open realm of the tundra for the first time. In Colorado, this alpine zone varies from above an altitude of 10,500 feet in the northern part of the state to more than 12,000 feet near the border with New Mexico. Above tree line, a harsh environment exists—one where summer lasts a fleeting 30 to 40 frost-free days, and in winter, temperatures can fall to well below zero. In essence, the tundra is a cold desert with precipitation levels of 20 inches per year or less, mainly in the form of snow. How this snow is distributed by the wind dictates the distribution of hardy alpine plants.

Compared with other alpine regions in the lower 48 states, Colorado's alpine tundra is particularly rich in plant numbers and species, putting on a spectacular display beginning with the first alpine forget-me-nots (*Eritrichium elongatum*) in June and lasting until arctic gentians (*Gentiana algida*) in early September signal the rapid approach of fall. Most species are "cushion" plants or miniature versions of species common at lower altitudes—a concession to the severe environment. Their growth rate is slow, with some plants taking up to a century to produce a mat only a foot or so in diameter, and is all the more reason to stay on the trail to avoid damaging them.

As you progress westward on the CT, the display of wildflowers becomes even more striking in the deeper soils of the moister western ranges, reaching a climax in the high alpine basins of the San Juan Mountains.

Tiny blue alpine forget-me-nots.
PHOTO BY BILL MANNING

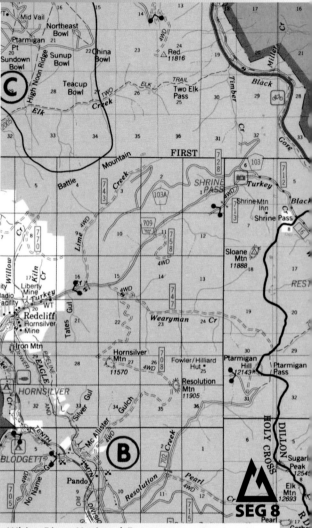

SCALE: Squares in grid approx. 1 Mile x 1 Mile

CT (current segment)

CT (adjacent segment)

CT Bicycle Wilderness Detour

1.8 CT Feature Mileage & Location

Trail

Paved Road

Improved Road

Unimproved Road

Unimproved Road and 4WD

National Forest Boundary

Wilderness Boundary

Continental Divide

Trailhead

Parking

Camping

lighter greens = National Forest

darker greens = Wilderness Area

orange or tan = BLM Land

purples = State Land

white = Private Land

SEGMENT 7 FEATURES TABLE   White River National Forest

Mileage	Features & Comments	Elevation (feet)	Mileage from Denver	Mileage to Durango	UTM-E	UTM-N (NAD83)	Zone
0.0	Begin Segment 7	9,197	104.4	380.2	410,455	4,377,354	13
1.0	Go left at intersection	9,659	105.4	379.2	409,065	4,377,498	13
1.6	Cross logging road	9,990	106.0	378.6	408,702	4,376,653	13
2.0	Turn right at logging road	10,158	106.4	378.2	408,383	4,376,950	13
3.2	Turn left onto Peaks Trail	9,952	107.6	377.0	407,049	4,376,983	13
3.4	Turn right onto Miners Creek Trail	10,018	107.8	376.8	407,121	4,376,548	13
4.8	Continue on Miners Creek Trail	10,555	109.2	375.4	405,670	4,376,507	13
8.0	Crest ridge of Tenmile Range	12,495	112.4	372.2	404,219	4,373,364	13
9.9	Descend to tree line	11,720	114.3	370.3	404,055	4,370,864	13
10.4	Switchback right onto Wheeler Trail	11,249	114.8	369.8	404,066	4,370,149	13
12.4	Bridge then Copper Far East Lot	9,767	116.8	367.8	402,368	4,372,579	13
12.8	End Segment 7	9,820	117.2	367.4	402,335	4,372,046	13

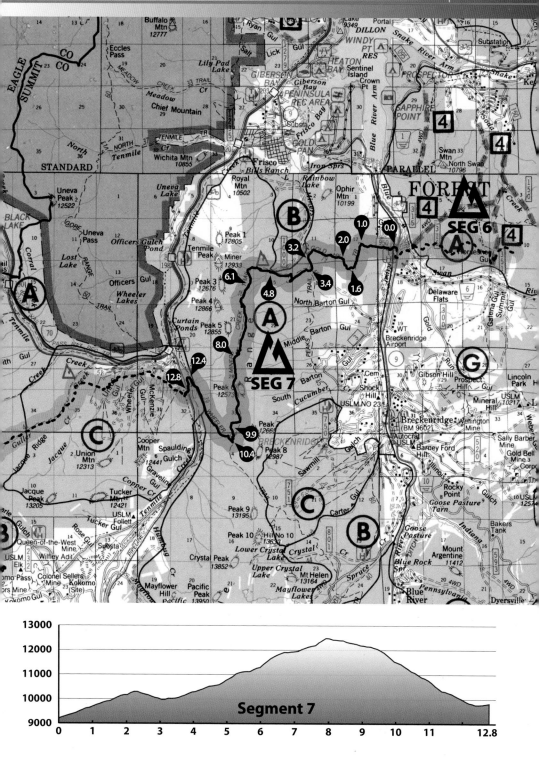

Segment 8: Copper Mountain to Tennessee Pass

Forest Service workers pack in supplies for a volunteer crew. PHOTO BY BILL BLOOMQUIST

Distance: 25.4 miles

Elevation gain: Approx. 4,417 feet

Elevation loss: Approx. 3,810 feet

USFS map: White River National Forest, pages 126–127

The Colorado Trail Databook 6: pages 26–27

The CT Map Book: pages 21–24

National Geographic Trails Illustrated map: No. 109

Latitude 40° map: Summit County Trails

Jurisdiction: Holy Cross and Dillon Ranger Districts, White River National Forest

Access from Denver end:

Access from Durango end: 🚗

Availability of water: ☕

Bicycling: 🚲

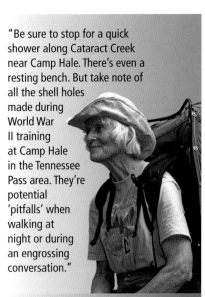

"Be sure to stop for a quick shower along Cataract Creek near Camp Hale. There's even a resting bench. But take note of all the shell holes made during World War II training at Camp Hale in the Tennessee Pass area. They're potential 'pitfalls' when walking at night or during an engrossing conversation."

Gudy's TIP

ABOUT THIS SEGMENT

The beginning of Segment 8 is much different from the preceding segments. The CT passes through Copper Mountain Resort, traversing ski slopes, edging along a golf course, and skirting the Copper Mountain Village Center, where there are restaurants, outdoor shops, lodging, and limited grocery shopping. While convenient for resupply, this area can be pricier than other resupply spots.

Somewhere on the slopes of Copper Mountain the CT crosses the Gore fault, a major fault active during uplift of the Ancestral Rockies. Rocks west of the fault were displaced downward 10,000 feet or more relative to basement rocks of the Tenmile Range. Both the fault and the bedrock on either side are concealed beneath glacial deposits, but west of the fault redbeds deposited during rise of the Ancestral Rockies are exposed as the trail climbs toward Searle Pass. On the ridges near the pass, the redbeds are cut by irregular bodies and sheetlike layers of porphyry that were injected during the Laramide Orogeny.

Elk Ridge, the high point of Segment 8. Behind looms the Tenmile Range.
PHOTO BY DAN MILNER

The middle of this segment takes trail users back into the tundra after a long climb from the resort. Again, the views of the surrounding mountains are impressive. After crossing Searle Pass, there are many opportunities for side trips to nearby peaks. The descent to Eagle Park and Camp Hale provide an entirely different feel from Copper Mountain. This abandoned training ground for the 10th Mountain Division is steadily deteriorating under the extreme weather conditions, but retains its rich military legacy.

The CT passes the ruins of

Cataract Falls at the edge of the Camp Hale valley, next to the CT at mile 17.2.
PHOTO BY DAVID DOLTON

several coking ovens just before reaching Tennessee Pass, capping a scenic walk through a variety of eras that have left their mark on this stretch of the trail.

TRAILHEAD/ACCESS POINTS

Trailhead access to The Colorado Trail in this area is a bit unusual. Parking is prohibited on the wide shoulders of CO Hwy 91 where Segment 8 begins. Nevertheless, there are convenient parking areas.

Copper Far East Lot: This large parking area is adjacent to Segment 7, mile 12.4, a nearly flat, 0.4-mile trail walk from the beginning of Segment 8. Drive west from Denver on I-70 for 80 miles to exit 195 (Copper Mountain/Leadville/CO Hwy 91). Drive beyond the stoplight and entrance to Copper (on the right) and, less than a half mile farther, turn left into the large Copper Far East Parking Lot where there

West of Kokomo Pass descending toward Camp Hale.
PHOTO BY SCOTT RYBERG

are bathrooms, though at times they are locked. Mid-lot on the east edge, find the CT (and CDT) trailhead with sign. To reach the start of CT Segment 8, beyond the trailhead sign and paved rec path, follow the CT south 0.4 mile to where it crosses CO Hwy 91. Segment 8 begins on the west side of the highway. Use caution when crossing the highway; traffic comes very fast from both directions.

Chapel Parking Lot Access: From Denver, drive I-70 west 80 miles to exit 195. Turn right into Copper Mountain Resort. Continue approximately 1 mile, then turn left into the chapel parking lot. Walk south and west to the Village Center Plaza in the area of the American Eagle chairlift. To intersect the CT, go about 150 yards diagonally southeast between the condos on the left and the American Eagle lift on the right, Segment 8, mile 1.6.

Union Creek Ski Area Access: Instead of parking at the chapel lot, continue through

Copper Mountain Village to the Union Creek drop-off parking area. (Parking is permitted here during off-ski-season months.) Cross over the covered bridge, go past the ticket office and under the elevated walkway, turn right on a gravel road, pass under a ski lift, and go about 200 yards on the road. Turn left up the road, around a green security gate, and follow the road east uphill about 400 yards to a wide area in the road. Pick up the single-track of the CT to the right, by a painted white rock, mile 2.1 of CT Segment 8.

Tennessee Pass Trailhead Access: See Segment 9 on page 128.

SERVICES, SUPPLIES, AND ACCOMMODATIONS – COPPER MOUNTAIN

The Colorado Trail passes close by **Copper Mountain Resort** near the start of this segment. Resort accommodations and restaurants may be pricey. There is a convenience store/gas station 0.5 mile north of Copper Far East Lot accessible by either the rec path or CO Hwy 91.

Distance from CT: 0 miles
Elevation: 9,600 feet
Zip code: 80443
Area code: 970

Bus
Summit Stage
(970) 668-0999

Groceries
McCoy's Mountain Market
Village Square
(970) 968-2182

Info
Copper Mountain Resort Association
Village Square
(970) 968-6477

Lodging
Copper Mountain Lodging Services
(800) 458-8386

Medical
Closest services in Frisco
(970) 668-3300

Post Office
West Lake Lodge
800 Copper Road
(970) 968-2318 ext. 41873
(Self-service only; full service available in Frisco)

TRAIL DESCRIPTION

Begin Segment 8 on the west side of CO Hwy 91 (no parking) at **mile 0.0** (9,820). Camping is prohibited the next 4 miles. The trail enters the forest southwest and follows a few switchbacks uphill as it skirts the golf course, crosses a bridge, and passes under a power line. The CT then heads northwest and traverses ski runs, goes under a ski lift, and passes nearest the Copper Mountain Resort at **mile 1.6** (9,768). There are restaurants, sporting goods shops, and some grocery shopping at the base of the ski hill. The trail passes underneath the American Eagle Ski Lift and then becomes single-track at **mile 2.1** (9,988), following a few roundabout switchbacks up the hill. There are two streams ahead, followed by great views of the Tenmile Range.

At **mile 3.4** (10,345), bear sharply to the right and leave the horse trail the CT was following. A cross-country ski trail merges from the left at **mile 5.0** (10,519), but the CT continues straight ahead. At **mile 5.2** (10,480), pass Jacque Creek, immediately followed

The CT crosses beneath the ski lifts at Copper Mountain Resort. PHOTO BY JULIE VIDA AND MARK TABB

by Guller Creek. There is a campsite just up the hill between the two. Continue upstream along Guller Creek following an elongated meadow to **mile 6.2** (10,854) for additional camping and water. Janet's Cabin, a popular ski hut, comes into view as the trail climbs out of the canyon.

Leave the trees at **mile 8.7** (11,708), cross Guller Creek headwaters at **mile 9.2** (11,804), and continue to the top of Searle Pass at **mile 9.7** (12,043). In the next few miles, the trail undulates across tundra and crosses seasonal streams with exposed campsites. Climb to the top of Elk Ridge at **mile 12.3** (12,282), then descend to Kokomo Pass at **mile 12.9** (12,023). From here, continue down to Cataract Creek headwaters at **mile 13.2** (11,841) and tree line at **mile 13.5** (11,639). Down farther find switchbacks and potential campsites as the trail travels along Cataract Creek.

At **mile 16.4** (10,085), ford Cataract Creek and bear right at a fork in the road 0.1 mile farther. Continue to **mile 17.1** (9,668), where the trail turns right at the intersection just above the road. Cross Cataract Creek on a bridge by Cataract Falls at **mile 17.2** (9,700). Camping is not allowed between this point and **mile 20.1**, due to possible unexploded munitions. At **mile 17.9** (9,438), the trail comes to FS Rd 714. Take a right onto the road and walk 0.1 mile, picking up the trail again on the right. Rejoin the road at the Camp Hale Trailhead, where there is a small parking area at **mile 18.6** (9,362). Beyond the parking area, continue to the right on FS Rd 714, looking for the next road on the left. Turn left on an intersecting road at **mile 18.8** (9,349). The road ends at **mile 19.2** (9,326) near some old concrete bunkers. Here the trail resumes, crossing a footbridge and heading uphill. At **mile 20.1** (9,671), meet FS Rd 726. (There is a campsite about 0.1 mile north of this intersection and river water 0.1 mile farther northwest.) Cross the road and continue south and uphill.

After re-entering the forest, the trail begins a steady climb, reaching a bench at an overlook at **mile 20.4** (9,778). Cross a jeep road at **mile 21.2** (9,863). There are several potential campsites in this area. Walk over a footbridge at Fiddler Creek, **mile 21.7** (9,967), then continue south until reaching US Hwy 24 at **mile 22.1** (9,966). Cross the highway, then a set of railroad tracks, followed by footbridges over three small creeks.

After leaving the swampy area, the CT turns to the southwest and follows Mitchell Creek in a wide grassy meadow, which features several potential campsites. At **mile 23.6** (10,180), the trail turns east and begins following an old railroad grade. After bending to the south, the trail crosses a footbridge over a seasonally wet area and a railroad bridge before reaching the remains of old coke ovens at **mile 25.2** (10,382). Reach the parking area for Tennessee Pass and US Hwy 24 at **mile 25.4** (10,424). Camping is allowed more than 100 feet from the trail and parking lot. This is the end of Segment 8.

Dense woods surround the trail between Copper Mountain and Guller Creek.

PHOTO BY CARL BROWN

Mount of the Holy Cross

From several vantage points on Segment 8, hikers have excellent views to the west of the photogenic Mount of the Holy Cross. Nearly a century ago, this was perhaps the most famous and revered mountain in America.

In the early 1800s, explorers brought back rumors of a great mountain in the West that displayed a giant cross on its side, but the exact location was shrouded in mystery. The search for the peak became one of the most intriguing in the history of the West. F. V. Hayden made it his top priority in the 1873 field session of his topographic survey. Hayden's team determined that the peak lay somewhere north and west of Tennessee Pass. After several arduous days of travel, Hayden reached the summit on August 22. From Notch Mountain across the valley, famed photographer W. H. Jackson captured an image of the immense snowy cross.

W. H. JACKSON'S FAMOUS IMAGE.

It's hard to imagine today the sensation Jackson's photo caused around the country. Henry Wadsworth Longfellow was moved to write a poem after viewing the image, and well-known artists such as Thomas Moran journeyed to Colorado to paint the peak. Hundreds of people made pilgrimages up Notch Mountain to view the cross, faith healings were reported, and Congress established it as a national monument in 1929.

The mountain was used for mountain-eering training by troops from nearby Camp Hale during World War II, including a first-ever winter ascent of the 1,200-foot-high cross in December 1943. But as time passed, religious interest faded and the mountain's monument status was rescinded shortly after the war.

A later USGS survey determined that the 14,005-foot peak just barely qualified as a fourteener (Hayden had listed it at 13,999 feet), and today, Mount of the Holy Cross is a favorite with peak-baggers.

Camping is NOT permitted between Cataract Creek and the South Fork of the Eagle River (due to unexploded munitions). White arrows mark the travel corridor.

The Short Life and Long Legacy of Camp Hale

Camp Hale bunkers.

PHOTO BY BERNARD WOLF

The storied history of the U.S. Army's 10th Mountain Division began in 1942 at Camp Hale, nestled in a large valley north of Tennessee Pass along U.S. Highway 24 between Leadville and Minturn. Surrounded by mountains at an altitude of 9,200 feet, it offered an ideal location to train troops for mountain and winter warfare during World War II.

In 1942, the valley was transformed in a matter of months into a military camp with more than 1,000 buildings, including barracks, administrative offices, stables, a hospital, movie theater, and field house, capable of accommodating some 14,000 troops. Little evidence of the buildings remains, but visitors to the site can still wander the streets that made up the main camp area—three major north-south roads labeled A, B and C, and 21 cross streets numbered 1st through 21st —and read scattered plaques containing historical information about the camp's construction and activities.

The first troops, members of the First Battalion of the 87th Mountain Infantry Regiment, began arriving at Camp Hale in November 1942. This all-volunteer unit consisted of recreational skiers, cowboys, trappers, forest rangers, and other outdoorsmen, who began their training at Fort Lewis in Washington. In 1943, the 85th and 86th Infantry Regiments were activated at Camp Hale, joining the 87th in forming a unit that ultimately became the 10th Mountain Division in 1944. In addition to regular military training, the men of the 10th also became experts in winter survival, skiing, and rock climbing.

Attached to the 5th Army, the 10th fought bloody battles up the spine of Italy's Apennine Mountains in 1945, culminating in the taking of the strategic Riva Ridge and Mount Belvedere in February of that year. The division suffered nearly 25 percent casualties, one of the highest of any unit in the war. Among the wounded was Robert Dole, who went to become a longtime U.S. senator from Kansas and Republican presidential candidate. The division was still fighting in Italy when German forces surrendered in May, 1945, ending the war in Europe.

After the war, many veterans of the 10th, drawn by their experiences in Colorado, returned to the state and were instrumental in developing its ski industry. Among them was Pete Seibert, who founded the nearby Vail Ski Resort in 1962.

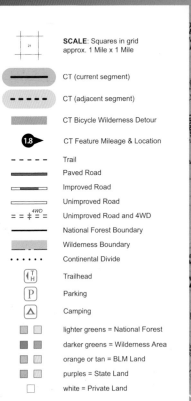

SCALE: Squares in grid approx. 1 Mile x 1 Mile

CT (current segment)

CT (adjacent segment)

CT Bicycle Wilderness Detour

1.8 CT Feature Mileage & Location

Trail

Paved Road

Improved Road

Unimproved Road

Unimproved Road and 4WD

National Forest Boundary

Wilderness Boundary

Continental Divide

Trailhead

Parking

Camping

lighter greens = National Forest

darker greens = Wilderness Area

orange or tan = BLM Land

purples = State Land

white = Private Land

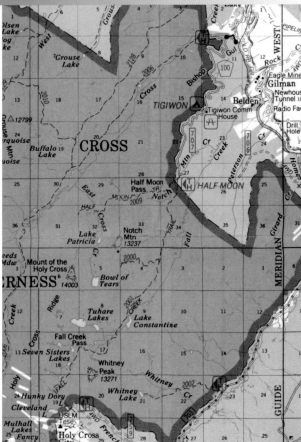

SEGMENT 8 FEATURES TABLE White River National Forest

Mileage	Features & Comments	Elevation (feet)	Mileage from Denver	Mileage to Durango	UTM-E	UTM-N (NAD83)	Zone
0.0	Begin Segment 8	9,820	117.2	367.4	402,335	4,372,046	13
5.2	Cross Jacque Creek	10,480	122.4	362.2	397,633	4,371,608	13
8.7	Reach tree line	11,708	125.9	358.7	394,006	4,369,297	13
9.7	Reach Searle Pass	12,043	126.9	357.7	394,332	4,368,348	13
12.3	Elk Ridge high point	12,282	129.5	355.1	395,116	4,365,436	13
12.9	Kokomo Pass	12,023	130.1	354.5	394,405	4,365,068	13
13.5	Tree line	11,639	130.7	353.9	393,632	4,365,845	13
16.4	Ford Cataract Creek then right	10,085	133.6	351.0	390,731	4,364,642	13
17.1	Turn right, pass Cataract Falls	9,668	134.3	350.3	390,543	4,364,366	13
17.9	Go right on road 0.1 mile	9,438	135.1	349.5	389,339	4,364,312	13
18.6	Camp Hale Trailhead then roads	9,362	135.8	348.8	388,229	4,364,653	13
20.1	Cross FS Rd 726	9,671	137.3	347.3	386,859	4,363,442	13
20.4	Reach bench and overlook	9,778	137.6	347.0	386,799	4,363,011	13
21.2	Cross jeep road	9,863	138.4	346.2	386,601	4,361,960	13
21.7	Cross Fiddler Creek	9,967	138.9	345.7	386,751	4,361,352	13
22.1	Cross US Hwy 24	9,966	139.3	345.3	386,556	4,360,752	13
23.6	Left onto old railroad grade	10,180	140.8	343.8	385,625	4,359,709	13
25.2	Pass by coke ovens	10,382	142.4	342.2	386,477	4,358,073	13
25.4	End Segment 8	10,424	142.6	342.0	386,983	4,357,913	13

Segment 9: Tennessee Pass to Timberline Lake Trailhead

Wetlands in the Holy Cross Wilderness Area.

PHOTO BY ROGER FORMAN

Distance: 13.6 miles

Elevation gain: Approx. 2,627 feet

Elevation loss: Approx. 3,004 feet

USFS map: San Isabel National Forest, pages 134–135

The Colorado Trail Databook 6: pages 28–29

The CT Map Book: pages 24–26

National Geographic Trails Illustrated maps: Nos. 109, 126

Latitude 40° map: Summit County Trails

Jurisdiction: Leadville Ranger District, San Isabel National Forest

Access from Denver end:

Access from Durango end:

Availability of water:

Bicycling: See page 132

"There is a fascinating tundra walk between Longs Gulch and the St. Kevin Lake Trail in the Holy Cross Wilderness Area."

There are several lakes and ponds, ideal for camping, situated just off the trail and glaciated headwalls of the Continental Divide, exemplified by Porcupine Lakes (mile 7.7), a beautiful spot for high-altitude camping.

Gudy's TIP

A sign marks the wilderness boundary, Segment 9, mile 6.7.
PHOTO BY BERNIE KRAUSSE

ABOUT THIS SEGMENT

In Segment 9, The Colorado Trail turns south, passing through gneiss and 1.4 billion-year-old granite that forms the eastern flank of the Sawatch Range. Alternating between ascents to passes and ridges and descents to creeks or rivers at the bottom of drainages, elevations in the segment range between 10,000 and 12,000 feet. Much of this section of the CT follows the path of the old Main Range Trail, which was built by the Civilian Conservation Corps in the 1930s for both recreation and fire protection. There are great views along the trail of the Arkansas River Valley and the Mosquito Range to the east. This part of the Arkansas Valley marks the northern end of the Rio Grande Rift. Equally dramatic are the views of the Sawatch Range peaks to the west. Toward the end of the segment, the CT passes through the southeast corner of the Holy Cross Wilderness Area. Here there are some great views of Mount Massive, the second-highest mountain in Colorado at 14,421 feet, to the south.

TRAILHEAD/ACCESS POINTS

Tennessee Pass Trailhead: Travel north from Leadville on US Hwy 24 for approximately 9 miles to the top of Tennessee Pass. A parking area with bathrooms on the west side of the highway is the start of this segment.

Wurts Ditch Road Trail Access: 🚗 Drive north from Leadville on US Hwy 24 for about 7.5 miles to Wurtz Ditch Road (FS Rd 705). It's easy to identify by the old-fashioned yellow road grader parked beside the road. Proceed about 1 mile on the gravel road to an intersection. Turn right. Proceed 0.3 mile to the CT crossing. Parking space is limited.

Timberline Lake Trailhead: 🚗 See Segment 10 on pages 136.

SERVICES, SUPPLIES, AND ACCOMMODATIONS

Sunrise at Porcupine Lakes.
PHOTO BY AARON LOCANDER

These amenities are available in Leadville; see Segment 10 on pages 136–145.

TRAIL DESCRIPTION

Segment 9 begins at the Tennessee Pass parking area with bathrooms on the west side of US Hwy 24, **mile 0.0** (10,424 feet). Camping is allowed more than 100 feet from the trail and parking lot. From the trailhead sign, follow the CT into the forest in a southwesterly direction. At **mile 0.6** (10,510) stay left at a side trail to Point Breeze and Continental Divide Cabins (reservations required, 8-person minimum, huts.org). Enjoy the swing seat with view of Mount Elbert, Colorado's highest summit, at 14,433 feet. At **mile 1.1** (10,440), continue straight at intersection with Treeline Trail on right and 0.1 mile farther pass a seasonal spring. At **mile 2.5** (10,422), cross Wurts Ditch and a creek (both often dry) on two bridges. Then pass over Wurts Ditch Road 0.3 mile farther on where cyclists diverge to detour around the Holy Cross and Mount Massive Wilderness areas. (Right, northwest 3 miles and 1,000 feet uphill, is 10th Mountain Division Hut, reservations required, huts.org.) There are good campsites in this area. Cross a jeep trail called Lily Lake Road at **mile 3.4** (10,396), then cross the North Fork of Tennessee Creek at **mile 3.5** (10,390) and West Tennessee Creek 0.2 mile after that. More campsites are nearby. At **mile 4.1** (10,502), the single-track inconspicuously joins a very old jeep road.

After a gentle climb, there is an intersection at **mile 4.9** (10,704). Take a right here. The trail enters the Holy Cross Wilderness Area at **mile 6.7** (10,875). There is a boundary

Southbound in the Holy Cross Wilderness, looking toward the Continental Divide.
PHOTO BY BERNARD WOLF

sign and trail register. At **mile 6.9** (10,917) cross the stream in Longs Gulch. Climb to Porcupine Lakes at **mile 7.7** (11,451), where there are potential campsites. At **mile 8.0** (11,252) cross Porcupine Creek and then a seasonal stream at **mile 8.3** (11,214). After a short descent, climb to a high point on the tundra at **mile 8.8** (11,702). Head downhill, ignoring an unmarked side trail heading down the valley to the left, and bear right at a sharp bend at **mile 9.6** (11,498). At **mile 10.1** (11,255), turn right at a junction with the trail to Bear Lake Trailhead plus Uncle Bud's Hut (reservations required, huts.org). Cross a small stream on a footbridge and turn right at the intersection with the trail to Bear Lake at **mile 10.5** (11,128). Pass an unnamed lake to the right of the trail, then pass another unnamed lake to the right at **mile 10.9** (11,041). There are more good campsites here.

Climb to another saddle at **mile 11.4** (11,422) that has a dry campsite. The trail goes above tree line briefly here, then descends steeply on a series of switchbacks, re-enters the trees, and passes two small seasonal streams. Leave the Holy Cross Wilderness Area at **mile 12.6** (10,561). Pass under a power line at **mile 12.9** (10,434) and again at **mile 13.3** (10,141). Continue downhill to the parking area for the Timberline Lake Trailhead at **mile 13.6** (10,043) and the end of Segment 9.

Holy Cross/Mount Massive Wilderness Bicycle Detour

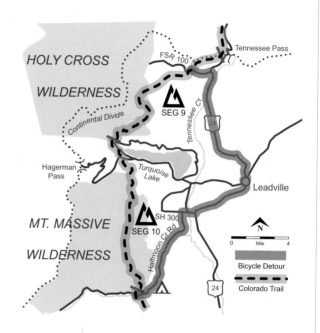

This detour bypasses both the Holy Cross and Mount Massive wilderness areas, beginning at mile 2.5 of CT Segment 9.

At **mile 0.0** (10,488), turn left (downhill) on Wurts Ditch Road (dirt). At **mile 0.3** (10,385), turn left on FS Rd 100 (Meadows Drive, gravel). At **mile 1.3** (10,146), turn right (south) along US Highway 24. At **mile 8.4** (10,137) reach an intersection and bear right onto CO Hwy 91/US Hwy 24. At **mile 10.0** (10,132) is downtown Leadville, a great place to stop and spend a night and resupply. The historic town has a post office, lodging, restaurants, Safeway grocery store, outfitter, laundromat, and mining museum.

Leave Leadville south on US Hwy 24. At **mile 14.0** (9,563), turn right on paved CO Hwy 300. At **mile 14.8** (9,559), turn left on FS Rd 160, also known as County Road 11 and Halfmoon Creek Road. At **mile 16.0** (9,482), curve right (southwest) and cycle past numerous campsites and Forest Service campgrounds. At **mile 21.5** (10,065), just before a bridge on Halfmoon Creek, rejoin The Colorado Trail where it takes off to the left, the beginning of Segment 11.

Sign at north end of detour.

PHOTO BY BILL MANNING

10th Mountain Division Hut System

For backcountry skiing, snowshoeing, and snowboarding enthusiasts, there are a number of winter access points to the CT, usually where the trail crosses a major pass at a regularly plowed highway. Undoubtedly, the best of these is the Tennessee Pass access, at the start of Segment 9, which is smack in the middle of a network of mountain huts run by the 10th Mountain Division Hut Association.

The hut association is a nonprofit founded in 1980 by a group of backcountry recreationalists, including several veterans of the U.S. Army's famed 10th Mountain Division, which trained at nearby Camp Hale in the 1940s.

PHOTO BY BILL MANNING

The hut system lies within a large triangle roughly formed by Vail, Breckenridge, and Aspen. In the style of traditional European hut-to-hut travel, thirty-four huts provide overnight shelter for backcountry skiers, snow boarders, snowshoers, mountain bikers, and backpackers. Six of the huts were built with donations from

Janet's Cabin.

PHOTO BY BILL BLOOMQUIST

family and friends to honor individuals who died while serving in the 10th Mountain Division during World War II.

The huts are situated between 9,700 and 11,700 feet and are designed for experienced backcountry travelers. Most operate in the winter between late November and late April, and then again for three months in the summer.

Accommodations are best described as comfortably rustic, with bunks sleeping about fifteen people in a communal setting. Huts are equipped with wood stoves for heat, propane for cooking, photovoltaic lighting, mattresses, and utensils. You bring your own sleeping bag, food, and clothing. Users melt snow for water in winter and collect it from streams in summer.

More than 300 miles of trails link the huts and several are close to The Colorado Trail, including Janet's Cabin, Vance's Cabin, and Uncle Bud's Hut. Reservations are required. Contact the 10th Mountain Division Hut Association at (970) 925-5775 or visit its website at huts.org. Note that this website administers a system of huts, including those of the 10th as well as the Summit Huts Association, the Alfred A. Braun Huts, Grand Huts Association, Friends Huts, and privately owned huts.

SCALE: Squares in grid approx. 1 Mile x 1 Mile

CT (current segment)

CT (adjacent segment)

CT Bicycle Wilderness Detour

1.8 CT Feature Mileage & Location

Trail

Paved Road

Improved Road

Unimproved Road

Unimproved Road and 4WD

National Forest Boundary

Wilderness Boundary

Continental Divide

Trailhead

Parking

Camping

lighter greens = National Forest

darker greens = Wilderness Area

orange or tan = BLM Land

purples = State Land

white = Private Land

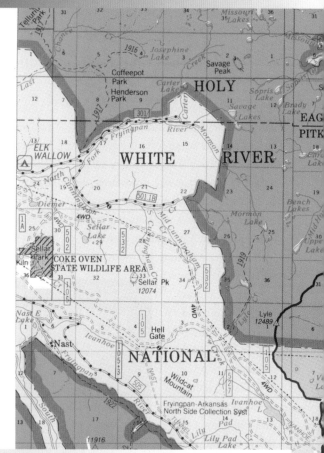

SEGMENT 9 FEATURES TABLE San Isabel National Forest

Mileage	Features & Comments	Elevation (feet)	Mileage from Denver	Mileage to Durango	UTM-E	UTM-N (NAD83)	Zone
0.0	Begin Segment 9	10,424	142.6	342.0	386,983	4,357,913	13
2.5	Cross Wurtz Ditch plus creek then road	10,422	145.1	339.5	383,769	4,356,745	13
3.4	Cross Lily Lake Road	10,396	146.0	338.6	382,932	4,356,261	13
3.5	Cross North Fork Tennessee Creek	10,390	146.1	338.5	382,809	4,356,185	13
3.7	Bridge over West Tennessee Creek	10,365	146.3	338.3	382,825	4,355,876	13
4.1	Bear right joining old jeep road	10,502	146.7	337.9	382,169	4,355,712	13
4.9	Turn right at intersection	10,704	147.5	337.1	381,244	4,355,702	13
6.7	Enter Holy Cross Wilderness	10,875	149.3	335.3	379,060	4,354,324	13
7.7	Pass Porcupine Lakes	11,451	150.3	334.3	378,148	4,353,381	13
9.6	Bear right	11,498	152.2	332.4	378,890	4,351,836	13
10.5	Go right past Bear Lake Trail	11,128	153.1	331.5	377,760	4,350,973	13
10.9	Pass second lake	11,041	153.5	331.1	377,200	4,350,635	13
11.4	Tree line	11,422	154.0	330.6	376,655	4,350,577	13
12.6	Leave Holy Cross Wilderness Area	10,561	155.2	329.4	375,610	4,350,011	13
13.6	End Segment 9	10,043	156.2	328.4	375,190	4,349,393	13

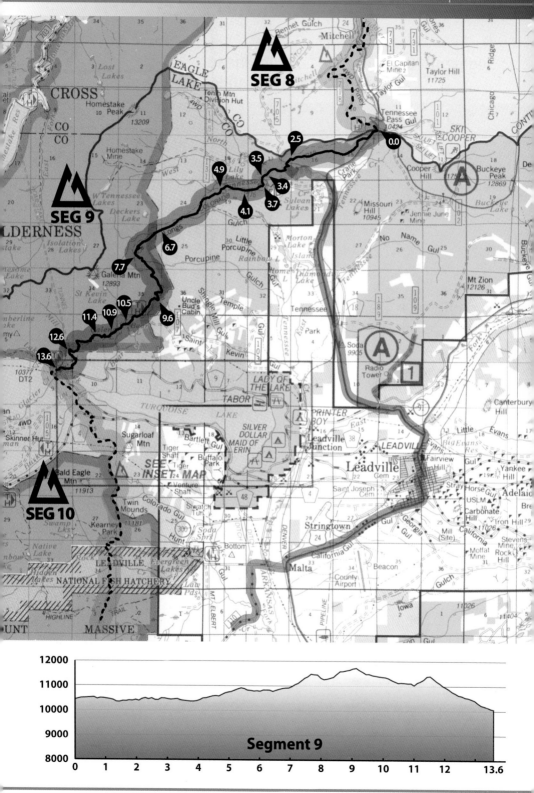

Segment 10: Timberline Lake Trailhead to Mount Massive Trailhead

A stout bridge crosses Busk Creek near the start of Segment 10.

PHOTO BY PETE TURNER

Distance: 13.1 miles

Elevation gain: Approx. 2,690 feet

Elevation loss: Approx. 2,676 feet

USFS map: San Isabel National Forest, pages 144–145

The Colorado Trail Databook 6: pages 30–31

The CT Map Book: pages 26–28

National Geographic Trails Illustrated maps: Nos. 126, 127

Latitude 40° map: Summit County Trails

Jurisdiction: Leadville Ranger District, San Isabel National Forest

Access from Denver end: 🚗

Access from Durango end: 🚗

Availability of water: ☕

Bicycling: 🚲 See page 132

"If your goal is to climb Mount Elbert or Mount Massive, get a very early start. Thunderstorms and lightning can roll in by noon during the summer. By starting early, you'll also avoid the crowd of peak-baggers."

There is camping near the Mount Massive Trailhead, which serves as a good base camp for climbing both of these fourteeners.

Gudy's TIP

ABOUT THIS SEGMENT

This segment has seen many changes through the nine versions of *The Colorado Trail Guidebook*. The trailhead location has been changed and the trailhead and segment break is now at the Timberline Lake Trailhead, which has ample parking, water sources nearby, and potential campsites. It used to be called the Timberline Lake and CT Trailhead, but now has been simplified and shortened to the Timberline Lake Trailhead. The segment ends at the Mount Massive Trailhead, formerly known as the Halfmoon Creek Trailhead.

Airing out one's feet is delightful! PHOTO BY PETE TURNER

Segment 10 takes trail users into the Mount Massive Wilderness Area and features multiple long climbs and descents. In the vicinity of mile 6.2, the CT passes through the Leadville National Fish Hatchery, one of the oldest hatcheries in the federal system. It was established by Congress in 1889 and is still active. The hatchery buildings are about 2 miles east of where the CT crosses Rock Creek. At about mile 10.0, a side trail leads to the top of Mount Massive (14,421), the second-highest mountain in Colorado. For those interested in the side trip, it is 3.5 miles each way, with about 3,350 feet of climbing. This segment ends as you leave the wilderness area at the Mount Massive Trailhead.

Mt. Massive climbers diverge here.
PHOTO BY BILL MANNING

During the last ice age, the Sawatch Range was festooned with glaciers and icefields. Glaciers in the major valleys advanced beyond the mountain front and into the Arkansas Valley, leaving massive terminal moraines composed of glacial debris that accumulated as the ice melted at their snouts. Turquoise Lake lies behind one of these moraines. The valley of Halfmoon Creek was also occupied by a glacier that built a similar moraine.

TRAILHEAD/ACCESS POINTS

Timberline Lake Trailhead:  This access road seems to have several names, depending or your source: Turquoise Lake Road, Lake County Rd 9, and FS Rd 104. Turquoise Lake Road seems to be the most comprehensive, since it applies to the road starting from the end of the 1000 block of West 6th Street in downtown Leadville, all the way around Turquoise Lake, and back to its starting point on West 6th Street. Access to the CT is at the westernmost point of Turquoise Lake Road. To get to the trailhead from US Hwy 24, which runs through the center of Leadville, turn west on West 6th Street and follow it to the end of the 1000 block. Curve right around the Lake County Recreation Center, then almost immediately turn left onto Turquoise Lake Road. Follow it to its westernmost point and turn west onto the access road for the 100-yard drive to the parking area. It makes no difference whether you drive around the north side of the lake or the south, but the south is a bit shorter.

Hagerman Pass Road Access (no parking): Follow the aforementioned instructions to Turquoise Lake Road. Follow it around the south side of the lake. After crossing Sugarloaf Dam, at mile 3.1, Hagerman Pass Road exits at a shallow angle to the left. The CT crosses 0.9 mile up this road. There is no parking space here.

Mount Massive Trailhead: See Segment 11 on page 146.

A green carpet of groundcover surrounds the path.
PHOTO BY ROGER FORMAN

SERVICES, SUPPLIES, AND ACCOMMODATIONS – LEADVILLE

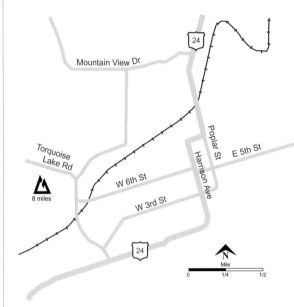

Info
Chamber of Commerce
809 Harrison Ave.
(719) 486-3900

Laundry
Mountain Laundry
1707 Poplar Ave.
(719) 486-0551

Lodging (several)
Leadville Hostel & Inn
500 E. 7th St.
(719) 486-9334

Medical
St. Vincent General Hospital
4th and Washington Sts.
(719) 486-0230

Post Office
Leadville Post Office
130 W. 5th St.
(719) 486-9397

Showers
Lake County Aquatic Center
1000 W. 6th St.
(719) 486-6986

Shuttle
Leadville Hostel & Inn
500 E. 7th St.
(719) 486-9334

Leadville, a historic mining and railroad town, is about 8 miles east of the trail access points by way of Turquoise Lake Road.

Distance from CT: 8 miles
Elevation: 10,152 feet
Zip code: 80461
Area code: 719

Dining
Several locations in town

Gear (including fuel canisters)
Bill's Sport Shop
225 Harrison Ave.
(719) 486-0739

Sawatch Backcountry
480 Harrison Ave.
(719) 486-2271

Groceries
Safeway
1900 US Hwy 24 North
(719) 486-0795

Looking north at peaks in the Holy Cross Wilderness Area.
PHOTO BY CARL BROWN

TRAIL DESCRIPTION

Segment 10 begins at the Timberline Lake Trailhead parking area above Turquoise Lake, **mile 0.0** (10,043 feet). Just after leaving the parking area, take a left at the well-marked intersection with the trail to Timberline Lake. Cross Lake Fork of the Arkansas River on a bridge shortly after this intersection. Cross Glacier Creek at **mile 0.4** (10,115) on a good bridge with campsites nearby, then cross Busk Creek on another good bridge at **mile 1.2** (10,039). Ignore the small fishing trail that heads to the left and climb steeply to Hagerman Pass Road at **mile 1.8** (10,341). Just after the trail crosses Hagerman Pass Road, there is a good, dry campsite above the road. Continue climbing until reaching the Sugarloaf Mountain saddle at **mile 3.1** (11,094), where the trail crosses an old logging road. Great views of Mount Elbert open up when the CT reaches the high point on the ridge. Enter the Mount Massive Wilderness Area at **mile 3.2** (11,073). There is a trail register here. Several small streams and good camping lie just ahead.

Pass under the summits of Bald Eagle Mountain to the west, eventually reaching the Twin Mounds saddle at **mile 4.8** (11,009). After a short descent, bear to the right at the intersection at **mile 5.4** (10,644). There is a good, dry campsite here. There is a Forest

Service sign identifying the CT and the Kearney Park Trail at **mile 5.5** (10,660). The Colorado Trail goes to the left (south) here, while the Kearney Park Trail heads east across the meadow. Cross Fish Hatchery Road, then a bridge over Rock Creek at **mile 6.2** (10,269). At **mile 6.5** (10,353) cross South Rock Creek on a corduroy bridge. Climb to the Highline Trail at **mile 7.8** (11,009). Continue in a southerly direction.

At **mile 8.8** (11,107), the CT crosses a bridge over North Willow Creek. There are potential campsites in this area. Climb to the top of a ridge at **mile 9.2** (11,310), where there is an exposed, dry campsite. Head downhill to **mile 10.0** (11,069), where the CT intersects the trail to Mount Massive. Shortly thereafter, cross Willow Creek at **mile 10.1** (11,040) and continue descending until crossing South Willow Creek at **mile 10.7** (10,816). Leave the Mount Massive Wilderness Area at **mile 12.9** (10,123) and reach the Mount Massive Trailhead parking area near Halfmoon Creek at **mile 13.1** (10,065), the end of Segment 10. (Cyclists rejoin here after Holy Cross/Mount Massive Wilderness detour.) Just east on Halfmoon Creek Road, FS Rd 110, is Elbert Creek Campground, a fee campground with potable water, highly popular with Mount Elbert and Mount Massive climbers.

Rock Creek in the Mount Massive Wilderness Area.
PHOTO BY BILL MANNING

The Fourteeners and Climbing Mount Elbert and Mount Massive

Of the 54 peaks in Colorado that rise above 14,000 feet, nearly two-thirds are within 20 miles of The Colorado Trail. They are a common and inspiring sight from many a ridgetop along the trail. The CT's closest encounter with a fourteener, however, comes when it passes San Luis Peak (14,014 feet) in Segment 20.

All of Colorado's fourteeners lie within a radius of 120 miles, centered in the Sawatch Range near Buena Vista. None of the other Rocky Mountain states has even one fourteener, despite their related geologic history. The reason why may rest with two geological features unique to Colorado: the Colorado Mineral Belt and the Rio Grande Rift. The Colorado Mineral Belt is a northeast-southwest band of igneous rock that roughly follows the same line as the CT. The Rio Grande Rift is a narrow rift valley that includes the San Luis and Arkansas valleys. Both of these features tend to push overlaying rock upward. All but one or two of the fourteeners are along these two features, and the highest and most numerous lie at the intersection of the two.

It is thought that although the entire Rocky Mountain region, including Colorado, Wyoming, and New Mexico, went through a broad uniform uplift, the fourteeners appear to be the result of an additional localized growth spurt involving these two geological features.

The results of this happy coincidence have captured the imagination of climbers ever since Carl Blaurock and Bill Ervin became the first to climb all of the fourteeners in 1923. A growing number of people have followed in their footsteps. The Colorado Mountain Club reported that by the end of 2015, well over 1,600 people had reported climbing all 54 fourteeners.

Mount Elbert and Mount Massive are the two highest peaks in the state and are tempting side trips on this stretch of the CT. No technical skills are required for either climb. Nevertheless, one must regard these as serious undertakings due to potentially adverse weather conditions and the strenuous high-altitude hiking. Be prepared—start early; carry warm clothing, rain gear, and plenty of water; and turn back if you encounter bad weather or experience symptoms of altitude sickness.

The Hayden Survey named Mount Massive (14,421) in the 1870s, and despite several subsequent attempts to rename it after various individuals, the descriptive appellation has stuck. Mount Elbert (14,433) was not so lucky. Like so many other mountains in Colorado, it was named for a politician, Samuel H. Elbert, who was appointed by President Abraham Lincoln in 1862 as secretary of the new Colorado Territory. After a succession of posts, Elbert became a Supreme Court justice when Colorado achieved statehood. Elbert the mountain is the highest peak in Colorado and second highest in the contiguous United States. Mount Whitney in California tops it by only 60 feet.

Each summit is about a 6-mile round trip hike from the CT and both can be reached from the Mount Massive Trailhead parking area on Halfmoon Creek Road (the end of Segment 10 and start of Segment 11). The Mount Massive Trail begins 3 miles from the end of Segment 10, proceeding west and then north to the summit. To scale Mount Elbert, go south on Segment 11 for 1.3 miles, then take the Mount Elbert Trail another 2.5 miles west to the top. The elevation gain from the trailhead for both summits is about 4,500 feet.

Kearney Park offers some welcome openness.
PHOTO BY SCOTT RYBERG

SCALE: Squares in grid approx. 1 Mile x 1 Mile

CT (current segment)

CT (adjacent segment)

CT Bicycle Wilderness Detour

1.8 CT Feature Mileage & Location

Trail

Paved Road

Improved Road

Unimproved Road

Unimproved Road and 4WD

National Forest Boundary

Wilderness Boundary

Continental Divide

Trailhead

Parking

Camping

lighter greens = National Forest

darker greens = Wilderness Area

orange or tan = BLM Land

purples = State Land

white = Private Land

SEGMENT 10 FEATURES TABLE   San Isabel National Forest

Mileage	Features & Comments	Elevation (feet)	Mileage from Denver	Mileage to Durango	UTM-E	UTM-N (NAD83)	Zone
0.0	Begin Segment 10	10,043	156.2	328.4	375,190	4,349,393	13
1.2	Cross Busk Creek	10,039	157.4	327.2	375,857	4,348,201	13
1.8	Cross Hagerman Pass Road	10,341	158.0	326.6	376,382	4,347,675	13
3.1	Reach saddle, cross dirt road	11,094	159.3	325.3	377,283	4,346,593	13
3.2	Enter Mount Massive Wilderness	11,073	159.4	325.2	377,117	4,346,272	13
4.8	Reach Twin Mounds saddle	11,009	161.0	323.6	377,348	4,344,261	13
5.4	Bear right	10,644	161.6	323.0	377,345	4,343,350	13
5.5	Go left at intersection	10,660	161.7	322.9	377,205	4,343,382	13
6.2	Cross Rock Creek	10,269	162.4	322.2	377,093	4,342,766	13
6.5	Cross South Rock Creek	10,353	162.7	321.9	377,012	4,342,367	13
7.8	Cross Highline Trail	11,009	164.0	320.6	376,757	4,340,864	13
8.8	Cross North Willow Creek	11,107	165.0	319.6	376,448	4,339,375	13
9.2	Top of ridge	11,310	165.4	319.2	376,647	4,338,783	13
10.0	Intersect trail to Mount Massive	11,069	166.2	318.4	376,889	4,337,789	13
10.1	Cross Willow Creek	11,040	166.3	318.3	376,858	4,337,696	13
10.7	Cross South Willow Creek	10,816	166.9	317.7	376,992	4,336,884	13
13.1	End Segment 10	10,065	169.3	315.3	377,387	4,334,528	13

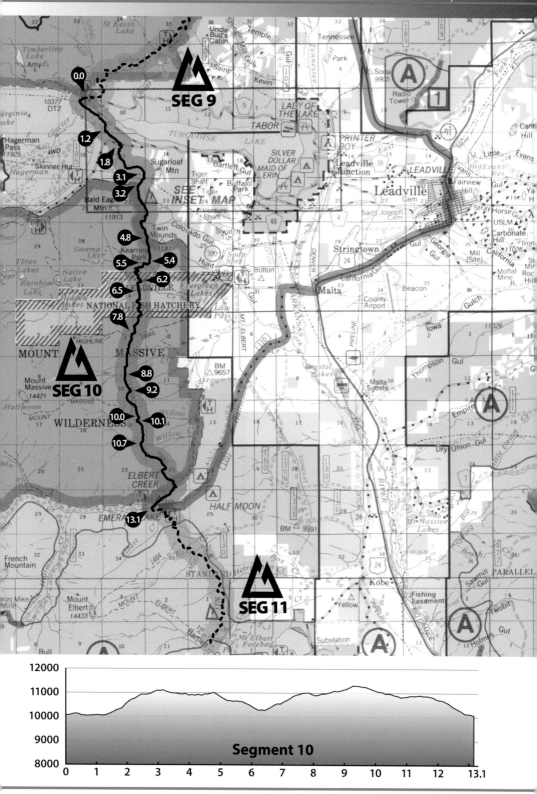

Massive Trailhead to Marshall Pass (Segments 11–15)

Segment 11: Mount Massive Trailhead to Clear Creek Road

Sunset over Twin Lakes. PHOTO BY JEFF SELLENRICK

Distance: 21.5 miles

Elevation gain: Approx. 2,910 feet

Elevation loss: Approx. 4,042 feet

USFS map: San Isabel National Forest, pages 152–153

The Colorado Trail Databook 6: pages 32–33

The CT Map Book: pages 28–30

National Geographic Trails Illustrated maps: Nos.110, 127

Jurisdiction: Leadville Ranger District, San Isabel National Forest

Access from Denver end:

Access from Durango end:

Availability of water: 🍵

Bicycling: 🚲

"The previous route over Hope Pass has been replaced by a more direct one, eliminating 4 miles of road travel. Those still choosing to climb Hope Pass know why it is so named: 'Hope I will never have to pack over that again.'"

In 2000, access issues were finally resolved and the current lower-elevation route between the Lake Creek and Clear Creek drainages opened. The old Hope Pass route is now part of the Continental Divide National Scenic Trail.

Gudy's TIP

ABOUT THIS SEGMENT

Segment 11 starts with a steep climb up a moraine ridge that marks the edge of the Halfmoon Creek Glacier to a side trail that continues up Mount Elbert (14,433), the highest mountain in Colorado. The CT skirts the eastern flank of the peak, then descends past several creeks and beautiful displays of summer wildflowers to Twin Lakes, which lie behind another

Cyclists along the south shore of Twin Lakes.
PHOTO BY DAN MILNAR

conspicuous terminal moraine. This reservoir, which is part of the Pan-Ark Project, diverts water from the Arkansas River to Colorado's Front Range cities via tunnels.

The trail wraps around the eastern lake and crosses the dam. Along the lake's southern edge, users encounter the decision point and must choose whether to turn left or right. This point is where the CT Collegiate West alternative diverges from the CT Collegiate East. Each route is roughly 80 miles. Turn left to continue Segment 11, Collegiate East, or right for Collegiate West. The western route is co-located with the Continental Divide National Scenic Trail, as The Colorado Trail has been from Georgia Pass in Segment 6.

Segment 11, Collegiate East, travelers may want to take a one-mile side trip to the historic Interlaken to see restored resort buildings of days gone by. After Segment 11 climbs away from the reservoir, there are a lot of intersections. Be sure to keep an eye out for confidence markers and signs at trail junctions.

TRAILHEAD/ACCESS POINTS

Mount Massive Trailhead: 🚗 Drive south from Leadville on US Hwy 24 for about 3.5 miles. Turn right (west) onto CO Hwy 300. Drive 0.8 mile, turn left (south), and continue 1.2 miles to an intersection. Take the righthand branch (FS Rd 110). Continue 5.5 miles to the trailhead on the righthand side of the road, just after passing over a large culvert.

Interlaken Trailhead: 🚗 Drive south from Leadville on US Hwy 24 for approximately 15 miles to CO Hwy 82, or north from Buena Vista 19.5 miles. Turn west onto Hwy 82 and drive 0.6 mile. Turn left onto graveled Lake County Rd 25 and proceed about 1 mile to end-of-the-road, spacious parking lot.

Clear Creek Road Trailhead: 🚗 See Segment 12 on page 154.

SERVICES, SUPPLIES, AND ACCOMMODATIONS – TWIN LAKES

Twin Lakes, an old mining town and perhaps Colorado's oldest resort town, is 1.5 miles southwest of where The Colorado Trail crosses CO Hwy 82. The Twin Lakes General Store is delightfully historic and provides the more than the basics.

Distance from CT: 1.5 miles
Elevation: 9,210 feet
Zip code: 81251
Area code: 719

Dining
Punky's Smokehouse BBQ Trailer
Hwy 82 just west of General Store

The Twin Lakes Inn
6435 E State Hwy 82
(719) 486-7965

Gear & Groceries
Twin Lakes General Store
6451 CO Hwy 82
(719) 486-2196

Laundry
Win-Mar Cabins
(6 miles) CO Hwy 82 and US Hwy 24
(719) 486-0785

Lodging
Win-Mar Cabins (see above)

Windspirit Cottage & Cabins
6559 CO Hwy 82
(719) 486-8138

Twin Lakes Roadhouse Lodge
6411 CO Hwy 82
(888) 486-4744

Medical
Nearest facilities in Leadville

Showers
Win-Mar plus Windspirit
(see above)

TRAIL DESCRIPTION

Segment 11 starts at the south side of the Mount Massive Trailhead parking area next to Halfmoon Creek, **mile 0.0** (10,065 feet). This is the re-entry point for mountain bikers after their detour around the Holy Cross and Mount Massive wilderness areas. Cross a bridge over the creek and continue to **mile 0.3** (10,141), where the Mount

Cache Creek in Lost Canyon, 4 miles west of the CT.
PHOTO BY DALE ZOETEWEY

Elbert Trailhead access merges into the CT from the left. Keep going straight. Pass by the remains of an old log cabin and begin climbing a series of switchbacks at **mile 0.6** (10,135). At **mile 1.3** (10,590), the Mount Elbert Trail takes off to the right. The CT stays to the left at this intersection. Continue in a generally southeasterly direction, crossing another old trail.

Aspens in the area of North Willow Creek.
PHOTO BY ROGER FORMAN

A few hundred feet beyond is a stream with a few potential campsites nearby.

Cross Box Creek at **mile 1.8** (10,468). Pass an old jeep trail, then cross the bridge over Mill Creek at **mile 2.1** (10,358). There are good campsites here. At **mile 2.3** (10,284), meet and follow an old logging road. Cross Herrington Creek at **mile 3.3** (10,320) and continue south. Reach an intersection marked by a post at **mile 4.8** (10,513) with campsite nearby. Take a right here, joining the Mount Elbert Trail (south access) for 300 feet until that trail leaves to the right. After a descent through an aspen forest, pass by some beaver ponds, where there are a few potential campsites.

After passing the ponds, the CT comes to another intersection marked with a post and a Mount Elbert sign. Go right and cross a bridge. Just after crossing the bridge, the trail turns to the right, avoiding the road at **mile 5.2** (10,522). At **mile 5.4** (10,396), the trail crosses a small stream. At **mile 5.9** (10,012) is an intersection with a sometimes poorly maintained, one-mile path (right) to Twin Lakes Village. Stay left on the CT and cross a bridge over a fast-moving creek below a small waterfall at **mile 6.0** (10,051).

Follow the CT in an easterly direction to an intersection with the trail to the Mount Elbert Trailhead parking area. Bear right and then straight ahead, and follow the trail along the southwestern edge of Lake View Campground. The trail continues just below Lake View Campground, then crosses another side trail. From this point, the trail descends a long radius switchback to **mile 7.2** (9,320), where it crosses under CO Hwy 82 via a culvert. This culvert has the distinction of being the only pedestrian underpass on The Colorado Trail. This is also where many CT users will diverge to Twin Lakes Village, 1.5 miles west along Hwy 82. Beyond here on the trail is the beginning of a long, and potentially hot, hike along the shoreline of Twin Lakes.

The trail passes through a forest of large ponderosa pines on the south side of CO Hwy 82 and goes past the Mount Elbert Power Plant at **mile 7.8** (9,295). Cross through a log fence and over five roads in the next 3 miles. After the fifth road, the CT turns to the right and crosses Twin Lakes Dam at **mile 11.4** (9,221). This route was closed following the 2001 terrorist attacks because of security concerns. It was reopened in 2009 with the stipulation that trail users must not stop or loiter on the dam.

Follow the dam road to an intersection with a gravel road and go straight. After a few hundred feet, turn left at **mile 12.1** (9,242) and follow a small jeep trail 400 feet uphill to a gate that serves as a barricade to motorized traffic. Just past the gate at **mile 12.2** (9,257), turn right on a trail and follow it west along the south shore. Reach the signed trail intersection where the CT Collegiate East and Collegiate West diverge (north end) at **mile 13.7** (9,222). The trail for Segment 11, Collegiate East, turns sharply to the left and climbs away from the lake. The CT Collegiate West, co-located with the CDNST, splits off and follows the trail along the lake, eventually crossing Hope Pass. For Collegiate West directions, skip to page 282 of the Guidebook.

Segment 11, near its south end, descends toward the Clear Creek Reservoir.

PHOTO BY BERNIE KRAUSSE

Follow the trail to the ridge, then descend to a jeep trail at **mile 14.6** (9,710), where the CT turns to the right. Ignore a logging trail to the left at **mile 14.7** (9,740) and continue ahead to another intersection at **mile 15.0** (9,819). Turn left here. Cross a seasonal stream with potential campsites, then a small stream, where there is good camping. Cross a road at **mile 16.6** (9,857), then enter a spectacular aspen forest. After crossing another small stream, turn left on a well-used jeep road at **mile 17.4** (9,803). For northbound hikers, it is especially important to note this junction because it is easy to overlook. At **mile 17.7** (9,787), turn right on a jeep road and then turn left 100 feet later to follow the CT.

There is an irrigation ditch to cross at **mile 18.2** (9,449), followed by another intersection with an old logging road. Take a right and continue ahead, passing another logging trail that enters from the left shortly afterward. After crossing a seasonal stream, go right on the power line road at **mile 18.8** (9,371). Turn to the right at **mile 19.2** (9,515), leaving the power line road. Turn left at an intersection marked with a post at **mile 19.7** (9,729) and continue climbing to **mile 19.8** (9,837), where the CT bears to the right on a single-track trail, gaining the top of a ridge several hundred feet later. Begin a big-view descent into the Clear Creek drainage, where the trail crosses an old canal, turns right at the jeep road, and stays below the road for the next few hundred feet. Cross Clear Creek Road to the tiny, road shoulder parking area at **mile 21.5** (8,937), the end of Segment 11.

When East Meets West

Collegiate East or Collegiate West? It's a question every thru-hiker, biker or rider faces on the way to or from Durango. Some have a plan going in after carefully considering the virtues of each. Others make a decision only after reaching Twin Lakes in the north or the Fooses Creek turnoff in the south, letting inspiration be their guide. Still others gather opinions from those they meet along the Trail and make their decision en route.

Whatever you decide, there is, of course, no right or wrong answer.

Neither is a "short-cut." Lengthwise, they differ by only about 5 miles, the western route being longer. As for elevation gain and loss, Collegiate East gains roughly 17,800 and loses 15,100 feet. For Collegiate West, it's 19,800 and 17,100 feet. Not a major difference over an 80-mile stretch.

Here, however, are some factors that may sway your decision one way or the other:

1. Collegiate East is the "classic" route. It has been part of The Colorado Trail since 1987, the year the Trail from Denver to Durango was officially linked. Collegiate West is the "new" route. Though long a part of the Continental Divide National Scenic Trail, it was added to The Colorado Trail only in 2012. Furthermore, the "High 23" miles of the route weren't completed until 2014.

2. East is a bit more "civilized," with higher foot and rider traffic and good access to three major resupply points: Buena Vista, about 10 miles on a well-traveled road, Mount Princeton Hot Springs, which is right on the trail, and Salida, 13 miles from the trail crossing on U.S. Highway 50. West is wilder and resupply is trickier, with less convenient access to a full range of services until reaching Monarch Pass and access to Salida, 22 miles to the east on U.S. Highway 50 or Gunnison, 42 miles to the west.

3. Thunderstorm activity can be a factor. The East is lower in average elevation, more distant from the Collegiate ridge line, and may offer better safety when there's lightning. The West is higher overall, closely tracks the Continental Divide, and has much more above-tree line exposure where the storms are most intense.

4. Want to climb a Fourteener? Take your pick. East provides relatively close and straightforward access to Mounts Yale, Princeton, Antero and Shavano, and Tabeguache Peak. From the West, you don't have to go too far off-trail to access good climbing routes to Mounts Oxford and Belford, Missouri Mountain, and La Plata and Huron Peaks.

5. The vast majority of bike riders take the East route because it offers the only practical detour around sections where bicycles are prohibited including the Collegiate Peaks Wilderness Area.

More and more Trail users, thru-hikers especially, are avoiding the choice altogether by including the Collegiate Loop in their planning, taking one side, then the other, before resuming their trip north or south.

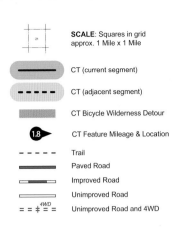

SCALE: Squares in grid approx. 1 Mile x 1 Mile

CT (current segment)

CT (adjacent segment)

CT Bicycle Wilderness Detour

1.8 — CT Feature Mileage & Location

- - - - - Trail

Paved Road

Improved Road

Unimproved Road

4WD — Unimproved Road and 4WD

National Forest Boundary

Wilderness Boundary

· · · · · · Continental Divide

Trailhead

Parking

Camping

lighter greens = National Forest

darker greens = Wilderness Area

orange or tan = BLM Land

purples = State Land

white = Private Land

SEGMENT 11 FEATURES TABLE   San Isabel National Forest

Mileage	Features & Comments	Elevation (feet)	Mileage from Denver	Mileage to Durango	UTM-E	UTM-N (NAD83)	Zone
0.0	Begin Segment 11	10,065	169.3	315.3	377,387	4,334,528	13
0.3	Trail merges from left, stay right	10,141	169.6	315.0	377,835	4,334,396	13
1.3	Left for CT right for Mt Elbert	10,590	170.6	314.0	378,314	4,333,707	13
1.8	Cross Box Creek	10,468	171.1	313.5	378,600	4,333,054	13
2.1	Cross Mill Creek	10,358	171.4	313.2	378,859	4,332,895	13
2.3	Meet and follow old logging road	10,284	171.6	313.0	379,251	4,332,743	13
3.3	Cross Herrington Creek	10,320	172.6	312.0	379,731	4,331,547	13
4.8	Turn right at intersection	10,513	174.1	310.5	379,535	4,329,861	13
5.2	Trail leaves road to the right	10,522	174.5	310.1	379,358	4,329,376	13
5.9	Stay left at intersection	10,012	175.2	309.4	379,922	4,328,344	13
6.0	Cross creek	10,051	175.3	309.3	379,924	4,328,451	13
7.2	Pass under Hwy 82	9,320	176.5	308.1	381,986	4,328,090	13
7.8	Pass by power plant	9,295	177.1	307.5	382,842	4,328,171	13
11.4	Turn right and cross dam	9,221	180.7	303.9	387,250	4,326,731	13
11.9	Straight onto gravel road	9,218	181.2	303.4	387,196	4,325,904	13
12.1	Turn left and go 400 feet to a gate	9,242	181.4	303.2	387,085	4,325,634	13
12.2	Past gate turn right on single-track	9,257	181.5	303.1	387,039	4,325,596	13
13.7	Left for Seg 11 right for Collegiate West	9,222	183.0	301.6	384,754	4,325,974	13
14.6	Turn right at intersection	9,710	183.9	300.7	385,315	4,325,204	13
15.0	Turn left at intersection	9,819	184.3	300.3	384,718	4,325,219	13
16.6	Cross a road	9,857	185.9	298.7	385,728	4,323,538	13
17.4	Turn left on jeep road	9,803	186.7	297.9	386,074	4,322,442	13
18.2	Cross irrigation ditch	9,449	187.5	297.1	386,881	4,321,979	13
19.2	Turn right	9,515	188.5	296.1	387,148	4,320,651	13
19.7	Turn left at intersection	9,729	189.0	295.6	387,022	4,320,092	13
19.8	Bear right	9,837	189.1	295.5	387,109	4,319,959	13
21.5	End Segment 11	8,937	190.8	293.8	388,946	4,319,961	13

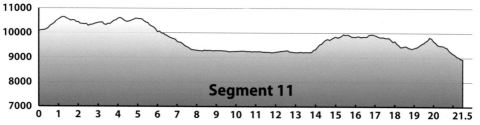

Segment 12: Clear Creek Road to Silver Creek Trailhead

Beginning of Segment 12 along Clear Creek Road.
PHOTO BY DAVID DOLTON

Distance: 18.5 miles

Elevation gain: Approx. 4,866 feet

Elevation loss: Approx. 4,364 feet

USFS map: San Isabel National Forest, pages 158–159

The Colorado Trail Databook 6: pages 34–35

The CT Map Book: pages 30–32

National Geographic Trails Illustrated maps: Nos. 110, 129

Jurisdiction: Leadville Ranger District, San Isabel National Forest

Access from Denver end:

Access from Durango end:

Availability of water:

Bicycling: See page 157

"If you have the time, a hike up Pine Creek into Missouri Basin is a rewarding side trip. In this emerald-clad basin, you are seemingly in the very heart of the sky-touching Collegiates, surrounded by four fourteeners: Harvard, Missouri, Belford, and Oxford."

This long day trip into Missouri Basin, one of the largest alpine basins in the Sawatch Range, is about 5.5 miles each way.

Gudy's TIP

ABOUT THIS SEGMENT

The beginning of Segment 12 was rerouted by the CTF and partners in 2007 to avoid the private property of Clear Creek Ranch. This required almost 3 miles of new trail construction and preparations for the 80-foot-long bridge across Clear Creek—work that was accomplished by eight crews of volunteers organized by The Colorado Trail Foundation, with bridge funding from partners and individuals.

Clear Creek Reservoir is cradled within the massive terminal moraine of the Clear Creek Glacier. At its maximum extent this glacier advanced far enough to dam the Arkansas River, forming a large temporary lake.

After entering the Collegiate Peaks Wilderness Area, the CT climbs into tundra, gains a ridge, then descends into another drainage. Without a doubt, this is the defining characteristic of this segment: A steep up and down, followed by another steep up and down. There are three fourteeners (Mounts Oxford, Harvard, and Columbia) within 3 miles of the trail through this segment. With a little planning, it is possible to climb all three of these peaks in a relatively short period of time. There are many great campsites throughout this segment and plenty of water sources.

TRAILHEAD/ACCESS POINTS

Clear Creek Road Trailhead Access: Drive north from Buena Vista for approximately 17 miles. Turn left on Chaffee County Rd 390. Drive 2.5 miles to a small, rough parking area, just west of the Colorado Division of Wildlife Campground. Three large boulders on the south side of the road mark this trailhead. There are Colorado Trail markers on both sides of the road.

Silver Creek Trailhead Access: See Segment 13 on page 160.

A major winter blowdown from 2012 in wilderness was cleared with hand saws by CTF volunteers. PHOTO BY TOM PARCHMAN

SERVICES, SUPPLIES, AND ACCOMMODATIONS

These amenities are available in Buena Vista; see Segment 13 on pages 160–169.

TRAIL DESCRIPTION

Segment 12 begins by the three boulders at the Clear Creek Trailhead, **mile 0.0** (8,937 feet). The trailhead is just to the east of a pole fence marking the boundary of Clear

Creek Ranch. At mile 0.3 begins a campground and possible confusion. Head east to the middle of the campground then south toward the creek. At **mile 0.5** (8,916), the trail crosses Clear Creek on a steel bridge that was built by volunteer trail crews. Begin a steady climb, passing under a power line at **mile 1.4** (9,365) and crossing an old road in Columbia Gulch at **mile 1.8** (9,655). Shortly thereafter, enter the Collegiate Peaks Wilderness

An eighty-foot steel bridge over Clear Creek was installed by CTF volunteers in 2007.
PHOTO BY KEITH EVANS

Area. There are several small seasonal streams in the next few miles.

Gain the ridge off Waverly Mountain at **mile 4.8** (11,653) in a stand of bristlecone pines mixed with firs. Descend via a series of steep switchbacks. In the valley bottom, Pine Creek Trail joins the CT from the northwest. (Diverge here for a major side trip possible to Missouri Basin and/or to climb Fourteeners Oxford, Belford and Missouri.) Continue south and cross a bridge over Pine Creek at **mile 6.4** (10,430). There are several good campsites along the creek corridor. Follow the CT as it bears right, leaves Pine Creek Trail, and climbs away from Pine Creek. Climb several steep switchbacks before coming to a side trail that goes right to Rainbow Lake at **mile 8.1** (11,561). Continue straight ahead. Shortly after entering the tundra, gain a ridge off Mount Harvard at **mile 9.0** (11,845) and descend to Morrison Creek at **mile 9.8** (11,573).

At **mile 10.5** (11,520), the CT crosses the Wapaca Trail, which comes in from the east, and leads to the old Lienhart Mine and road. Continue straight, heading downhill and crossing Frenchman Creek on a good bridge at **mile 11.8** (11,031). There is a good campsite on the south side of the creek. Shortly after passing this creek, cross Frenchman Creek Trail (also known as the Harvard Trail) and continue in a southeasterly direction. Gain a ridge below Mount Columbia at **mile 12.6** (11,142), then descend to **mile 14.2** (10,646), where the CT passes an old mine and road. Cross Three Elk Creek and Trail where there's a campsite 200 feet south at **mile 15.2** (10,280), pass by Harvard Lakes, and exit the Collegiate Peaks Wilderness Area at **mile 15.4** (10,246).

The CT continues to descend, crossing Powell Creek at **mile 15.9** (10,048) and passing a side trail to the A/U Ranch at **mile 16.5** (9,953). At **mile 17.8** (9,855), there is another side trail to the A/U Ranch, followed by a trail register and a right turn onto North

Cottonwood Creek Road at **mile 18.3** (9,422). Head west on the road for 0.2 mile, where you will come to the Silver Creek Trailhead at **mile 18.5** (9,430), the end of Segment 12. There is a large parking lot with interpretive signs and a bathroom here.

Collegiate Peaks Wilderness Bicycle Detour

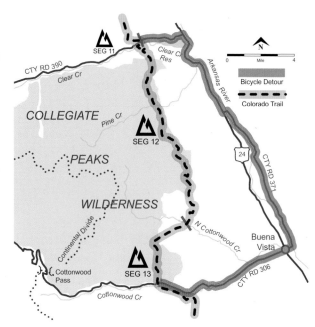

This mandatory detour bypasses the Collegiate Peaks Wilderness Area. Cyclists will enjoy majestic views of the Collegiate Peaks to the west. Although riders can stay on US Hwy 24 that has a reasonably good shoulder, it is more pleasant to turn onto the side roads below for the 10-mile pedal into Buena Vista.

Start this detour, **mile 0.0** (8,937), at the end of Segment 11 and ride east on the graveled Chaffee County Rd 390 past Clear Creek Reservoir. At **mile 3.0** (8,903), turn right (south) onto US Highway 24. Continue along the highway to **mile 9.5** (8,476) then turn left onto the graveled Chaffee County Rd 371 and cross over the Arkansas River. At **mile 9.7** (8,488), curve south onto an abandoned railroad bed of the Colorado Midland Railroad, still County Rd 371, that follows the Arkansas River and passes through short tunnels as it heads toward Buena Vista. Entering neighborhoods at **mile 18.7** (7,969), the road becomes North Colorado Avenue.

At **mile 18.9** (7,946) turn right (west) onto Main Street, cross the Arkansas River, and ride through downtown Buena Vista. At **mile 19.1** (7,943), Main Street crosses US Hwy-24. Continue cycling west on Main Street as it becomes County Rd-306, Cottonwood Pass Rd. At **mile 28.3** (9,395), reach Avalanche Trailhead (bathrooms), where cyclists rejoin the CT at Segment 13, mile 6.6.

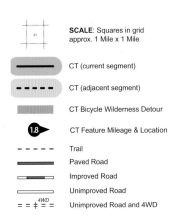

SCALE: Squares in grid approx. 1 Mile x 1 Mile

— CT (current segment)

- - - - - CT (adjacent segment)

CT Bicycle Wilderness Detour

1.8 CT Feature Mileage & Location

- - - - - Trail

— Paved Road

Improved Road

Unimproved Road

= = ‡ = = *4WD* Unimproved Road and 4WD

National Forest Boundary

Wilderness Boundary

...... Continental Divide

(T/H) Trailhead

(P) Parking

(A) Camping

lighter greens = National Forest

darker greens = Wilderness Area

orange or tan = BLM Land

purples = State Land

white = Private Land

SEGMENT 12 FEATURES TABLE   San Isabel National Forest

Mileage	Features & Comments	Elevation (feet)	Mileage from Denver	Mileage to Durango	UTM-E	UTM-N (NAD83)	Zone
0.0	Begin Segment 12	8,937	190.8	293.8	388,944	4,319,963	13
0.5	Cross Clear Creek Bridge	8,916	191.3	293.3	389,331	4,319,541	13
1.4	Cross under power line	9,365	192.2	292.4	388,825	4,318,814	13
1.8	Enter Collegiate Peaks Wilderness	9,655	192.6	292.0	388,839	4,318,542	13
4.8	Gain ridge	11,653	195.6	289.0	388,613	4,314,810	13
6.4	Cross Pine Creek	10,430	197.2	287.4	389,384	4,313,657	13
8.1	Straight for CT or right for lake	11,561	198.9	285.7	389,731	4,312,397	13
9.0	Gain ridge	11,845	199.8	284.8	389,867	4,311,574	13
9.8	Cross Morrison Creek	11,573	200.6	284.0	389,916	4,310,752	13
10.5	Pass Wapaca Trail on left	11,520	201.3	283.3	390,901	4,310,460	13
11.8	Cross Frenchman Creek	11,031	202.6	282.0	391,074	4,308,881	13
12.6	Gain ridge	11,142	203.4	281.2	392,078	4,308,530	13
14.2	Pass neglected mine and old road	10,646	205.0	279.6	391,994	4,306,883	13
15.2	Cross Three Elk Creek and Trail	10,280	206.0	278.6	392,448	4,305,664	13
15.4	Exit Collegiate Peaks Wilderness	10,246	206.2	278.4	392,432	4,305,358	13
15.9	Cross Powell Creek	10,048	206.7	277.9	392,331	4,304,736	13
16.5	Pass side trail to A/U Ranch	9,953	207.3	277.3	392,844	4,304,163	13
17.8	Pass 2nd side trail to A/U Ranch	9,855	208.6	276.0	392,589	4,302,792	13
18.3	Turn right on road	9,422	209.1	275.5	392,535	4,302,469	13
18.5	End Segment 12	9,430	209.3	275.3	392,346	4,302,593	13

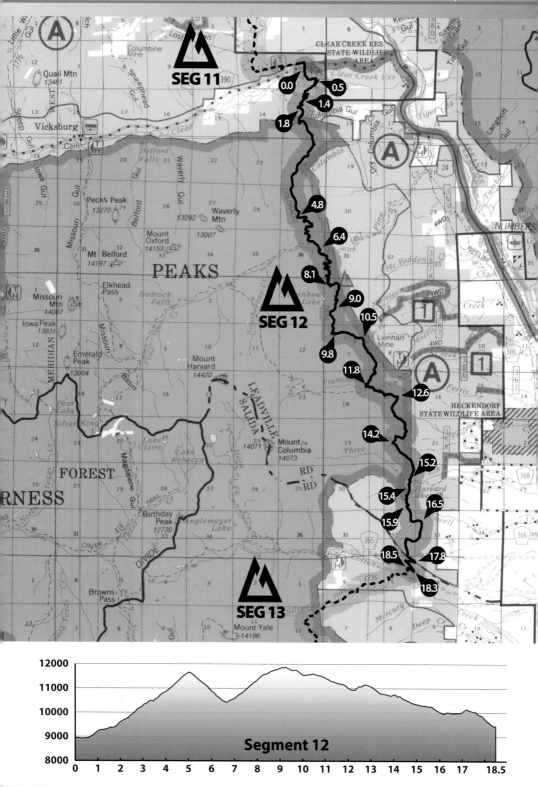

Segment 13: Silver Creek Trailhead to Chalk Creek Trailhead

Mount Princeton from Mount Yale.

PHOTO BY JEFF SELLENRICK

Distance: 22.8 miles

Elevation gain: Approx. 4,296 feet

Elevation loss: Approx. 5,343 feet

USFS map: San Isabel National Forest, pages 168–169

The Colorado Trail Databook 6: pages 36–37

The CT Map Book: pages 32–34

National Geographic Trails Illustrated map: No. 129

Jurisdiction: Salida Ranger District, San Isabel National Forest

Access from Denver end:

Access from Durango end:

Availability of water:

Bicycling: See page 157

"Be respectful of the long stretch of private property as the trail descends into the Chalk Creek Valley."

Although CT travel here is primarily on public corridors, there is no public camping available on the surrounding private land.

Gudy's TIP

ABOUT THIS SEGMENT

Segment 13 begins at the Silver Creek Trailhead. Begin south beyond the sign and cross North Cottonwood Creek on a bridge, then commence a long climb that passes into the Collegiate Peaks Wilderness Area before topping out on a saddle on the east ridge of Mount Yale (14,196). The views from here are outstanding, and a short jaunt up the knoll to the east of the saddle brings the Arkansas Valley into view. It is possible and straightforward to climb Mount Yale via this ridge, although the faint trail disappears and it's necessary to do some scrambling. Allow about four hours for the round trip and don't be discouraged by the false summits along the route. The descent to the Avalanche Trailhead is very steep—one trail user noted he wouldn't have minded a belay in a few spots! Trekking poles come in handy here.

There is NO camping for the next 6.5 miles after encountering private property at the youth camp at mile 17.

The CT leaves the wilderness area just before reaching the trailhead, allowing mountain bikers to rejoin the trail. Eventually, the trail contours around the base of Mount Princeton. As it approaches Chalk Creek it descends along a moraine ridge that marks the edge of the Chalk Creek Glacier; the terminal moraine of the glacier and the broad aprons of gravel spread by its melt water are conspicuous in the valley below. Where it joins County Rd 321, the CT begins a 5.7-mile road walk to bypass private land. The Colorado Trail Foundation has been searching for a way to realign this onto trail

West along one of the county roads near Segment 13's end with part of Mt. Princeton behind.

PHOTO BY JEFF SELLENRICK

for years, but has not had any luck yet. A soak at the Mount Princeton Hot Springs Resort can help ease the monotony of road walking, though. West of the resort the road route skirts the base of the Chalk Cliffs, which are not chalk at all, but 65 million-year-old granite largely altered to white clay by water from the hot springs. Staying on the trail-route roads in this area can be tricky, so be alert and consult your *Guidebook, Map Book,* or *Databook* to ensure you go the right way at each road junction.

Chalk Cliffs from near Mount Princeton Hot Springs.

PHOTO BY JULIE VIDA AND MARK TABB

TRAILHEAD/ACCESS POINTS

Silver Creek Trailhead: From US Hwy 24 at the north end of Buena Vista, 7 blocks north of the traffic light, turn west on Crossman Street, also known as Chaffee County Rd 350. Follow it for 2 miles to its end, where it intersects Chaffee County Rd 361. Turn right (north), proceed 0.9 mile, and make a sharp left turn (south) onto Chaffee County Rd 365, a gravel road. The road soon turns west and continues for 3.5 miles (sometimes rough and rutted) to the *northbound* CT trailhead. A trail register and sign identify it and there is a small informal parking area on the south side of the road. Continue 0.1 mile to the *southbound* trailhead on the south side of the road, the official end of Segment 12 and beginning of Segment 13. There is a large gravel parking lot, interpretive signs, and a Forest Service toilet here. On the north side of the road, there is an even larger parking lot, suitable for horse trailers.

Avalanche Trailhead: From US Hwy 24 in Buena Vista, turn west at the traffic light onto the Cottonwood Pass Road (Main Street, which becomes Chaffee County Rd 306 at the edge of town). Drive 9.5 miles to the Avalanche Trailhead on the north side of the highway. You may spot Colorado Trail signs on both sides of the highway about 0.2 mile before the trailhead entrance sign on the righthand side. The CT crosses the parking area.

Cottonwood Lake Road Access: From the traffic light in Buena Vista, proceed west on the Cottonwood Pass Road for approximately 8 miles. Turn left onto the

Cottonwood Lake Road (Chaffee County Rd 344). After about 0.2 mile, the CT crosses the road. There is a small primitive parking area on the lefthand side.

Chalk Creek Trailhead: See Segment 14 on page 170.

SERVICES, SUPPLIES, AND ACCOMMODATIONS – BUENA VISTA

Buena Vista, as might be gathered from its Spanish name, is a beautiful place to visit because of its striking location in the Arkansas Valley between the mineralized Mosquito Range and the towering Sawatch Range. The town, approximately halfway between Denver and Durango on The Colorado Trail, is an ideal resupply point for long-distance trekkers. The most direct way to reach Buena Vista from the CT is to follow Chaffee County Rd 306. It is approximately 9.5 miles east of the Avalanche Trailhead.

Distance from CT: 9.5 miles
Elevation: 7,954 feet
Zip code: 81211
Area code: 719

Dining
Several locations in town

Gear (including fuel canisters)
The Trailhead
402 East Main St
(719) 395-8001

Groceries
City Market
438 US Hwy 24 North
(719) 395-2431

Info
Chamber of Commerce
343 US Hwy 24 South
(719) 395-6612

Laundry
Missing Sock Laundry
522 Antero Cir.
(719) 395-6757

Lodging
Several locations in town

Medical
Mountain Medical Center
36 Oak St.
(719) 395-8632

Post Office
Buena Vista Post Office
110 Brookdale Ave.
(719) 395-2445

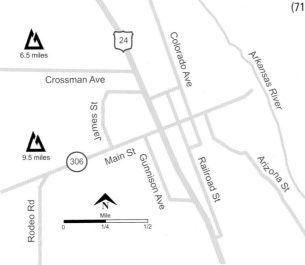

TRAIL DESCRIPTION

Segment 13 begins at the Silver Creek Trailhead on FS Rd 365, **mile 0.0** (9,430 feet), with toilets and plenty of parking. Begin south beyond the signs and cross North Cottonwood Creek on a good bridge, pass a trail register, and climb through a mixed spruce and fir forest. There are potential campsites with accessible water in the first couple miles. Eventually follow Silver Creek to **mile 2.5** (11,098), where the CT crosses the creek. Enter the Collegiate Peaks Wilderness Area at **mile 2.7** (11,269) and climb to the saddle on the east ridge of Mount Yale at **mile 3.4** (11,889). There is a potential campsite on the right. A short uphill trail east leads to an expansive view. A faint trail west leads to Mount Yale (14,196). Descend from the pass into a forest of bristlecone pine and fir in Avalanche Gulch. Leave the wilderness area near a small stream at **mile 6.3** (9,502) and arrive at the Avalanche Trailhead at **mile 6.6** (9,395).

Cross the parking lot to single-track, then cross Cottonwood Pass Road (Chaffee County Rd 306) and then through a small dirt parking area at **mile 6.7** (9,335). This is a good place for mountain bikers to rejoin the CT after detouring around the wilderness

Trekking through a grove of mature aspen.
PHOTO BY KEITH EVANS

Approach to climb Mt. Yale from the CT.
PHOTO BY JEFF SELLENRICK

area. Turn left on the trail and cross Middle Cottonwood Creek on a bridge. The trail bends to the southeast and follows along private property and above Rainbow Lake. Trail users are asked to stay on the trail and respect the private property. After passing a small stream, take the fork to the left when the trail splits at **mile 8.8** (9,018). From here, the trail crosses Chaffee County Rd 344 at **mile 8.9** (8,967).

The CT crosses a bridge over South Cottonwood Creek, which is the last reliable water source for the next 4.2 miles, at **mile 9.0** (8,921). There are a lot of good campsites in this area. The trail follows the creek for about 0.5 mile, then crosses a dirt road (County Rd 343) at **mile 9.5** (8,862). There is another trail register here. From the register, the CT climbs a series of switchbacks to a trail junction at **mile 11.0** (9,641). Take a left turn here. At **mile 11.6** (9,885), gain the saddle southwest of Bald Mountain. After passing two creeks, cross Silver Prince Creek at **mile 13.2** (9,925) and Maxwell Creek at **mile 14.0** (10,003). There is a good campsite 300 feet south of Maxwell Creek. Cross Dry Creek on a bridge at **mile 15.9** (9,526), then join a dirt road (FS Rd 322) at **mile 17.1** (9,497) where climbers of Mount Princeton diverge uphill. Stay left and downhill; the CT follows roads for the next 5.7 miles to avoid private land.

Pass under the Mount Princeton Trail Junction sign at **mile 18.2** (8,924) and walk through the parking lot of a private camp. The paved road begins here. Follow the road to the east until **mile 18.8** (8,681), where it bends to the northeast. Turn right (south) on

Chaffee County Rd 321, another paved road, at **mile 19.1** (8,615). Continue following the road, bending to the east, then turning hard to the southwest. Keep an eye out for the trail markers along the side of the road. At **mile 20.3** (8,194), the CT turns right at the junction onto Chaffee County Rd 162. After another 1.4 miles, veer to the left onto Chaffee County Rd 291 at **mile 21.7** (8,303). This dirt road goes through a neighborhood to the Chalk Creek Trailhead on the left at **mile 22.8** (8,389). This is the end of Segment 13.

Mount Princeton Hot Springs

This spot was long frequented by American Indians before being taken over and developed by whites, beginning in 1860. The fortunes of the Mount Princeton Hot Springs Hotel rose and fell with the fortunes of area mines and the coming of the railroad and its subsequent departure in 1926. The elaborate hotel on the site was demolished for scrap lumber in 1950. The resort has been rebuilt, and promises to "melt your cares away." Pools are a delight and open every day of the year (admission required). The resort store (maildrop and modest resupply) and the lodging are also of interest to CT travelers.

End of Segment 13 follows roads, like this Chaffee Cty Rd 162 that passes Mount Princeton Hot Springs.
PHOTO BY JEFF SELLENRICK

The Collegiate Peaks

Collegiate Wilderness boundary sign. The CT passes through six wilderness areas.
PHOTO BY AARON LOCANDER

This impressive collection of skyscraping fourteeners, with names such as Harvard, Columbia, Yale, and Princeton, are collectively known as the Collegiate Peaks, a subset of the greater Sawatch Range. These peaks were first surveyed by a team led by Harvard Professor Josiah Dwight Whitney (for whom California's Mount Whitney is named). They started the tradition of naming the fourteeners in this area for universities after climbing Mount Harvard (14,420) in 1869. Mount Yale (14,196) was named after Whitney's alma mater. Later climbers continued the practice, adding Princeton, Oxford, and Columbia.

Despite their proximity, some of the Collegiate fourteeners don't lend themselves to a day climb from The Colorado Trail. Possibly the best opportunity comes with Mount Yale in Segment 13. At about mile 3.4 of that segment, the CT gains the long east ridge of Yale, offering a moderate, though without well-defined trail, route to the summit with a bit of rock hopping and a few false summits along the way.

Another Fourteener, Mount Princeton, also offers relatively direct access from the CT, though the round-trip is 12 miles and the peak 4,700 feet above the trail. At mile 17.1 of Segment 13, diverge from the CT and hike 3 miles uphill on a dirt road open to vehicles. (It might be feasible to trim your hiking miles by soliciting a ride from one of the many peak-baggers, especially easy very early on a weekend morning.) Beyond where vehicles must park, hike 3 more miles on good trail to the summit.

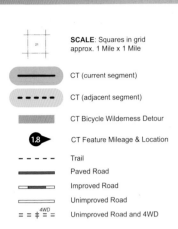

SCALE: Squares in grid approx. 1 Mile x 1 Mile

CT (current segment)

CT (adjacent segment)

CT Bicycle Wilderness Detour

1.8 CT Feature Mileage & Location

Trail

Paved Road

Improved Road

Unimproved Road

Unimproved Road and 4WD

National Forest Boundary

Wilderness Boundary

Continental Divide

Trailhead

Parking

Camping

lighter greens = National Forest

darker greens = Wilderness Area

orange or tan = BLM Land

purples = State Land

white = Private Land

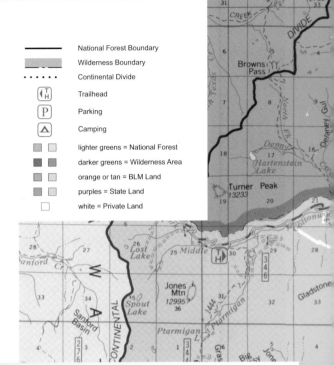

SEGMENT 13 FEATURES TABLE   San Isabel National Forest

Mileage	Features & Comments	Elevation (feet)	Mileage from Denver	Mileage to Durango	UTM-E	UTM-N (NAD83)	Zone
0.0	Begin Segment 13	9,430	209.3	275.3	392,346	4,302,593	13
2.5	Cross Silver Creek	11,098	211.8	272.8	389,394	4,301,379	13
2.7	Enter Collegiate Peaks Wilderness	11,269	212.0	272.6	389,134	4,301,149	13
3.4	Gain saddle	11,889	212.7	271.9	388,760	4,300,634	13
6.3	Leave Collegiate Peaks Wilderness	9,502	215.6	269.0	389,007	4,297,155	13
8.8	Turn left then cross County Rd 344	9,018	218.1	266.5	391,624	4,295,488	13
9.0	Cross South Cottonwood Creek	8,921	218.3	266.3	391,866	4,295,419	13
9.5	Cross the dirt County Rd 343	8,862	218.8	265.8	392,508	4,295,787	13
11.0	Turn left at intersection	9,641	220.3	264.3	392,797	4,294,759	13
11.6	Gain saddle	9,885	220.9	263.7	393,425	4,294,630	13
13.2	Cross Silver Prince Creek	9,925	222.5	262.1	394,002	4,292,735	13
14.0	Cross Maxwell Creek	10,003	223.3	261.3	394,537	4,292,200	13
15.9	Cross Dry Creek	9,526	225.2	259.4	395,798	4,290,627	13
17.1	Join the dirt FS Rd 322	9,497	226.4	258.2	396,774	4,289,482	13
18.2	Mount Princeton Trail Junction sign	8,924	227.5	257.1	397,846	4,288,577	13
19.1	Turn right on paved County Rd 321	8,615	228.4	256.2	399,035	4,288,820	13
20.3	Turn right on paved County Rd 162	8,194	229.6	255.0	398,830	4,287,780	13
21.7	Left onto dirt County Rd 291	8,303	231.0	253.6	397,328	4,286,598	13
22.8	End Segment 13	8,389	232.1	252.5	395,669	4,286,022	13

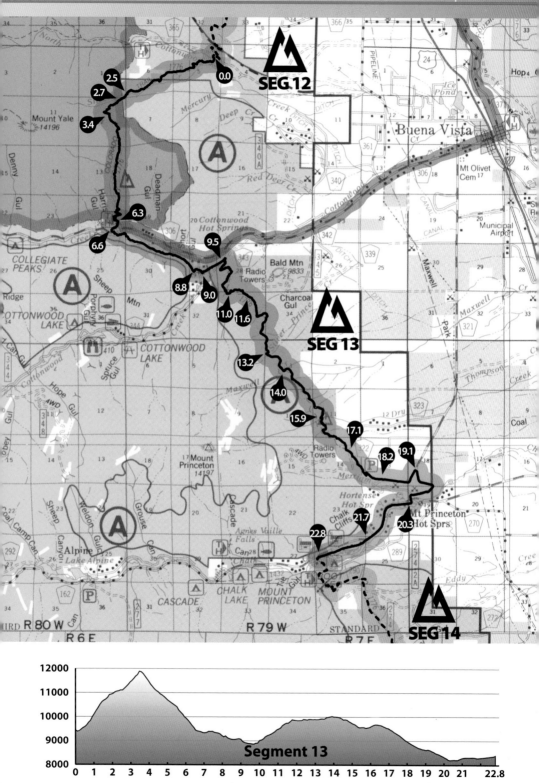

Segment 14: Chalk Creek Trailhead to US Hwy 50

Chalk Cliffs north of Segment 14.

PHOTO BY CARL BROWN

Distance: 20.4 miles

Elevation gain: Approx. 4,007 feet

Elevation loss: Approx. 3,531 feet

USFS map: San Isabel National Forest, pages 176–177

The Colorado Trail Databook 6: pages 38–39

The CT Map Book: pages 34–37

National Geographic Trails Illustrated map: No. 130

Jurisdiction: Salida Ranger District, San Isabel National Forest

Access from Denver end:

Access from Durango end:

Availability of water:

Bicycling:

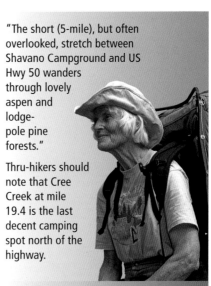

"The short (5-mile), but often overlooked, stretch between Shavano Campground and US Hwy 50 wanders through lovely aspen and lodge-pole pine forests."

Thru-hikers should note that Cree Creek at mile 19.4 is the last decent camping spot north of the highway.

Gudy's TIP

ABOUT THIS SEGMENT

Segment 14 travels through the southern end of the Sawatch Range, passing Mounts Antero and Shavano and Tabeguache Peak, all fourteeners. The trail climbs steeply at the start of the section, but soon levels off and travels through forested areas before reaching the first water source since Chalk Creek, a distance of 6.6 miles. After this, there are several water sources and good camping as the northern part of the Sangre de Cristo Range comes into view ahead. The big descent at the end of the segment comes out on US Hwy 50, a good place for thru-hikers to arrange a ride to the nearby town of Salida for rest and resupply.

Waterfall on Browns Creek 1.5 miles west of the CT.
PHOTO BY DALE ZOETEWEY

TRAILHEAD/ACCESS POINTS

Chalk Creek Trailhead: 🚗 Drive south from Buena Vista on US Hwy 285 to Nathrop. Turn right (west) onto Chaffee County Rd 162 for approximately 7 miles. The trailhead is on the left side of the road, slightly below road level.

Browns Creek Trailhead: 🚗 Drive south from Nathrop on US Hwy 285 for about 3.2 miles. Turn right (west) on Chaffee County Rd 270 for 2 miles to where it turns north. Continue straight ahead onto Chaffee County Rd 272 for 2 miles to where it turns left (south) at an intersection. Continue south on 272 for 1.6 more miles to the Browns Creek Trailhead. Walk west on the trail for 1.4 miles to intersect the CT.

Angel of Shavano Trailhead: 🚗 From the intersection of US Hwy 285 and US Hwy 50 at Poncha Springs, drive west on US Hwy 50 for about 6 miles. Turn right (north) onto Chaffee County Rd 240 (North Fork South Arkansas River Road). Proceed on 240 for 3.8 miles to the trailhead parking area opposite the Angel of Shavano Campground.

US Hwy 50 Trailhead Access: 🚗 See Segment 15 on page 178.

SERVICES, SUPPLIES, AND ACCOMMODATIONS – SALIDA

Salida, an old railroad town and now a commercial center for the Arkansas Valley, is about 13 miles east of the CT crossing at US Hwy 50. Poncha Springs, 8 miles east of the crossing, has a small restaurant and a small convenience store. Monarch Spur RV Park, about a mile east of the CT on US Hwy 50, has camping and showers. Monarch Mountain Lodge, about 4.5 miles west of the CT on US Hwy 50, has lodging, mail drop, showers, and laundry.

Distance from CT: 13 miles
Elevation: 7,036 feet
Zip code: 81201
Area code: 719

Bus
Chaffee Shuttle
54 Jones Ave.
(719) 530-8980

Dining
Several locations in town

Gear (including fuel canisters)
Salida Mountain Sports
110 North F St.
(719) 539-4400

Groceries (several including)
Walmart Supercenter
7865 W Hwy 50
(719) 539-3566

PloughBoy
311 H St
(719) 539-5292

Info
Chamber of Commerce
406 W. Rainbow Blvd.
(719) 539-2068

Laundry
Salida Laundromat
1410 E St.
(719) 530-1263

Lodging
The Simple Lodge & Hostel
224 E. First St.
(719) 650-7381

Salida Hostel
225 W Hwy 291
(719) 530-1116

Medical
Heart of the Rockies Regional Medical Center
1000 Rush Dr
(719) 530-2200

Post Office
Poncha Springs Post Office
6500 US Hwy 285
(719) 539-2117

Salida Post Office
310 D St.
(719) 539-2548

Showers
Salida Hot Springs Aquatic Center
410 W. US Hwy 50
(719) 539-6738

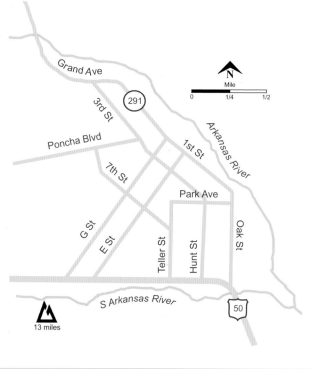

TRAIL DESCRIPTION

Segment 14 begins at the Chalk Creek Trailhead, **mile 0.0** (8,389 feet). Chalk Creek is the last reliable water until Little Browns Creek, 6.6 miles ahead. Go south across a bridge and begin hiking uphill. Pass the Bootleg Trail at **mile 0.1** (8,430). There is a fee campground if you take this trail left about 100 yards. At **mile 0.4** (8,506) cross County Rd 290. The intersection is marked with a Forest Service sign for Raspberry Gulch. In a half mile reach a campsite with a small seasonal stream in a ravine at **mile 0.9** (8,870). Ascend several switchbacks to the top of a knoll at **mile 1.4** (9,310). After heading downhill to the east, turn to the right at **mile 2.1** (9,021) and head down a steep, rocky hillside, crossing Eddy Creek at **mile 2.2** (8,920). Cross another road (FS Rd 274) at **mile 2.4** (8,901).

Contour along the northeast side of Peak 11,038, eventually crossing Raspberry Gulch Road (FS Rd 273) at **mile 3.9** (8,906), with dry camping in the area. The CT crosses an eroded jeep trail at **mile 4.5** (8,963) and climbs until reaching **mile 6.1** (9,664), where the trail bears left at the junction with the Little Browns Creek Trail. At **mile 6.4** (9,546) turn right at the intersection. Cross Little Browns Creek on a bridge at **mile 6.6** (9,615)

Northbound hikers in Segment 14. Mount Princeton is in the background.
PHOTO BY KEITH EVANS

then turn left. (Go straight 1.5 miles to the waterfall pictured on page 171.) Then cross another small stream before passing over Browns Creek on a log bridge at **mile 6.8** (9,590). There are potential campsites in this area.

Bridge over Chalk Creek at the Segment 14 trailhead.
PHOTO BY KEITH EVANS

Cross the Wagon Loop Trail at **mile 7.0** (9,615) and head in a generally southerly direction until reaching Fourmile Creek at **mile 8.7** (9,757). Cross Sand Creek at **mile 10.0** (9,621) and Squaw Creek at **mile 12.2** (9,833). Both creeks offer camping possibilities. There is an intersection with the Mount Shavano Trail at **mile 12.7** (9,880). Continue straight ahead. Pass through a Forest Service gate and into an open meadow. A log fence prevents motor vehicles from accessing the trail at **mile 13.0** (9,812). Cross a jeep road (FS Rd 254) at **mile 13.2** (9,832), continuing southwest. Descend to **mile 14.9** (9,208), where the CT reaches the Angel of Shavano Trailhead. The trail briefly re-enters some trees before crossing road (Chaffee County Rd 240) at **mile 15.0** and continues to a bridge over the North Fork of the Arkansas River at **mile 15.2** (9,133). There are several confidence markers on trees in this area. Trail users may decide to stay at the nearby Angel of Shavano Campground for a fee.

Begin a climb up several switchbacks, eventually reaching the top of the ridge at **mile 16.7** (9,743). From here, the CT skirts the edge of an old logging area that has been replanted. There is a spring-fed, seasonal pond with campsites at about **mile 17.5** (9,575). At **mile 18.0** (9,442), the trail crosses Lost Creek and then the Lost Creek jeep road. Follow the CT to the southwest, crossing a road next to a huge circular meadow and another road (FS Rd 248) just past the meadow. At **mile 19.5** (9,210), cross Cree Creek, the last campsite area until about a mile into Segment 15. Go under a double power line at **mile 19.8** (9,316), then leave the power line road at **mile 20.0** (9,223) on a single-track trail to the left. Cross an old railroad grade at **mile 20.2** (8,960). Segment 14 ends at US Hwy 50 at **mile 20.4** (8,861). There is a large trail marker on the north side of the highway.

Mount Shavano and Tabeguache Peak

Want to climb a Fourteener (or two) as part of your Colorado Trail trek? This side trip opportunity is very straightforward. The Mount Shavano Trail, which intersects the CT at mile 12.7 (9,880), is the Colorado Fourteeners Initiative's recommended route. Follow the Mount Shavano Trail west about 4 miles, first to a saddle and then along the ridge to top of Mount Shavano (14,229). If you're still feeling strong and the weather is favorable, from the top of Shavano, travel northwest along the connecting ridge to Tabeguache Peak's summit (14,155), less than a mile and 500 feet of climbing away. Return via the same route. Although technically easy, don't underestimate the difficulties. Get an early start and be prepared for 5,000 feet of elevation gain and an arduous 10-mile round trip.

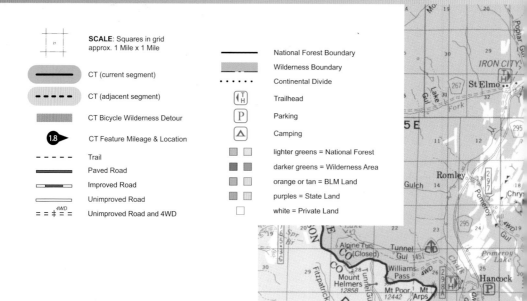

SCALE: Squares in grid approx. 1 Mile x 1 Mile

CT (current segment)

CT (adjacent segment)

CT Bicycle Wilderness Detour

1.8 CT Feature Mileage & Location

Trail

Paved Road

Improved Road

Unimproved Road

Unimproved Road and 4WD

National Forest Boundary

Wilderness Boundary

Continental Divide

Trailhead

Parking

Camping

lighter greens = National Forest

darker greens = Wilderness Area

orange or tan = BLM Land

purples = State Land

white = Private Land

SEGMENT 14 FEATURES TABLE White River and Pike National Forests

Mileage	Features & Comments	Elevation (feet)	Mileage from Denver	Mileage to Durango	UTM-E	UTM-N (NAD83)	Zone
0.0	Begin Segment 14	8,389	232.1	252.5	395,669	4,286,022	13
0.1	Pass Bootleg Trail	8,430	232.2	252.4	395,719	4,285,900	13
0.4	Cross County Rd 290	8,506	232.5	252.1	395,932	4,285,586	13
1.4	Top out on knoll	9,310	233.5	251.1	396,291	4,285,071	13
2.1	Turn right	9,021	234.2	250.4	397,268	4,285,280	13
2.2	Cross Eddy Creek	8,920	234.3	250.3	397,196	4,285,103	13
2.4	Cross FS Rd 274	8,901	234.5	250.1	397,202	4,284,870	13
3.9	Cross Raspberry Gulch Road 273	8,906	236.0	248.6	398,183	4,282,952	13
4.5	Cross eroded jeep road	8,963	236.6	248.0	398,446	4,282,224	13
6.1	Bear left at junction	9,664	238.2	246.4	397,219	4,280,808	13
6.4	Turn right at intersection	9,546	238.5	246.1	397,292	4,280,441	13
6.6	Cross Little Browns Creek	9,615	238.7	245.9	397,123	4,280,132	13
6.8	Cross Browns Creek	9,590	238.9	245.7	397,277	4,279,953	13
7.0	Pass Wagon Loop Trail on left	9,615	239.1	245.5	397,387	4,279,866	13
8.7	Cross Fourmile Creek	9,757	240.8	243.8	397,062	4,277,860	13
10.0	Cross Sand Creek	9,621	242.1	242.5	397,283	4,276,298	13
12.2	Cross Squaw Creek	9,833	244.3	240.3	396,242	4,273,962	13
12.7	Pass Mount Shavano Trail on right	9,880	244.8	239.8	395,880	4,273,299	13
13.0	Pass through Forest Service gate	9,812	245.1	239.5	395,703	4,272,954	13
13.2	Cross side trail and FS Rd 254	9,832	245.3	239.3	395,515	4,272,626	13
14.9	Reach Angel of Shavano Trailhead	9,208	247.0	237.6	393,792	4,271,443	13
15.2	Cross North Fork of Arkansas River	9,133	247.3	237.3	393,618	4,271,144	13
16.7	Reach top of ridge	9,743	248.8	235.8	393,610	4,270,555	13
18.0	Cross Lost Creek then jeep road	9,442	250.1	234.5	392,870	4,269,234	13
19.5	Cross Cree Creek	9,210	251.6	233.0	391,787	4,267,794	13
19.8	Cross under double power line	9,316	251.9	232.7	391,859	4,267,336	13
20.2	Cross railroad grade	8,960	252.3	232.3	391,698	4,267,018	13
20.4	End Segment 14	8,861	252.5	232.1	391,720	4,266,827	13

Segment 15: US Hwy 50 to Marshall Pass Trailhead

On the Continental Divide above South Fooses Creek, Segment 15.

PHOTO BY BEN KRAUSHAAR

Distance: 14.3 miles

Elevation gain: Approx. 3,576 feet

Elevation loss: Approx. 1,608 feet

USFS maps: San Isabel and Gunnison National Forests, pages 182–183

The Colorado Trail Databook 6: pages 40–41

The CT Map Book: pages 37–39

National Geographic Trails Illustrated maps: Nos. 130, 139

Jurisdiction: Salida and Gunnison Ranger Districts, San Isabel and Gunnison National Forests

Access from Denver end:

Access from Durango end:

Availability of water: 🍵

Bicycling: 🚴

"Once up on the Divide, you'll have unobstructed views in every direction. Three of our mightiest mountain ranges—the Sawatch, the San Juan, and the Sangre de Cristo—reach for the sky."

The Divide is lofty and remote. There are no towns close by for convenient resupply, and cell phones are unlikely to work in an emergency. The next 100 miles is the least-traveled portion of the CT.

Gudy's TIP

ABOUT THIS SEGMENT

After leaving US Hwy 50 and beginning this segment, there are no convenient resupply points for the next 100 miles until the town of Creede. *Be prepared.* The first few miles climb gently southwest on a dirt road passing campsites. The route becomes single-track and turns south as it climbs steeply in the South Fooses Creek drainage, eventually reaching the Continental Divide. This is the south junction of the Collegiate East and Collegiate West, and where Segment 15 rejoins the Continental Divide National Scenic Trail (CDNST). It is also a well-known mountain bike route known as the Monarch Crest Trail. (See the sidebar in Segment 16 on page 187). Be on the alert for mountain bikers approaching from behind, as well as the motorcycles also allowed here, especially numerous on weekends.

From here, the trail follows the Divide closely until the end of the segment at Marshall Pass and beyond. Just north of Marshall Pass the trail passes out of basement rocks and into gray volcanic rocks, part of the San Juan volcanic field that covers almost 10,000 square miles and includes at least 10,000 cubic miles of volcanic rocks.

TRAILHEAD/ACCESS POINTS

US Hwy 50 and South Fooses Creek Trailhead: From the intersection of US Hwy 285 and US Hwy 50 at Poncha Springs, drive west on US Hwy 50 for approximately 9 miles to the Fooses Creek Road (Chaffee County Rd 225). There is a wide shoulder on the south side of US Hwy 50 that provides limited parking. This is the official beginning of Segment 15. The CT follows Fooses Creek Road for 2.8 miles (left at junctions) to the South Fooses Creek Trailhead and additional limited parking. The road to the trailhead is rather primitive, but usually most cars can make it.

Marshall Pass Trailhead: See Segment 16 on page 184.

SERVICES, SUPPLIES, AND ACCOMMODATIONS

These amenities are available in Salida; see Segment 14 on pages 170–177.

TRAIL DESCRIPTION

Segment 15 begins at the intersection of US Hwy 50 and Fooses Creek Road (FS Rd 225), **mile 0.0** (8,861 feet). Follow the dirt road through a stretch where camping is prohibited, taking a fork to the left at **mile 0.2** (8,830), and crossing the South Fork of the Arkansas River. The road bends back to the west and eventually heads in a southwesterly direction. Pass by Fooses Lake, a small reservoir that is part of a hydroelectric project that

Mountain bikers take on the famous Monarch Crest.
PHOTO BY ANTHONY SLOAN

produces power for the Salida area, at **mile 0.8** (8,960) beyond which camping is allowed and several good sites exist. Stay on this main road until reaching **mile 2.7** (9,553).

At **mile 2.7** (9,553), turn left onto another small road and reach the South Fooses Creek Trailhead at **mile 2.8** (9,551) where there are hard-packed campsites. Turn right, cross the creek on a bridge, and begin single-track. From this point until mile 8.2, the trail stays near the creek, passes campsites, and crosses multiple times on bridges well built by CTF volunteers and the US Forest Service. The final crossing of South Fooses Creek comes at **mile 8.2** (11,450). Begin a climb that ascends 668 feet in a half mile, one of the steepest grades on the entire CT. Gain the crest of the Continental Divide at **mile 8.6** (11,909) and reach the southern junction of the CT Collegiate East and Collegiate West. Here you'll resume following the co-located Continental Divide National Scenic Trail and encounter the famed Monarch Crest bicycle route. Expect southbound bicycles, especially numerous on weekends, as well as the motorcycles allowed here. To continue to the end of Segment 15, turn left at this well-marked intersection.

Follow the Monarch Crest in a generally southeasterly direction, turning right at the intersection at **mile 10.3** (11,501), where the CT heads to the south. The Green Creek Shelter is just east of and visible from the CT, with water available 0.3 mile north and below along the Green Creek Trail. Cross a trail, Agate Creek Trail on the right and Cochetopa Creek Trail on the left, at **mile 11.4** (11,814). (The summit of 13,971-foot Mount Ouray is to the east and most often climbed by following the Cochetopa Creek Trail to the Divide and traversing the ridge to the peak.) Continue ahead until joining an old jeep trail at **mile 12.8** (11,364). There is a piped spring that flows reliably at **mile 13.0** (11,260). After **mile 14.0** (10,850) and about 200 yards before Marshall Pass Rd, cross a large ditch culvert where there is water available. Take a right turn onto Marshall Pass Road (Chaffee County Rd 200) at **mile 14.1** (10,820) and cross the road to the Marshall Pass restrooms and parking. Water from Poncha Creek is available in a large swampy area 0.25 mile east of the restrooms—either follow the road to the east or just head downhill past the restrooms. If you don't mind a little road traffic, Marshall Pass is good for camping given the restrooms and water. In dry periods, this may be the last water available for the next 10 or 12 miles. To reach the end of Segment 15, walk up the road 0.2 mile to Marshall Pass Trailhead. Turn left on a jeep trail heading south. Follow the jeep trail up the hill to **mile 14.3** (10,864) where a sign marks the trail and end of Segment 15.

Continental Divide National Scenic Trail (CDNST)

The Continental Divide National Scenic Trail, commonly known as the Continental Divide Trail, passes through five Western states as it winds through the majestic Rocky Mountains from Canada to Mexico, encountering some of America's most dramatic scenery.

The Colorado Trail and the CDNST are co-located for about 314 miles. The two trails join from Georgia Pass in CT Segment 6, continue as co-located along the entire Collegiate West, and finally diverge in CT Segment 24 atop the Divide near the Elk Creek descent.

First envisioned by several far-sighted groups and individuals, including Benton Mackaye, founder of the Appalachian Trail, the 3,100-mile CDNST is about 70 percent complete today. The Colorado portion has one of the highest completion rates at 90 percent. The trail achieves its highest point in Colorado, passing over 14,270-foot Grays Peak, and includes a network of trails 759 miles long, beginning in the Mount Zirkel Wilderness Area on the Wyoming border and entering New Mexico through the spectacular San Juans.

The Continental Divide Trail Coalition (CDTC) estimates that about 300 people undertake the entire 5-month journey from Canada to Mexico each year but far fewer finish. As with The Colorado Trail, thousands more enjoy CDNST day hikes or multiday backpack trips on sections of it.

The first complete hike of Colorado's Continental Divide National Scenic Trail was done by Carl Melzer, his son, Bob, and Julius Johnson in 1936. This was truly a pioneering trip, considering the incomplete maps and sketchy information available to them at that time. (The Melzers had a string of accomplishments. They also were the first to climb all of Colorado's fourteeners in one summer [1937] and the first to climb all of the fourteeners in the 48 states [1939]—all before Bob was 11 years old!)

For more information about the CDNST, contact the CDTC at (303) 996-2759 or visit the group's website at continentaldividetrail.org.

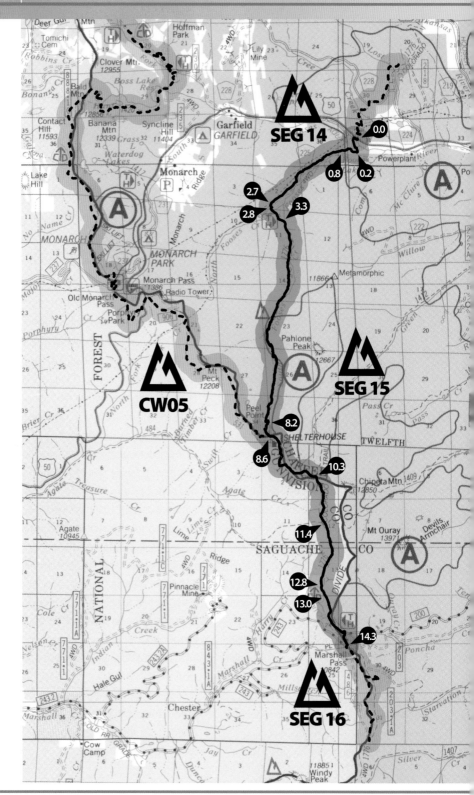

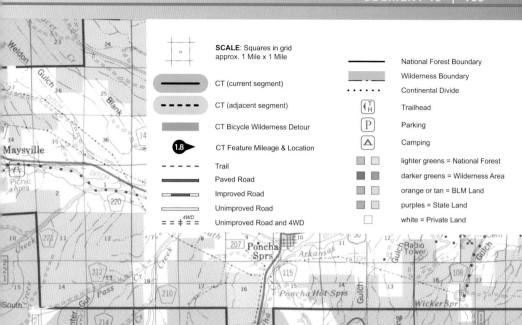

SCALE: Squares in grid approx. 1 Mile x 1 Mile

— CT (current segment)

- - - CT (adjacent segment)

CT Bicycle Wilderness Detour

1.8 CT Feature Mileage & Location

- - - Trail

Paved Road

Improved Road

Unimproved Road

= = ‡ = = Unimproved Road and 4WD

National Forest Boundary

Wilderness Boundary

• • • • • Continental Divide

[T/H] Trailhead

[P] Parking

[△] Camping

lighter greens = National Forest

darker greens = Wilderness Area

orange or tan = BLM Land

purples = State Land

white = Private Land

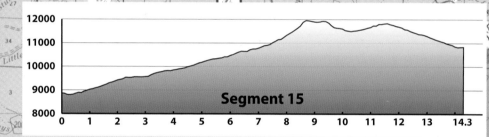

Segment 15

SEGMENT 15 FEATURES TABLE   San Isabel and Gunnison National Forests

Mileage	Features & Comments	Elevation (feet)	Mileage from Denver	Mileage to Durango	UTM-E	UTM-N (NAD83)	Zone
0.0	Begin Segment 15	8,861	252.5	232.1	391,720	4,266,827	13
0.2	Go left at fork and cross river	8,830	252.7	231.9	391,720	4,266,412	13
0.8	Pass by lake	8,960	253.3	231.3	391,203	4,266,465	13
2.7	Turn left	9,553	255.2	229.4	388,764	4,264,728	13
2.8	South Fooses Creek Trailhead	9,551	255.3	229.3	388,788	4,264,594	13
3.3	First creek crossing	9,769	255.8	228.8	389,274	4,263,844	13
8.2	Last creek crossing	11,450	260.7	223.9	388,469	4,257,493	13
8.6	Left for Seg 15 right for Collegiate West	11,909	261.1	223.5	388,578	4,257,017	13
10.3	Go right at intersection	11,501	262.8	221.8	390,165	4,255,630	13
11.4	Go straight at intersection	11,814	263.9	220.7	390,458	4,254,050	13
12.8	Join jeep road	11,364	265.3	219.3	390,299	4,252,010	13
13.0	Piped spring	11,260	265.5	219.1			
14.3	End Segment 15	10,864	266.8	217.8	391,128	4,250,001	13

Marshall Pass to San Luis Pass (Segments 16–20)
Segment 16: Marshall Pass Trailhead to Sargents Mesa

Distance: 15.2 miles

Elevation gain: Approx. 3,184 feet

Elevation loss: Approx. 2,405 feet

USFS maps: San Isabel, Gunnison, and Rio Grande National Forests, pages 188–189

The Colorado Trail Databook 6: pages 42–43

The CT Map Book: pages 39–41

National Geographic Trails Illustrated map: No. 139

Jurisdiction: Salida, Gunnison, and Saguache Ranger Districts; San Isabel, Gunnison, and Rio Grande National Forests

Access from Denver end: 🚗

Access from Durango end: 🚗

Availability of water: 🍵

Bicycling: 🚲

Jerry Brown in camp warming up for another long day of surveying the CT.

PHOTO BY CARL BROWN

"Beyond Marshall Pass for over 50 miles, backpackers need to sharpen their focus on water sources, carry enough, and stay hydrated."

Sargents Mesa and the rolling uplands along this section of the Continental Divide are known as the Cochetopa Hills. The area receives less snow than other ranges and water sources are widely scattered. Still, CT travelers who plan and are careful typically don't go dry.

Gudy's TIP

ABOUT THIS SEGMENT

Most of this segment of The Colorado Trail and the next two segments are open to motorized travel. As the CT Foundation's goal since inception has been an entirely non-motorized route, the organization and others are collaborating on possible alternative routes through this area. Trail users should stay alert for dirt bikes approaching at high speeds.

The trail through here stays very close to the Continental Divide, which means water sources are few and scattered. There is water at Silver Creek about a quarter mile below the trail, 4.1 miles from the Marshall Pass Trailhead. About 11 miles in, you will cross Tank Seven Creek, which is also a good source of water. While walking up the meadow onto Sargents Mesa near the end of Segment 16 is a metal stock tank where travelers might choose to filter and "camel up." Just beyond is *Soldierstone,* an interesting backcountry memorial to fallen soldiers in Indochina, including Vietnam.

TRAILHEAD/ACCESS POINTS

Marshall Pass Trailhead: Drive about 5 miles south of Poncha Springs on US Hwy 285 and turn right (west) at the Marshall Pass and O'Haver Lake Campground turnoff. The road starts out as Chaffee County Rd 200 and toward the top of the pass morphs into FS Rd 200. It is about 13 miles from the highway to the summit of Marshall Pass. About 0.2 mile short of the pass is a parking area for about a dozen cars with a Forest Service toilet nearby. There is also limited parking at the top of the pass itself. The trailhead for Segment 16 is at the top of the hill just above the road, where a sign marks the CT trailhead.

Sargents Mesa Access: See Segment 17 on page 190.

SERVICES, SUPPLIES, AND ACCOMMODATIONS

There is no convenient resupply point for this segment.

TRAIL DESCRIPTION

Begin Segment 16 at the smaller parking area atop Marshall Pass, **mile 0.0** (10,864), where a sign marks the trail. Follow the single-track trail south to **mile 2.4** (11,137), where the CT merges with a jeep trail. Veer left. Motorized vehicles are allowed on this portion of the CT and beyond, so be alert for fast approaching motorcycles and ATVs.

At **mile 4.1** (11,238), intersect the Silver Creek Trail that leads to the Rainbow Trail. Down this side trail about a quarter mile there is water and a campsite. Monarch Crest cyclists will diverge here. Stay right to continue on the CT. The jeep track narrows to single-track at **mile 4.5** (11,408). Cross a seasonal stream, and pass through a Forest Service gate on the Continental Divide at **mile 5.2** (11,560). The trail continues in

Hikers use trekking poles to keep balance and momentum on trail.
PHOTO BY BILL MANNING

a westerly direction, traversing the south flanks of Windy Peak, reaching a high point of 11,570 feet and then steeply descending. Cross a jeep trail at **mile 7.1** (10,903) and continue downhill until reaching **mile 8.9** (10,629), where the trail follows a pipeline cut for 200 feet then exits to the right.

At **mile 11.0** (10,569) begin descending. Reach campsites and Tank Seven Creek at **mile 11.6** (10,351), the last reliable water source until reaching Baldy Lake 11 miles ahead. After crossing the creek, turn left and begin climbing into Cameron Park. Cross FS Rd 578 at **mile 12.9** (10,796), where there are remains of crumbled buildings. Continue climbing to **mile 13.8** (11,101) and cross a road. At **mile 14.7** (11,394), intersect the Big Bend Creek Trail and stay left. Farther 0.2 mile, off to the left, is a metal stock tank (possible water) and beyond a 10-foot granite spire amongst trees that is *"Soldierstone."* Diverge from the CT southeast 0.2 mile for this interesting backcountry memorial to fallen soldiers in

Elk keep an eye on trail users. PHOTO BY PETE TURNER

Indochina, including Vietnam. Segment 16 ends on Sargents Mesa at **mile 15.2** (11,616), 0.4 mile from the end of FS Rd 855.

Monarch Crest Trail

The Monarch Crest Trail has been rated by *Bicycling Magazine* as one of the top-five mountain bike rides in the country. It descends an epic 3,500 feet from tundra to sagebrush desert, covering roughly 40 miles of mostly single-track trail.

Riders begin atop Monarch Pass, many having taken a commercial shuttle from Poncha Springs. They pedal (and coast) the CT Collegiate West / CDNST south, roll along CT Segment 15 to Marshall Pass, and travel 4.1 miles into Segment 16 before diverging on the Silver Creek and Rainbow Trail system to reach

Mountain bikers roll fast along the famous Monarch Crest. PHOTO BY GEORGE NESERKE

US Hwy 285 far below. A swift ride down the highway returns riders to Poncha Springs.

The Legacy of Marshall Pass

In 1873, troubled by a toothache and in a big hurry to get to a dentist in Denver, Army Lieutenant William Marshall "discovered" this shortcut. For centuries, of course, bands of Ute Indians had been using the several gaps in this relatively low section of the Continental Divide to travel between the intermountain parks on the east side of the Divide and their lands to the west. Famed road and rail builder Otto Mears constructed the first wagon road over the pass, following existing paths, then sold it to the Denver & Rio Grande Western railroad, which laid rails over it in 1881.

General William Palmer's D&RGW was in a battle with John Evans' Denver, South Park & Pacific Railroad to be the first to reach Gunnison and tap the mineral-rich San Juans. While the DSP&P took the shorter route on paper by tunneling under the Sawatch Range, Palmer chose the relatively low pass with modest grades for his route. The D&RGW won the race, pulling into Gunnison to an exuberant crowd on August 8, 1881. The DSP&P, meanwhile, labored for another year on its ill-fated Alpine Tunnel.

The rails are long gone today, but Chaffee County Rd 200 follows the old trackbed.

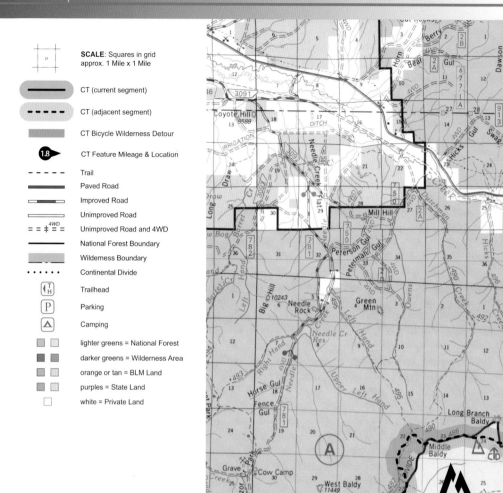

SCALE: Squares in grid approx. 1 Mile x 1 Mile

CT (current segment)

CT (adjacent segment)

CT Bicycle Wilderness Detour

1.8 CT Feature Mileage & Location

Trail

Paved Road

Improved Road

Unimproved Road

Unimproved Road and 4WD

National Forest Boundary

Wilderness Boundary

Continental Divide

Trailhead

Parking

Camping

lighter greens = National Forest

darker greens = Wilderness Area

orange or tan = BLM Land

purples = State Land

white = Private Land

SEG 17

SEGMENT 16 FEATURES TABLE   Gunnison National Forest

Mileage	Features & Comments	Elevation (feet)	Mileage from Denver	Mileage to Durango	UTM-E	UTM-N (NAD83)	Zone
0.0	Begin Segment 16	10,864	266.8	217.8	391,128	4,250,001	13
2.4	Go left onto jeep road	11,137	269.2	215.4	391,887	4,247,360	13
4.1	Pass Silver Creek Trail on left	11,238	270.9	213.7	391,513	4,245,781	13
4.5	Road ends, begin single-track	11,408	271.3	213.3	391,101	4,245,484	13
5.2	Pass through gate	11,560	272.0	212.6	390,112	4,245,353	13
7.1	Cross jeep road	10,903	273.9	210.7	387,754	4,245,241	13
8.9	Go right at intersection	10,629	275.7	208.9	385,322	4,244,687	13
11.0	Begin descending	10,569	277.8	206.8	384,087	4,241,934	13
11.6	Cross Tank Seven Creek then left	10,351	278.4	206.2	383,452	4,241,460	13
12.9	Cross dirt road	10,796	279.7	204.9	382,059	4,240,605	13
14.7	Stay left at Big Bend Creek Trail	11,394	281.5	203.1	379,958	4,239,637	13
15.2	End Segment 16	11,616	282.0	202.6	379,441	4,238,979	13

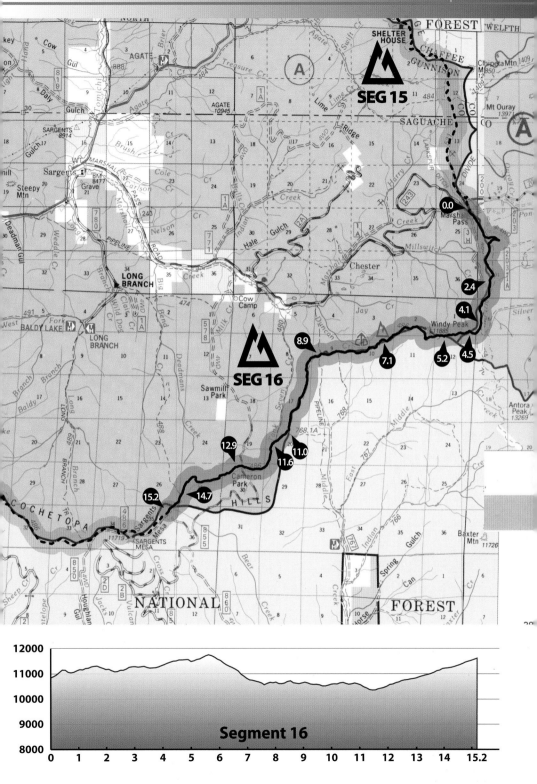

Segment 17: Sargents Mesa to CO Hwy 114

Baldy Lake. PHOTO BY JULIE VIDA AND MARK TABB

Distance: 20.4 miles

Elevation gain: Approx. 2,810 feet

Elevation loss: Approx. 4,810 feet

USFS maps: Rio Grande and Gunnison National Forests, pages 194–195

The Colorado Trail Databook 6: pages 44–45

The CT Map Book: pages 41–43

National Geographic Trails Illustrated map: No. 139

Jurisdiction: Saguache and Gunnison Ranger Districts; Rio Grande and Gunnison National Forests

Access from Denver end:

Access from Durango end:

Availability of water:

Bicycling: 🚲

"Baldy Lake after Sargents Mesa is worth the half-mile detour; it's a haven along a dry segment of the trail."

You'll need to plan your camping and water needs carefully for this segment. The only reliable water source is at Baldy Lake, north of mile 6.9. Livestock in this area is a reminder to purify all your water with a filter and/or chemicals.

Gudy's TIP

ABOUT THIS SEGMENT

In Segment 17 the CT continues to travel along the Continental Divide, relatively low in elevation and gentle through here. As in the previous segment, water sources can be scarce. Baldy Lake, north of mile 6.9, is the only reliable water source and it is well worth the short side trip. Early in the year or during particularly wet years, travelers may also find water in Razor or Lujan Creek.

Backpackers admire the broad expanse of Sargents Mesa.

PHOTO BY PETE TURNER

An expansive view can be enjoyed from Long Branch Baldy, 11,974', the highest peak for miles around and a great vantage point to identify distant mountains. From a high point at CT mile 7.3, diverge off trail, north and gently up a half mile along the rim towering above Baldy Lake until you reach the top.

TRAILHEAD/ACCESS POINTS

Sargents Mesa Access (via FS Rd 855): From the small town of Saguache on US Hwy 285 in the San Luis Valley, proceed northwest on CO Hwy 114 for 10.5 miles. Take the right-hand branch of the Y intersection here onto Saguache County Rd EE-38. Proceed 0.8 mile to the next Y and take the left branch, continuing on EE-38. Continue up Jacks Creek Valley for 5 miles and turn right on County Road 32JJ which morphs into FS Rd 855. From the right turn, proceed 9.5 miles to an intersection and bear left at a sign for Sargents Mesa. Continue another 0.5 miles to a Y intersection. Park here and walk west 0.4 mile farther to the signed division between CT Segments 16 and 17.

Lujan Creek Road Trail Access: From Saguache drive west on CO Hwy 114 for approximately 30 miles to North Pass. Continue 1.1 miles down from the pass to Lujan Creek Road (Saguache County Rd CC-31/FS Rd 785) on your right. Follow this narrow, slick-when-wet shelf road for 2 miles up Lujan Creek Valley, where it makes an abrupt right turn up a switchback. Avoid the jeep road that departs to the left. Continue 0.1 mile and cross a cattle guard. Branch left here for 0.1 mile to where the CT comes down from the mountain.

CO Hwy 114 Trailhead Access: See Segment 18 on page 196.

SERVICES, SUPPLIES, AND ACCOMMODATIONS

There is no convenient resupply point for this segment.

TRAIL DESCRIPTION

Segment 17 begins at the obscure Sargents Mesa, a 0.4-mile walk from the end of FS Rd 855, **mile 0.0** (11,616). The trail follows an old jeep route south and west to **mile 2.3** (11,176),

Trekkers enjoy easy hiking and big views on Sargents Mesa.
PHOTO COURTESY OF COLORADOTRAILHIKING.COM

where The Colorado Trail abruptly turns right and leaves the jeep route. Cross Long Branch Trail at **mile 2.4** (11,168) and continue climbing and descending along the Continental Divide. Reach the Baldy Lake Trail intersection at **mile 6.9** (11,517). A good place to camp and the only reliable Segment 17 water, the lake is just 0.5 mile north and 400 feet below the CT on well-traveled side trail.

At **mile 7.3** (11,769) ascend to the high point of Segment 17, then descend and reach a saddle at **mile 8.4** (11,422). Reach the summit of Middle Baldy Peak at **mile 9.2** (11,685). Bear to the left at the intersection with Dutchman Creek Trail at **mile 9.8** (11,378). Reach the usually-dry Razor Creek at **mile 10.5** (10,943). After following the creek bed for 0.3 mile, turn left at the intersection with Razor Creek Trail at **mile 10.8** (10,848).

Cattle graze in the Cochetopa Hills.
PHOTO BY JULIE VIDA AND MARK TABB

Continue straight at intersection with West Sheep Creek Trail on the left at **mile 11.2** (10,810). Regain the Divide at **mile 11.5** (10,819), then bear left at the intersection with Upper Razor Spur Trail at **mile 12.4** (11,073). The trail ascends to a minor summit at **mile 14.6** (10,964), then drops into a forested saddle at **mile 15.1** (10,602). There is a dry campsite at **mile 15.5** (10,694). The CT heads left onto an old jeep road at **mile 16.5** (11,019). Descend to Lujan Pass and turn right on Lujan Creek Road, FS Road 785, at **mile 17.8** (10,343), leaving the Divide.

After passing through a gate with a cattle guard, stay on the main road that curves sharply left at an intersection at **mile 18.0** (10,333). Begin following the seasonal headwaters of Lujan Creek at **mile 19.2** (10,043). Reach CO Hwy 114 at **mile 20.0** (9,729) and turn right, downhill, along the highway shoulder. On the left at **mile 20.4** (9,606) is a wide parking area on the south side of the highway, the end of this segment, and a fence gate where the trail continues into Segment 18.

Pocket Gophers

The long, sinuous casts packed with dirt that you see scattered over the grasslands and meadows of this and other segments of The Colorado Trail are evidence of pocket gophers at work.

This small, thickset, and mostly nocturnal animal is a regular biological excavation service, with burrow systems that may be more than 500 feet long, requiring the removal of nearly three tons of soil. Excess soil is thrown out in characteristic loose mounds. But it is the conspicuous winter casts that attract the attention of curious hikers. These are actually tunnels made during the winter through the snow and along the surface of the ground and packed with dirt brought up from below. Sometimes the endless burrowing activities of pocket gophers can undermine an area to such an extent that a passing hiker can be surprised when the ground suddenly gives way under foot.

In Colorado, pocket gophers are found well up into the meager soils of the alpine zone and are a major factor in the soil-building process in mountain areas.

Pocket gopher at work.
PHOTO COURTESY OF JIM HERD

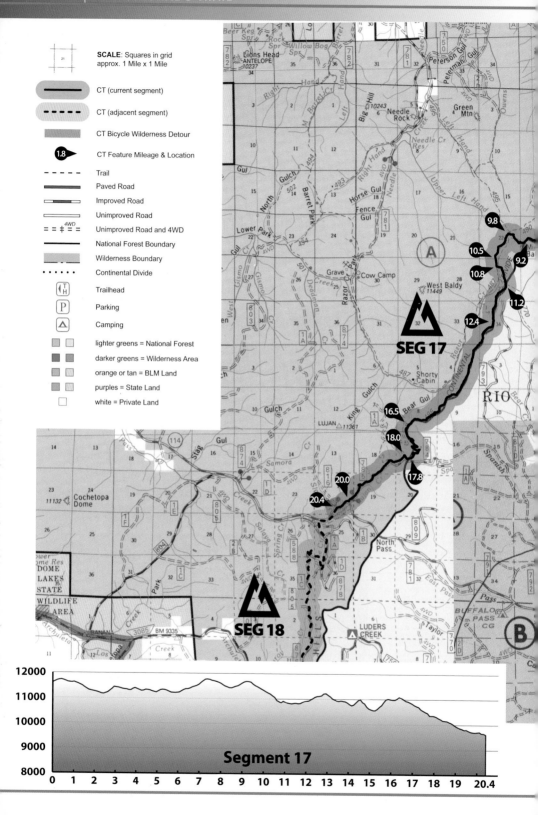

SCALE: Squares in grid approx. 1 Mile x 1 Mile

CT (current segment)

CT (adjacent segment)

CT Bicycle Wilderness Detour

1.8 CT Feature Mileage & Location

Trail

Paved Road

Improved Road

Unimproved Road

4WD Unimproved Road and 4WD

National Forest Boundary

Wilderness Boundary

Continental Divide

TH Trailhead

P Parking

△ Camping

lighter greens = National Forest

darker greens = Wilderness Area

orange or tan = BLM Land

purples = State Land

white = Private Land

SEG 17

SEG 18

Segment 17

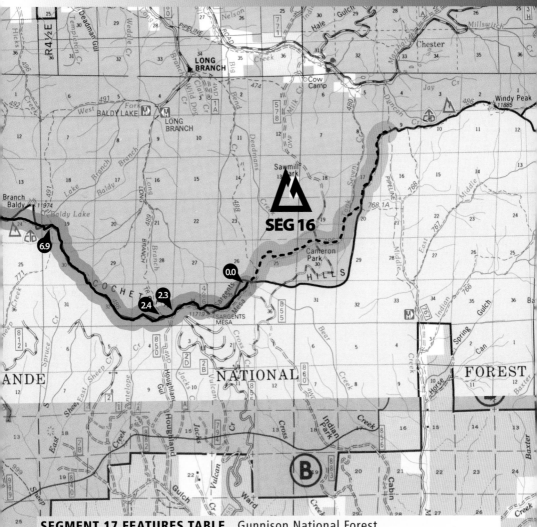

SEGMENT 17 FEATURES TABLE   Gunnison National Forest

Mileage	Features & Comments	Elevation (feet)	Mileage from Denver	Mileage to Durango	UTM-E	UTM-N (NAD83)	Zone
0.0	Begin Segment 17	11,616	282.0	202.6	379,441	4,238,979	13
2.3	Go right at intersection	11,176	284.3	200.3	376,575	4,238,035	13
2.4	Pass Long Branch Trail on right	11,168	284.4	200.2	376,345	4,237,950	13
6.9	Baldy Lake Trail intersection	11,517	288.9	195.7	371,858	4,241,633	13
9.2	Middle Baldy Peak summit	11,685	291.2	193.4	368,575	4,241,881	13
9.8	Bear left at intersection	11,378	291.8	192.8	367,802	4,242,074	13
10.5	Cross Razor Creek	10,943	292.5	192.1	367,273	4,241,134	13
10.8	Go left at intersection	10,848	292.8	191.8	367,292	4,240,849	13
12.4	Go left at intersection	11,073	294.4	190.2	367,087	4,238,717	13
16.5	Bear left onto jeep road	11,019	298.5	186.1	363,625	4,234,859	13
17.8	Turn right onto road	10,343	299.8	184.8	363,682	4,233,580	13
18.0	Go left past side road	10,333	300.0	184.6	363,421	4,233,706	13
20.0	Right along CO Hwy 114	9,729	302.0	182.6	361,204	4,232,024	13
20.4	End Segment 17	9,606	302.4	182.2	360,700	4,231,743	13

Segment 18: CO Hwy 114 to Saguache Park Road

Vast pastureland characterizes this part of the CT.

PHOTO BY CARL BROWN

Distance: 13.8 miles

Elevation gain: Approx. 1,447 feet

Elevation loss: Approx. 1,534 feet

USFS map: Gunnison National Forest, pages 202–203

The Colorado Trail Databook 6: pages 46–47

The CT Map Book: pages 43–45

National Geographic Trails Illustrated map: No. 139

Jurisdiction: Gunnison Ranger District, Gunnison National Forest

Access from Denver end:

Access from Durango end: 🚗

Availability of water: ☕

Bicycling: 🚲 See page 200

"Water sources on the ranch roads in this segment are few and far between, and what can be found is often besmirched by cow pies. However, spring water is available at Luders Creek Campground three miles east of the CT."

Also, Los Creek often flows and Lujan, Pine, and Archuleta Creeks may have small flows at times, but are unreliable in dry years and later in the summer.

Gudy's TIP

ABOUT THIS SEGMENT

Segment 18 guides travelers through the relatively gentle Cochetopa Hills where early summer wildflowers and easy walking can make it very enjoyable. This is ranch and cattle country; the views are expansive and have an entirely different feel from the forested ridges above. Visible to the north, Cochetopa Dome and the surrounding valley remain largely unchanged from a century before. The only on-trail water source that flows often is Los Creek. After that, the next truly reliable water source is Cochetopa Creek, 11.8 miles beyond. Be prepared for this, especially when temperatures are high. Much of the terrain in this segment is directly exposed to the sun.

A thru-hiker along Highway 114 hoping to resupply in Gunnison, 39 miles distant. Having a hiker sign often helps to secure a ride.   PHOTO BY LANE EARLY

TRAILHEAD/ACCESS POINTS

CO Hwy 114 Trailhead Access: From Saguache on US Hwy 285 in the San Luis Valley, drive west on CO Hwy 114 for approximately 30 miles to North Pass. Continue 1.1 miles down the pass to Lujan Creek Road (Saguache County Rd CC-31/FS Rd 785) on your right. Continue down CO Hwy 114 for 0.4 mile to a wide shoulder on the south side of the highway. Overnight parking here on the highway right-of-way has generated two tips from authorities: 1) place a visible "Do Not Tow. Using The Colorado Trail" so it's evident that the car is not abandoned, and 2) if parking for an extended time, longer than 72 hours, communicate the license plate number and plan to Montrose State Patrol at (970) 249-4392. This is the beginning of Segment 18 and the end of 17.

Cochetopa Pass Road (Saguache County Rd NN-14) Trail Access: From Saguache on US Hwy 285, go west on CO Hwy 114 for approximately 21 miles and take the left branch onto Saguache County Rd NN-14. Follow NN-14 for approximately 10 miles to Luders Creek Campground, which has a continuously flowing spring in the back (north end). Continue 1.8 miles to Cochetopa Pass and another 1.2 miles to where the CT joins NN-14 from the north. From this point, the CT follows NN-14 for 0.5 mile down two switchbacks and then leaves the road, heading south on a jeep trail. This crossing point is considered the access point. There is no formal parking area here, but there's little traffic, and an old Forest Service side road at the top of the switchbacks offers room to park a few cars.

Alternate Cochetopa Pass Road (Saguache County Rd NN-14) Trail Access: From Saguache on US Hwy 285, go west on CO Hwy 114 for approximately 5 miles. Turn left onto FS Rd 804 (BLM Rd 3089/Saguache County Rd GG-17) for approximately 5 miles

In this segment, parts of the CT follow old ranching roads.
PHOTO BY CARL BROWN

until it terminates at Saguache County Rd NN-14 (Cochetopa Pass Road/BLM Rd 3083). Turn left (east) on NN-14 for 6.5 miles. The access point is where the road starts to make a steep switchback turn to the left. The CT comes down the switchbacks and crosses NN-14, proceeding south.

Saguache Park Road Trail Access: See Segment 19 on page 204.

SERVICES, SUPPLIES, AND ACCOMMODATIONS

There is no convenient resupply point for this segment.

TRAIL DESCRIPTION

Begin Segment 18 on the south side of CO Hwy 114 where there is a large, wide shoulder and potential parking, **mile 0.0** (9,606 feet). Pass through the gate onto single-track and cross to the south side of often dry Lujan Creek at **mile 0.1** (9,553). Follow the trail to **mile 0.6** (9,533), where the trail bends to the south and follows Pine Creek, also often dry. At **mile 0.9** (9,529), join a logging road. Ignore a side road at **mile 1.0** (9,550) and cross Pine Creek at **mile 1.7** (9,680). Go right at the fork at **mile 1.8** (9,708), heading uphill in a northwesterly direction. The CT bends back to the south at **mile 2.5** (9,930). The road turns into single-track trail at **mile 3.6** (10,000) and heads steeply uphill.

Reach a saddle at **mile 3.8** (10,259) and pass through a Forest Service gate. Turn left on FS Rd 876, an old logging road, at **mile 4.0** (10,198). Follow this road until coming to another gate at **mile 6.4** (9,774). Pass through a third gate at **mile 6.6** (9,750), then turn right onto the Cochetopa Pass Road at **mile 6.7** (9,744). If you're up for a side trip to good water and camping, diverge here and go almost 3 miles east on Cochetopa Pass Road NN-14 to Luders Creek Campground where you'll find flowing spring water in the back end of the campground. To continue on the CT from where it meets the road, follow the NN-14 road west and downhill on two long switchbacks until coming to FS Rd 864-2A at **mile 7.2** (9,628). Take a sharp left here, following the trail as it heads slightly uphill. Pass through yet another gate at **mile 8.0** (9,769) and bend to the west. At **mile 8.3** (9,756) at an intersection, ignore the fork to the left.

Travel a jeep trail along Los Creek from **mile 8.6** to **mile 9.0** (9,628), where the jeep trail is closed off by several large boulders. Turn left and cross the creek. Water is likely here or possibly 0.1 mile downstream. Continue uphill to **mile 9.2** (9,666) where the CT turns right (west). There are good campsites farther uphill. At **mile 9.6** (9,619), the trail turns to the right down the hill. At **mile 9.7** (9,566), where you are again near Los Creek and possible last-chance water, turn left (west) and climb away from the creek valley. After con-touring around Peak 9,841, the trail descends and begins to follow a long, straight fence at **mile 10.5** (9,631).

Ignore a left fork at **mile 11.0** (9,425), pass through a gate at **mile 11.9** (9,366), and bear to the right at the intersection just beyond the gate. Take a sharp left onto Saguache Park Road 787 at **mile 12.3** (9,339). Cross a cattle guard at **mile 13.4** (9,500) and continue the gentle climb on the road to the intersection of FS Rd 787.2D and Saguache Park Road at **mile 13.8** (9,527), the end of Segment 18.

A thru-hiker heading west through the expanse of Segment 18.

PHOTO BY MARY PARLANGE

La Garita Wilderness Bicycle Detour

This long mandatory detour avoids the La Garita Wilderness Area. It is pleasant, passing through a remote part of Colorado, heavily timbered with aspen trees and spectacular in the fall. Part of the route was the planned itinerary of the infamous Alfred Packer, convicted for eating his snowbound companions in 1874. The detour passes the old Ute Indian Agency, which was Packer's destination.

The route beginning, **mile 0.0** (9,339), is where The Colorado Trail intersects the gravel Saguache Park Road, County Road 17FF, CT Segment 18 mile 12.3. Ride north on the 17FF to a T intersection with the gravel Saguache County Rd NN14, **mile 2.4** (9,243), where you turn left (west).

Pass an intersection with County Rd 17GG at **mile 3.6** (9,188). Before Dome Lakes, pass an intersection with County Rd 15GG at **mile 4.9** (9,128). Camping is allowed around the lakes. Continue following NN14 in a more northerly direction past the lakes to **mile 8.7** (8,995) and an intersection with BLM Rd 3084, also identified as County Rd KK14, George Bush Drive, also gravel. Turn left (southwest) and follow the road to **mile 14.3** (9,097), the old Ute Indian Agency location, now a Forest Service facility, where the road becomes FS Road 788, still George Bush Drive. Continue to an intersection with FS Road 790 at **mile 17.9** (9,342) and stay right, continuing on the main road. Ignore the second intersection with FS Road 790, on the left at **mile 26.4** (10,184), and continue following 788, George Bush Drive. Reach Los Pinos Pass at **mile 27.5** (10,508). Ignore FS Road 788 on the left at **mile 31.8** (9,099).

Head downhill to **mile 33.0** (8,917) and, at a T intersection, turn left to stay on the graveled FS Rd 788 (County Rd 50) and begin following Cebola Creek upstream. There's a Forest Service cattle guard at **mile 38.1** (9,178) and, 1 to 3 miles beyond, are three FS campgrounds along Cebolla Creek. After a prolonged climb, just beyond another FS campground, arrive at an intersection with the paved CO Hwy 149, **mile 47.9** (11,356). It is near this point where Packer and his party became snowbound. If visiting Lake City, turn right onto Hwy 149 for the 9.5-mile downhill.

To continue on the CT, turn left (east) onto Hwy 149 and ride over Slumgullion Summit to **mile 56.1** (10,908) at the top of Spring Creek Pass, the end of Segment 21 and the start of Segment 22.

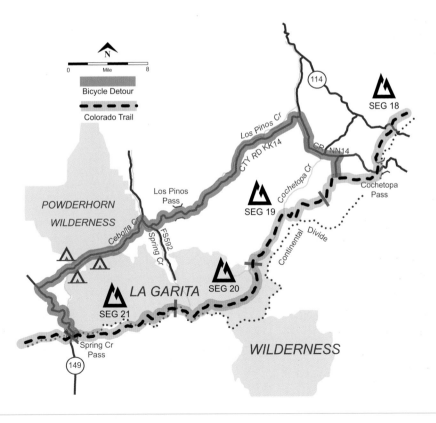

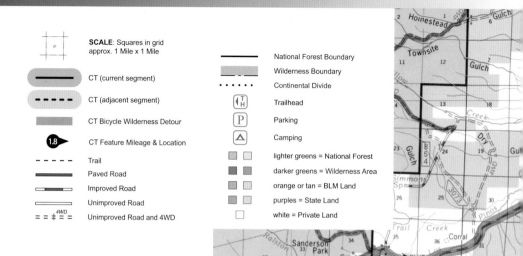

SCALE: Squares in grid approx. 1 Mile x 1 Mile

CT (current segment)

CT (adjacent segment)

CT Bicycle Wilderness Detour

1.8 CT Feature Mileage & Location

Trail

Paved Road

Improved Road

Unimproved Road

Unimproved Road and 4WD

National Forest Boundary

Wilderness Boundary

Continental Divide

(T/H) Trailhead

(P) Parking

(A) Camping

lighter greens = National Forest

darker greens = Wilderness Area

orange or tan = BLM Land

purples = State Land

white = Private Land

SEGMENT 18 FEATURES TABLE   Gunnison National Forest

Mileage	Features & Comments	Elevation (feet)	Mileage from Denver	Mileage to Durango	UTM-E	UTM-N (NAD83)	Zone
0.0	Begin Segment 18	9,606	302.4	182.2	360,700	4,231,743	13
0.1	Cross Lujan Creek	9,553	302.5	182.1	360,600	4,231,545	13
0.6	Trail turns south	9,533	303.0	181.6	359,973	4,231,245	13
0.9	Join logging road	9,529	303.3	181.3	360,046	4,230,889	13
1.0	Pass side road on left	9,550	303.4	181.2	360,175	4,230,731	13
1.7	Cross Pine Creek	9,680	304.1	180.5	360,104	4,229,678	13
1.8	Go right uphill at fork	9,708	304.2	180.4	360,083	4,229,501	13
3.6	Road narrows to single-track	10,000	306.0	178.6	359,592	4,228,767	13
3.8	Reach saddle and gate	10,259	306.2	178.4	359,441	4,228,335	13
4.0	Turn left	10,198	306.4	178.2	359,368	4,228,136	13
6.4	Pass through gate	9,774	308.8	175.8	358,310	4,225,269	13
6.7	Turn right onto Road NN-14	9,744	309.1	175.5	358,028	4,224,952	13
7.2	Turn left on FS Rd 864-2A	9,628	309.6	175.0	358,003	4,224,742	13
8.0	Pass through gate	9,769	310.4	174.2	357,933	4,223,755	13
8.3	Straight past fork on left	9,756	310.7	173.9	357,527	4,223,661	13
9.0	Turn left and cross Los Creek	9,628	311.4	173.2	356,417	4,223,655	13
9.2	Turn right	9,666	311.6	173.0	356,464	4,223,477	13
9.6	Turn down hill	9,619	312.0	172.6	355,898	4,223,488	13
9.7	Turn left uphill	9,566	312.1	172.5	355,763	4,223,681	13
11.0	Pass fork to left	9,425	313.4	171.2	353,785	4,223,851	13
11.9	Pass gate and bear right	9,366	314.3	170.3	352,329	4,223,622	13
12.3	Left on Saguache Park Rd 787	9,339	314.7	169.9	352,000	4,223,820	13
13.8	End Segment 18	9,527	316.2	168.4	351,270	4,221,765	13

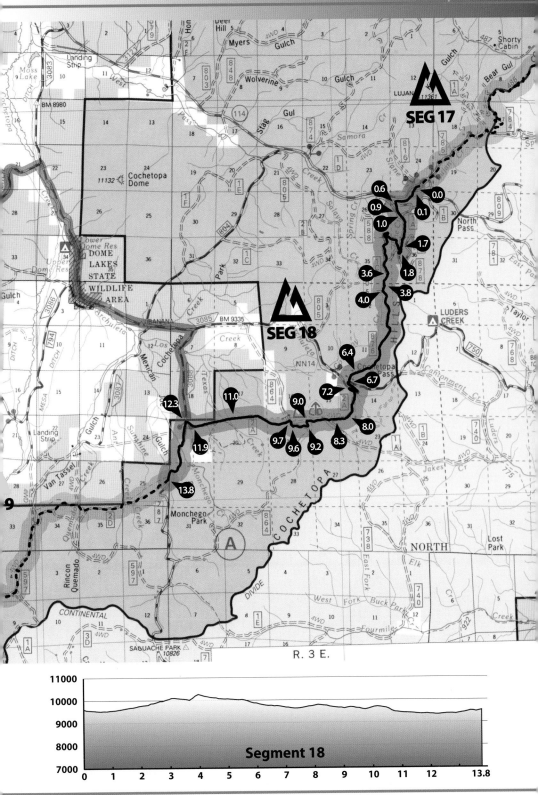

Segment 18

Segment 19: Saguache Park Road to Eddiesville Trailhead

Distance: 13.7 miles

Elevation gain: Approx. 2,239 feet

Elevation loss: Approx. 1,442 feet

USFS map: Gunnison National Forest, pages 208–209

The Colorado Trail Databook 6: pages 48–49

The CT Map Book: pages 45–47

National Geographic Trails Illustrated map: No. 139

Jurisdiction: Gunnison Ranger District, Gunnison National Forest

Access from Denver end:

Access from Durango end:

Availability of water:

Bicycling: See page 200

Southbound on Van Tassel Gulch Road.

PHOTO BY LUCI STREMME

"The La Garita Wilderness is remote and offers solitude. There are few day hikers and, if you meet others here, they are likely to be long-distance hikers."

If you seek solitude, this is one of the least-traveled segments of the CT. The trailheads are remote and can be difficult to reach in wet weather. Don't expect your cell phone to work out here.

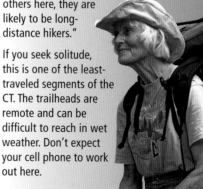

Gudy's TIP

ABOUT THIS SEGMENT

This segment rolls through cattle country, passing fields of summer wildflowers including paintbrush, larkspur, and various types of sunflowers. When the blooms are at peak, flatter areas around the trail appear like carpets of flowers. The segment is very dry until reaching Cochetopa Creek, one of the bigger waterways and a favorite of fishermen. You'll find grassy meadows along the east side of the creek. The trail continues in a southwesterly direction until it crosses the creek where you'll need to ford. Upstream along the west side, you'll enter the La Garita Wilderness Area and one of the most remote parts of the CT before reaching the end of the segment at the Eddiesville Trailhead.

At the old log bridge site, a hiker readies their footwear to ford Cochetopa Creek.   PHOTO BY MATT PIERCE

Many hikers have reported overlooking the intersection of the Saguache Park Road with FS Rd 787.2D. Pay close attention.

TRAILHEAD/ACCESS POINTS

Saguache Park Road Trail Access: From Saguache on US Hwy 285, go west on CO Hwy 114 for approximately 35 miles. Turn left onto County Rd 17GG (FS Rd 804) for approximately 5 miles until it terminates at Saguache County Rd NN14 (Cochetopa Park Road). Turn left (east) on NN14 and drive 1 mile. Then turn right (south) on Saguache Park Road (County Rd 17FF, FS Rd 787) for 3.5 miles. Keep your eyes peeled for the jeep road (FS Rd 787.2D) branching off to the right (southwest). This intersection is the end of Segment 18 and the beginning of Segment 19. There is no parking area at this trail access.

Eddiesville Trailhead: See Segment 20 on page 210.

SERVICES, SUPPLIES, AND ACCOMMODATIONS

There is no convenient resupply point for this segment.

TRAIL DESCRIPTION

Segment 19 begins along Saguache Park Road (County Rd 17FF) where FS Rd 787.2D intersects, **mile 0.0** (9,527 feet). At **mile 0.1** (9,527) go left at a fork continuing southwest. Continue to **mile 0.4** (9,525) where there is a dry campsite. The trail gradually

Old log fence.
PHOTO BY LUCI STREMME

Beaver dam on Cochetopa Creek.
PHOTO BY LUCI STREMME

Van Tassel Gulch Road.
PHOTO BY LUCI STREMME

bends to the west. Pass through gates and cross tiny, seasonal Ant Creek at **mile 1.2** (9,728). Continue straight at **mile 1.5** (9,784) where a road joins the CT on the left. Turn right at **mile 2.2** (9,773) and head toward the fenced area ahead. Turn left at **mile 2.4** (9,703), cross a small wetland area that is protected by a fence. Continue on the four-wheel-drive road to **mile 3.2** (9,949) ignoring a road from the left and passing through a Forest Service gate. Reach Van Tassel Gulch at **mile 3.6** (9,840) at a fenced-in spring, okay to use, where you might find water and replenish.

At **mile 3.8** (9,835), turn left and head uphill on the Van Tassel Gulch Road, FS Rd 597. Reach a high point and intersection at **mile 5.4** (10,404) and bear to the right on FS Rd 597.1A, descending. Pass through a gate at **mile 5.6** (10,280) and descend to **mile 6.6** (9,888), where the CT turns left at an intersection. Turn to the left again at **mile 6.8** (9,815), passing a stock pond and continuing in a southwesterly direction on the road closest to the water. The trail descends a steep hill, then leaves the road to the left and becomes single-track at **mile 7.0** (9,719), reaching campsites and Cochetopa Creek, a reliable water source and fishery. During the next 2.5 miles, the trail gradually climbs above the creek and then descends back to it.

Reach Cochetopa Creek again at **mile 9.7** (9,894) and ford upstream from old log bridges. Climb steeply up the west bank to **mile 9.8** (9,977) and turn left uphill to the southwest. At **mile 10.9** (10,047), cross Nutras Creek on a bridge and pass potential campsites before entering the La Garita Wilderness Area. At **mile 12.1** (10,217) is a grassy bench above the creek. Bear right at **mile 13.1** (10,278) where the trail splits. Leave the wilderness at **mile 13.7** (10,310) and proceed to the end of the segment at Eddiesville Trailhead where camping is limited to small sites.

Trekking with Llamas

Llamas have been used for centuries in South America as pack animals, as well as for their fiber and meat. Increasingly on long-distance trails, such as the CT, hikers are enjoying the advantages of these unique personal porters.

Llamas may be used for short hikes or may be fully loaded for traveling through the mountains on multiday outings. An adult animal (3 years or more) can carry about 20 percent of its body weight in rough terrain, or about 70 pounds. Llamas have two-toed padded feet, which do much less damage to the terrain because they do not tear up the ground the way hooves do. Llamas are browsers, not grazers, which limits overgrazing of delicate backcountry meadows.

Highly social animals, llamas travel well in a string and are easy to train. Most importantly, they are calm and trusting with people. The common stigma, that llamas spit, is true in the sense that they use that to gain advantage in their social structure. Just don't get stuck between two angry llamas.

With their panniers fully loaded, llamas can be expected to go 5 to 9 miles per day in the mountains. Smaller and far more maneuverable than other pack animals, their pace is perfectly suited for comfortable hiking. Being herd animals, llamas like to travel with companions and become anxious when separated from them. A good pack llama will follow its human leader willingly (nearly) anywhere, including areas where it might get hurt; so, the animal's welfare should be your primary concern at all times.

Several Colorado outfitters offer trekking services on the CT using llamas. As the price of pack stock continues to drop dramatically, they also are coming into use by individuals as well as by the Forest Service. Check with land management agencies in the segments you wish to travel about any restrictions regarding pack animals. The Colorado Trail Foundation's website (ColoradoTrail.org) also has a lot of good information about using llamas for pack stock.

Using llamas to haul camping gear is a great way to go.
PHOTO COURTESY OF DIANE GANSAUER

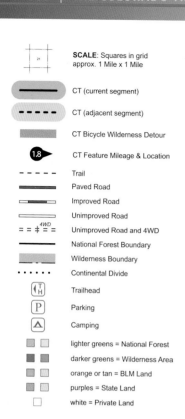

SCALE: Squares in grid approx. 1 Mile x 1 Mile

CT (current segment)

CT (adjacent segment)

CT Bicycle Wilderness Detour

1.8 — CT Feature Mileage & Location

Trail

Paved Road

Improved Road

Unimproved Road

Unimproved Road and 4WD

National Forest Boundary

Wilderness Boundary

Continental Divide

Trailhead

Parking

Camping

lighter greens = National Forest

darker greens = Wilderness Area

orange or tan = BLM Land

purples = State Land

white = Private Land

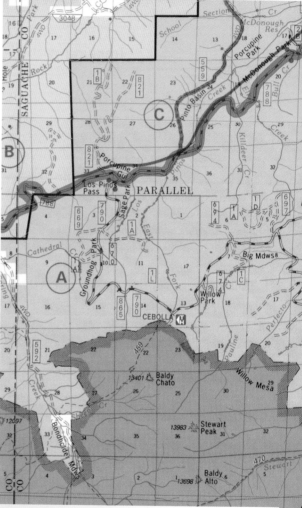

SEGMENT 19 FEATURES TABLE Gunnison National Forest

Mileage	Features & Comments	Elevation (feet)	Mileage from Denver	Mileage to Durango	UTM-E	UTM-N (NAD83)	Zone
0.0	Begin Segment 19	9,527	316.2	168.4	351,270	4,221,765	13
0.1	Go left at fork	9,527	316.3	168.3	351,057	4,221,625	13
2.2	Turn right at intersection	9,773	318.4	166.2	348,138	4,220,768	13
2.4	Turn left at intersection	9,703	318.6	166.0	347,924	4,221,028	13
3.2	Pass through gate	9,949	319.4	165.2	346,842	4,220,837	13
3.8	Turn left uphill on Road 597	9,835	320.0	164.6	346,235	4,220,294	13
5.4	Gain saddle, bear right	10,404	321.6	163.0	345,517	4,218,032	13
5.6	Pass through gate	10,280	321.8	162.8	345,139	4,217,871	13
6.8	Pass by stock pond	9,815	323.0	161.6	344,260	4,218,844	13
7.0	Leave road, left on single-track	9,719	323.2	161.4	344,115	4,218,569	13
9.7	Ford Cochetopa Creek	9,894	325.9	158.7	342,274	4,214,912	13
9.8	Turn left	9,977	326.0	158.6	342,142	4,214,923	13
10.9	Enter La Garita Wilderness	10,047	327.1	157.5	341,325	4,213,583	13
13.7	End Segment 19	10,310	329.9	154.7	339,005	4,210,354	13

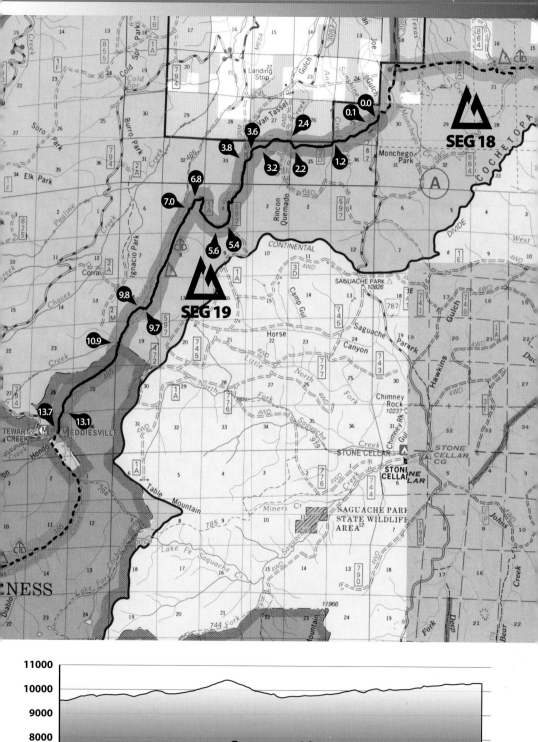

Segment 20: Eddiesville Trailhead to San Luis Pass

Hoodoos carved from layers of volcanic ash, remnants of volcanic activity 27 million years ago.

PHOTO BY ELLIOT FORSYTH

Distance: 12.7 miles

Elevation gain: Approx. 3,104 feet

Elevation loss: Approx. 1,478 feet

USFS maps: Gunnison and Rio Grande National Forests, pages 214–215

The Colorado Trail Databook 6: pages 50–51

The CT Map Book: pages 47–49

National Geographic Trails Illustrated map: No. 139

Jurisdiction: Gunnison Ranger District, Gunnison National Forest

Access from Denver end: 🚗

Access from Durango end: 🚙

Availability of water: ☕

Bicycling: 🚲 See page 200

"It is a temptation to climb 14,014-foot San Luis Peak, but the high incidence of lightning storms in that area can make it a dicey proposition. Be sure to check the cloud patterns and weather before ascending."

It's best to depart from the pass quite early. Drop the bulk of your gear on the pass for the jaunt to the top, then resume your trek before afternoon thundershowers move in.

Gudy's TIP

ABOUT THIS SEGMENT

Segment 20 immediately re-enters the La Garita Wilderness Area, detouring around private property. The trail slowly bends westward as it climbs up the Cochetopa Creek watershed, eventually reaching the saddle with San Luis Peak (14,014) to the north. It is a relatively short side trip to the top of the peak, consisting of a 1,400-foot climb in 1.25 miles, where climbers enjoy great views of the surrounding area. From the saddle, the CT descends and ascends two more

A hiker takes a break along the saddle beneath San Luis Peak.
PHOTO BY PETE TURNER

saddles before reaching the end of the segment at San Luis Pass. The trail is relatively steep throughout, but the views and summer wildflowers are terrific. After leaving tree line just above Cochetopa Creek, the trail crosses tundra until reaching the end of the segment.

San Luis Peak and the surrounding ridges are made up of volcanic tuff (consolidated volcanic ash). The ash was erupted about 27 million years ago from a huge volcanic depression known as the Nelson Mountain caldera. Much of the ash from the eruption spread out to form tuff layers that cap the surrounding ridges, but much of it fell back to fill the caldera and form the tuff that now forms San Luis Peak and its neighbors. It is only one of more than a dozen similar calderas in the San Juan volcanic field.

TRAILHEAD/ACCESS POINTS

Eddiesville Trailhead Access: From Saguache on US Hwy 285, go west on CO Hwy 114 for approximately 35 miles. Turn left onto FS Rd 804 (BLM Rd 3089/Saguache County Rd GG-17) for approximately 5 miles, until it terminates at Saguache County Rd NN-14 (Cochetopa Pass Rd/BLM-3083). Turn right (west) and follow NN-14 for 1.5 miles to Upper Dome Reservoir. Turn left (west) onto Saguache County Rd GG-15 (BLM Rd 3086/FS Rd 974). Follow it around the west side of the reservoir, where it curves and heads south. Proceed south for 3 miles to an intersection with Saguache County Rd DD-14 (FS Rd 794). This road may also be labeled as Stewart Creek. Follow it for about 21 miles to the Eddiesville Trailhead. This road can be very challenging when wet.

San Luis Pass Trail Access: See Segment 21 on page 216.

Climbing out of Cochetopa Creek toward the saddle beneath San Luis Peak.
PHOTO BY LEN GLASSNER

SERVICES, SUPPLIES, AND ACCOMMODATIONS

These amenities are available in Creede; see Segment 21 on pages 216–223.

TRAIL DESCRIPTION

Segment 20 begins at the well-marked trailhead in Eddiesville, **mile 0.0** (10,310), an old ranch inholding that is essentially a private island within the La Garita Wilderness Area. The trailhead is near the junction of Stewart and Cochetopa Creeks. There are small campsites in the area. From the trailhead sign, walk south along the dirt road (FS Rd 794) and at **mile 0.1** (10,346) turn left onto a dirt road and cross Stewart Creek on a bridge. At the end of the road and wilderness sign, turn right (uphill) onto a single-track trail at **mile 0.3** (10,358). Enter the La Garita Wilderness Area shortly afterward and pass through a gate at **mile 0.4** (10,412), where the trail turns sharply to the west and begins heading southeast along the edge of the private landholdings. There are small, seasonal streams at **mile 0.5** (10,417) and **mile 0.8** (10,351).

Pass through a gate at **mile 1.3** (10,348) and by another wilderness boundary sign. Intersect the Machin Basin Trail, which comes in from the east side of the valley at **mile 1.6** (10,362). The trail heads south, then bends to the southwest before passing through another Forest Service gate at **mile 3.7** (10,642). There are many small stream crossings between mile 3.7 and mile 7.6. Follow along the north side of Cochetopa Creek as the trail climbs and heads to the west, crossing the Stewart Creek Trail at **mile 7.5** (11,749) where there are good campsites. Cross Cochetopa Creek at **mile 7.6** (11,755), pass good alpine-meadow campsites, and climb to the high saddle at **mile 8.8** (12,612). From here, many people climb San Luis Peak (14,014) just 1,400 feet up and 1.25 miles north.

Descend from the saddle to a small spring at **mile 9.2** (12,549). Climb to another saddle just off the Continental Divide at **mile 10.1** (12,366). Pass a trail on the right to Bondholder Meadows at **mile 10.5** (12,146) and continue generally westward. Cross a stream at **mile 10.9** (12,029), ascend to another saddle on the Divide at **mile 12.1** (12,379), and head downhill to San Luis Pass at **mile 12.7** (11,944). There is an old sign marking the pass, the end of Segment 20.

Climbing San Luis Peak

The Colorado Trail's closest encounter with a fourteener comes when it passes gentle-giant San Luis Peak (14,014 feet) at mile 8.8 of Segment 20.

Despite the popularity of fourteener bagging, if you elect to climb San Luis Peak while passing by on your trek, you may be lucky enough to have it all to yourself. According to the Colorado Mountain Club, San Luis Peak is one of the least climbed of the fourteeners. The ascent is not a difficult one, with its Class 1 rating and 1,400 feet of elevation gain in about 1.25 miles. Proceed north from the saddle, following the gentle ridge to the top. Plan on an early start, though, to avoid afternoon storms. Allow about 2 to 3 hours round trip.

A climber ascends a talus-covered slope.
PHOTO COURTESY OF COLORADO MOUNTAIN EXPEDITIONS

From the saddle, a section-hiker points toward San Luis Peak and the climbing route from the CT.
PHOTO BY BILL MANNING

SCALE: Squares in grid approx. 1 Mile x 1 Mile

CT (current segment)

CT (adjacent segment)

CT Bicycle Wilderness Detour

1.8 CT Feature Mileage & Location

Trail

Paved Road

Improved Road

Unimproved Road

Unimproved Road and 4WD

National Forest Boundary

Wilderness Boundary

Continental Divide

Trailhead

Parking

Camping

lighter greens = National Forest

darker greens = Wilderness Area

orange or tan = BLM Land

purples = State Land

white = Private Land

SEGMENT 20 FEATURES TABLE   Gunnison National Forest

Mileage	Features & Comments	Elevation (feet)	Mileage from Denver	Mileage to Durango	UTM-E	UTM-N (NAD83)	Zone
0.0	Begin Segment 20	10,310	329.9	154.7	339,005	4,210,354	13
1.3	Pass through gate	10,348	331.2	153.4	339,553	4,208,767	13
1.6	Pass Machin Basin Trail on left	10,362	331.5	153.1	339,756	4,208,363	13
3.7	Pass through gate	10,642	333.6	151.0	337,996	4,205,956	13
7.5	Pass Stewart Creek Trail on right	11,749	337.4	147.2	332,659	4,204,819	13
8.8	Gain saddle below San Luis Peak	12,612	338.7	145.9	330,987	4,204,410	13
10.1	Gain saddle	12,366	340.0	144.6	329,719	4,203,859	13
10.5	Pass trail to Bondholder Meadows	12,146	340.4	144.2	329,568	4,203,352	13
12.7	End Segment 20	11,944	342.6	142.0	326,771	4,204,498	13

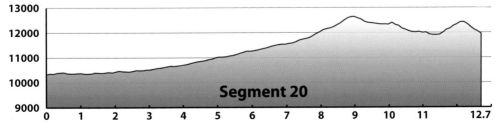

San Luis Pass to Junction Creek Trailhead (Segments 21–28)

Segment 21: **San Luis Pass to Spring Creek Pass Trailhead**

CT on Snow Mesa with 1,500 sheep and a cowboy.

PHOTO BY JEFF SELLENRICK

Distance: 14.8 miles

Elevation gain: Approx. 3,116 feet

Elevation loss: Approx. 4,157 feet

USFS maps: Gunnison and Rio Grande National Forests, pages 222–223

The Colorado Trail Databook 6: pages 52–53

The CT Map Book: pages 49–51

National Geographic Trails Illustrated maps: Nos. 139, 141

Latitude 40° map: Southwest Colorado Trails

Jurisdiction: Gunnison and Divide Ranger Districts, Gunnison and Rio Grande National Forests

Access from Denver end:

Access from Durango end:

Availability of water:

Bicycling: See page 200

"Take in the views from Snow Mesa above Spring Creek. You can see the Rio Grande Pyramid and the Uncompahgre Mountains, where Ute Indians once hunted."

Ahead is a great U-shaped bend of the Continental Divide that holds the headwaters of the mighty Rio Grande.

Gudy's TIP

Sheep herder on Snow Mesa.

PHOTO BY DON WALLACE

ABOUT THIS SEGMENT

This segment is quite the roller coaster. The Colorado Trail climbs in and out of the East, Middle, and West Mineral Creek drainages and traverses the Continental Divide to a maximum elevation of 12,785 feet. The views of the surrounding mountains are equally spectacular from the ridges and saddles as they are from the headwaters of the creeks below. There are many great potential campsites in the forests as the trail rolls in and out of the trees.

Segment 21 ends after crossing Snow Mesa. There is no shelter on Snow Mesa, so be cautious about crossing this 3.3-mile stretch if thunderstorms threaten. Even though the mesa looks relatively flat on the map, it does dip into several small creek drainages, oftentimes quite steeply. This is one of the most remote segments of The Colorado

A lamb checks out passing hikers.

PHOTO BY DON WALLACE

Trail and Snow Mesa can feel completely cut off from civilization. This can be a good thing on clear, windless days, but a scary prospect if there are lightning bolts flashing around you. The last 2 miles of the segment descend more than 1,200 feet to Spring Creek Pass and CO Hwy 149.

TRAILHEAD/ACCESS POINTS

San Luis Pass Trail Access: 🚙 From the north end of Creede in a vehicle such as a Subaru with moderate clearance and ruggedness, drive on the gravel and steep FS Road 503 north into a narrow canyon, about 7.5 miles to the closed Equity Mine and a small parking area. Vehicles like Jeeps that have high clearance and low range can continue an additional 1.5 miles. There is no formal parking available here. From this point, it's a 1-mile hike to San Luis Pass and the CT on a trail that prohibits motorized vehicles.

Spring Creek Pass Trailhead: 🚗 See Segment 22 on page 224.

SERVICES, SUPPLIES, AND ACCOMMODATIONS – CREEDE

It is about a 10-mile side trip into Creede from San Luis Pass. Walk 1 mile south, descending a side trail along the headwaters of West Willow Creek until you meet up with FS Rd 503. Continue on it downhill into town. About 1.5 miles down this road is a parking area at the Equity Mine. This area is often used by people climbing nearby San Luis Peak, hunters during hunting season, and people on a self-guided mine tour. On a busy weekend, a backpacker may find an easy hitch into town. Note that Creede can also be reached, if with difficulty due to the 33-mile distance and low traffic, from the Spring Creek Pass Trailhead that is described at the start of Segment 22 (page 224). Creede is an old mining town with various watering holes that recall the town's rip-roaring past.

Distance from CT: 10 miles
Elevation: 8,852 feet
Zip code: 81130
Area code: 719

Dining
Several locations in town

Gear (including fuel canisters)
San Juan Sports
102 S. Main St.
(719) 658-2359

Groceries
Kentucky Bell Market
2nd and Main streets
(719) 658-2526

Info
Chamber of Commerce
904 S. Main St.
(719) 658-2374

Laundry
Kip's Grill
101 E. 5th St.
(719) 658-0220

Lodging
Several locations in town

Medical
Mineral City Public Health/ Creede Family Practice
802 Rio Grande Ave.
(719) 658-2416
(719) 658-0929

Post Office
Creede Post Office
10 S. Main St.
(719) 658-2615

Showers
Snowshoe Motel
202 E. 8th St.
(719) 658-2315

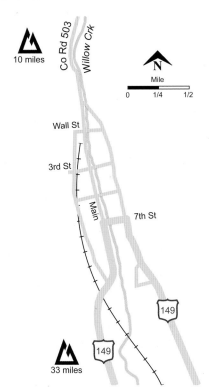

Trail users are treated to astounding views of fourteeners in the distance.

PHOTO BY ANDREW SKURKA

TRAIL DESCRIPTION

This segment begins at San Luis Pass, a point that is accessible only by hiking. It is separated from jeep access by 1 mile, car access by 2.5 miles, and Creede by 10 miles.

From the four-way trail junction at **mile 0.0** (11,944 feet), briefly head west, then south. Curve to the west again and, at **mile 1.0** (12,731), cross the Continental Divide and enter La Garita Wilderness. Climb steeply to a saddle just north of Peak 13,111 at **mile 1.3** (12,887). The trail then descends to the headwaters of East Mineral Creek at **mile 2.0** (12,139). At **mile 2.4** (11,917) is a campsite near tree line. Pass the East Mineral Creek Trail at **mile 2.6** (11,799) and cross East Mineral Creek at **mile 2.7** (11,678). Ascend to another saddle along the ridge that divides the East and Middle Mineral Creek drainages at **mile 3.3** (12,173).

Downhill from the saddle, cross Middle Mineral Creek at **mile 3.9** (11,617) with a campsite 0.1 mile east. The CT passes the Middle Mineral Creek Trail at **mile 4.3** (11,463) where there are campsites. After a series of uphill switchbacks, gain the ridge that separates the Middle and West Mineral Creek drainages at **mile 4.8** (11,852) where there's a good dry campsite. Descend again and cross a small stream at **mile 5.2** (11,977) where a small camp is possible below the trail, the last sheltered campsite until reaching the end of the segment at Spring Creek Pass Trailhead..

Climb to yet another saddle at **mile 5.8** (12,239) and continue west past the West Mineral Creek Trail at **mile 6.2** (12,323). Exit the La Garita Wilderness at **mile 6.9** (12,600). Climb gently and pass south of Peak 12813, reaching the high point of the segment at **mile 7.6** (12,785) where the view is stunning, including Snow Mesa and the white volcanic tuff beneath.

At a saddle on the Continental Divide at **mile 8.3** (12,558), pass the trail to Rough and Tumble Creeks. The CT stays to the left (south) here and descends toward Snow Mesa and a pond at **mile 9.5** (12,319). Head west across the expanse of Snow Mesa, climbing in and out of several small drainages. Cross the headwaters of Willow Creek at **mile 9.8** (12,290). There are potential campsites on top of Snow Mesa, but no shelter of any kind. Reach the edge of the mesa at **mile 12.8** (12,100). Drop off the mesa and reach tree line at **mile 13.2** (11,740). The segment ends at **mile 14.8** (10,908), when the CT reaches Spring Creek Pass on CO Hwy 149 where there's parking and a bathroom, but camping is not allowed. Cyclists rejoin here after the La Garita Wilderness detour.

The trail section is largely above tree line. Hikers should consider weather as a major factor when choosing campsites and determining hiking schedules. Snow Mesa can be a very unsettling experience during an electrical storm.

Wildflowers blanket a slope above Miners Creek.
PHOTO BY AARON LOCANDER

Viewing Ptarmigan

📷 The white-tailed ptarmigan is a small alpine grouse that inhabits open tundra in summer, resorting to willows and other sheltered areas in winter. It is the only bird species in Colorado to spend the entire year above tree line. The extensive alpine terrain along CT Segment 21 is perfect habitat for this hardy ground bird.

The ptarmigan's near-perfect seasonal camouflage helps it escape detection from predators (and even sharp-eyed trail users). Its mottled-brown summer plumage makes it almost invisible amid the scattered rocks and alpine plants. In winter, only the bird's black eyes and bill stand out against its pure white coloration.

Ptarmigan are weak flyers and are as likely to scurry away when disturbed as to burst into a short, low sail over the tundra. Despite that, they still manage to travel surprising distances in early winter to congregate in areas that harbor their favorite winter sustenance: dormant willow buds. In summer they add insects, seeds, and berries to their diet.

Nesting occurs in June with four to eight buff, spotted eggs laid in a lined depression in open ground. During breeding, males are sometimes aggressive toward interlopers passing through their territory, flying around erratically and making hooting noises, or approaching to peck comically at the boot of a resting hiker.

A study by ecologist James Larison of Cornell University raised a warning flag about the future of these fascinating birds. In areas of Colorado where metals from mining operations have leached into the soil, ptarmigan have accumulated high levels of cadmium in their bodies. Ultimately, this causes calcium loss and the birds can suffer broken bones in their brittle wings and legs.

Ptarmigan can be tricky to spot.
PHOTO BY TERRY ROOT

Photographers can sometimes get close.
PHOTO BY JULIE VIDA AND MARK TABB

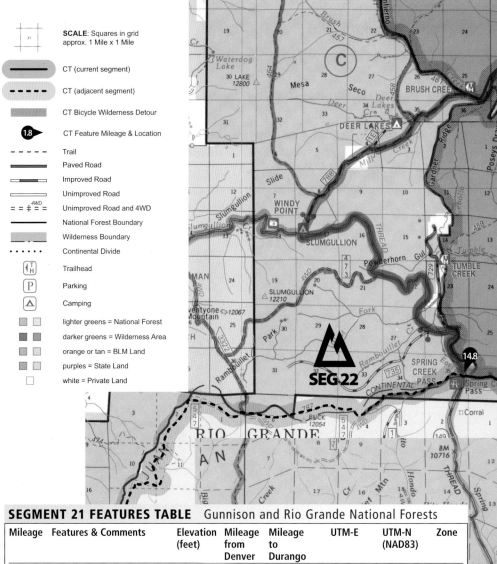

SCALE: Squares in grid approx. 1 Mile x 1 Mile

CT (current segment)

CT (adjacent segment)

CT Bicycle Wilderness Detour

CT Feature Mileage & Location

Trail

Paved Road

Improved Road

Unimproved Road

Unimproved Road and 4WD

National Forest Boundary

Wilderness Boundary

Continental Divide

Trailhead

Parking

Camping

lighter greens = National Forest

darker greens = Wilderness Area

orange or tan = BLM Land

purples = State Land

white = Private Land

SEGMENT 21 FEATURES TABLE   Gunnison and Rio Grande National Forests

Mileage	Features & Comments	Elevation (feet)	Mileage from Denver	Mileage to Durango	UTM-E	UTM-N (NAD83)	Zone
0.0	Begin Segment 21	11,944	342.6	142.0	326,771	4,204,498	13
2.6	Pass East Mineral Creek Trail	11,799	345.2	139.4	324,070	4,203,579	13
3.3	Gain saddle	12,173	345.9	138.7	323,431	4,203,260	13
3.9	Cross Middle Mineral Creek	11,617	346.5	138.1	322,627	4,203,077	13
4.3	Pass Middle Mineral Creek Trail	11,463	346.9	137.7	322,363	4,203,494	13
4.8	Gain ridge	11,852	347.4	137.2	321,838	4,203,572	13
5.2	Cross stream	11,977	347.8	136.8	321,604	4,203,060	13
5.8	Gain saddle	12,239	348.4	136.2	321,113	4,202,654	13
6.2	Pass West Mineral Creek Trail	12,323	348.8	135.8	320,568	4,202,190	13
7.6	High point of segment	12,785	350.2	134.4	319,013	4,202,624	13
8.3	Left past Rough & Tumble Trail	12,558	350.9	133.7	317,963	4,202,880	13
9.5	Pass by pond	12,319	352.1	132.5	317,755	4,201,168	13
12.8	Drop off Snow Mesa	12,100	355.4	129.2	312,771	4,200,710	13
14.8	End Segment 21	10,908	357.4	127.2	310,289	4,201,367	13

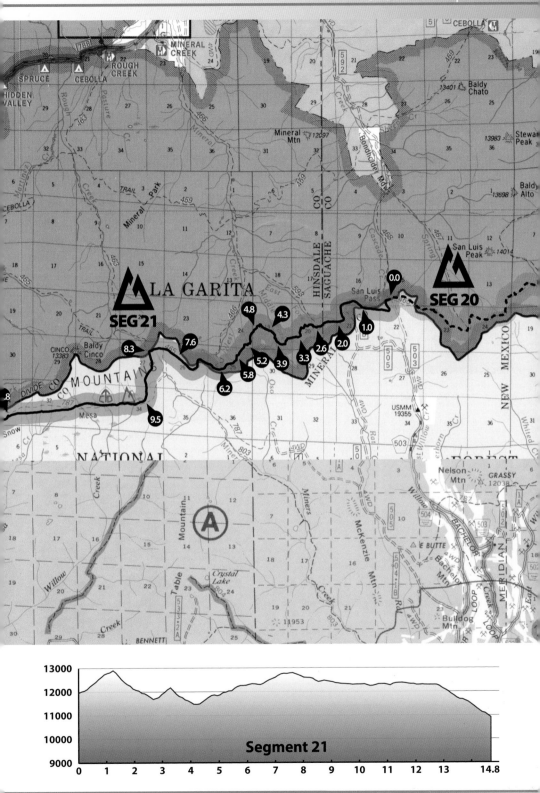

Segment 22: **Spring Creek Pass Trailhead to Carson Saddle**

The majestic San Juan Mountains.

PHOTO BY ROGER FORMAN

Distance: 17.2 miles

Elevation gain: Approx. 3,829 feet

Elevation loss: Approx. 2,385 feet

USFS maps: Gunnison and Rio Grande National Forests, pages 228–229

The Colorado Trail Databook 6: pages 54–55

The CT Map Book: pages 51–53

National Geographic Trails Illustrated maps: Nos. 139, 141

Latitude 40° map: Southwest Colorado Trails

Jurisdiction: Gunnison and Divide Ranger Districts, Gunnison and Rio Grande National Forests

Access from Denver end:

Access from Durango end:

Availability of water:

Bicycling:

"Don't miss the panoramas from Antenna Summit, just after Jarosa Mesa. The view overlooking the Uncompahgre Mountains is worth the climb. From Coney Summit to Carson Saddle there is a steep descent on the trail, but much better than on the jeep road. If your boot tread is worn, you'll probably slip and slide here."

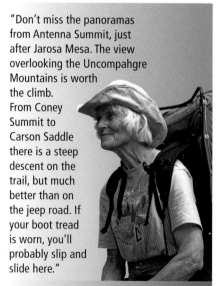

Gudy's TIP

ABOUT THIS SEGMENT

After crossing Spring Creek Pass, The Colorado Trail climbs again and crosses Jarosa Mesa on single-track. The trail across the mesa is rough with rocks sticking up out of soil that's in short supply. Afterwards, you'll proceed on jeep track through tundra and then through a forested area. The trail becomes single-track again. It climbs into the tundra and passes over two prominent hills as it heads toward Coney Summit and the high point on The Colorado Trail (13,271). Views from the Coney ridge are fantastic. The trail descends a steep hillside on switchbacks then steep four-wheel-drive road to Carson Saddle where there's rich mining history.

As the CT descends toward Carson Saddle it affords spectacular views of Lake San Cristobal, Red Mountain, and Redcloud and Sunshine Peaks. The arched course of the Lake Fork Valley marks the edge of the Lake City caldera, which erupted about 23 million years ago. High peaks beyond it are carved in volcanic tuff that fills the caldera. Lake San Cristobal first formed when a huge landslide (the Slumgullion Slide) dammed the river about 760 years ago. Parts of the slide are still moving.

TRAILHEAD/ACCESS POINTS

Above the clouds.
PHOTO BY PETE KARTSOUNES

Spring Creek Pass Trailhead: 🚗 This trailhead is located where CO Hwy 149 tops the Continental Divide at Spring Creek Pass. The pass is approximately 17 miles southeast of Lake City and 33 miles northwest of Creede. There is a Forest Service picnic area here with tables and fire rings, a toilet and an informative kiosk, as well as parking for another half-dozen or so cars. It is not unusual to see a camper or two in the picnic area. Water is usually available during the summer in a small irrigation ditch on the east side of the highway.

Carson Saddle/Wager Gulch Road Trail Access: 🚙 See Segment 23 on page 230.

SERVICES, SUPPLIES, AND ACCOMMODATIONS – LAKE CITY

It is approximately 17 miles north and west from Spring Creek Pass to the old mining town of **Lake City** on CO Hwy 149. That's probably too far for most backpackers to travel for resupply; nor is hitch-hiking especially good on this remote byway.

Distance from CT: 17 miles
Elevation: 8,671 feet
Zip code: 81235
Area code: 970

Dining
Several locations in town

Gear (including fuel canisters and shuttle)
The Sportsman
238 S. Gunnison Ave.
(970) 944-2526

Groceries
The Country Store
916 Hwy 149 North
(970) 944-2387

Info
Chamber of Commerce
3rd and Silver streets
(970) 944-2527

Laundry
The Lost Sock
808 N. Gunnison Ave.

Lodging (several)
Backcountry Basecamp
720 Gunnison Ave.
(970) 944-0181

The Raven's Rest Hostel
207 Gunnison Ave.
(970) 944-7119

Medical
Lake City Medical Center
700 Henson St.
(970) 944-2331

Post Office
Lake City Post Office
803 Gunnison Ave.
(970) 944-2560

Showers
Elkhorn RV Resort
713 N. Bluff St.
(970) 944-2920

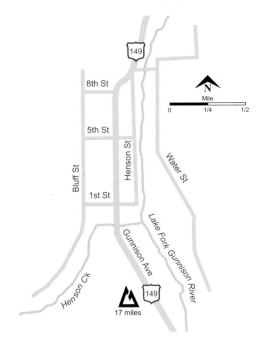

TRAIL DESCRIPTION

Segment 22 begins atop Spring Creek Pass on the Continental Divide, where there is a trailhead parking area, **mile 0.0** (10,908). Cyclists rejoin here after the La Garita Wilderness Detour. Previous guides have noted that this is a campground, but currently it is day-use only. Leave the parking area west on a Forest Service jeep trail (FS Rd 547). CT confidence markers help guide the way. Head uphill and, at about 2.5 miles, cross a small creek with potential campsites nearby. At **mile 2.6** (11,430), bear right off the jeep road onto the old La Garita Stock Driveway, mostly single-track. It is marked with rock cairns that support tall posts with CT confidence markers, helping guide you for the next 3 miles.

A sign marks the highest point on The Colorado Trail.
PHOTO BY FELECIA MORAN

At **mile 4.5** (12,027), reach the high point on Jarosa Mesa. Continue west to a three-way junction of jeep roads at **mile 5.6** (11,735). Stay left (west) here and head uphill, passing south of a mountain with a large antenna array on its summit. Reach a saddle at **mile 7.0** (12,074), then bend to the southwest. Take the right fork onto a single-track trail at **mile 7.9** (12,018). At **mile 8.7** (11,713) in a marshy valley, cross a jeep trail. Check out the Colorado Trail Friends Yurt (reservation, hinsdalehauteroute.org), 0.1 mile uphill. Camp Trail begins 0.2 mile west of yurt. Water is often available 0.3 mile downhill of this same intersection. Continue west on single-track.

Proceed to the right on a jeep trail through the willows at **mile 9.2** (11,924), then bear left and exit the willows to the west at **mile 9.5** (12,040). Climb a series of short switchbacks and follow the CT to the southwest. At **mile 11.5** (12,500) reach the head of cirque for Ruby Creek with water in ponds 400 feet below and 0.5 mile off the trail. Leave the trees and follow the Continental Divide. Climb several steep switchbacks to a high point and then another, enjoying great views. Descend to a saddle at **mile 14.4** (12,880) where Kitty Creek ponds can be seen a half-mile and 400 feet below (south).

The Colorado Trail reaches its highest point at **mile 15.6** (13,271) on the slope just beneath Coney Summit. The trail turns west, runs parallel to and crosses a jeep road, then joins the steep jeep road at **mile 16.0** (13,153). Descend to the bottom of the hill and turn right on an intersecting jeep road at **mile 17.1** (12,297). Head uphill to the intersection of three jeep trails and a small parking area at **mile 17.2** (12,366). This is Carson Saddle and the end of Segment 22.

SCALE: Squares in grid approx. 1 Mile x 1 Mile

CT (current segment)

CT (adjacent segment)

CT Bicycle Wilderness Detour

CT Feature Mileage & Location

Trail

Paved Road

Improved Road

Unimproved Road

Unimproved Road and 4WD

National Forest Boundary

Wilderness Boundary

Continental Divide

Trailhead

Parking

Camping

lighter greens = National Forest

darker greens = Wilderness Area

orange or tan = BLM Land

purples = State Land

white = Private Land

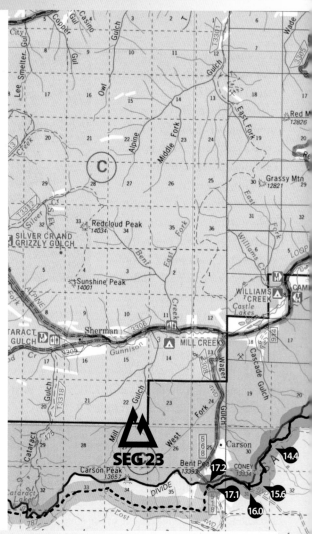

SEGMENT 22 FEATURES TABLE   Gunnison Rio Grande National Forests

Mileage	Features & Comments	Elevation (feet)	Mileage from Denver	Mileage to Durango	UTM-E	UTM-N (NAD83)	Zone
0.0	Begin Segment 22	10,908	357.4	127.2	310,289	4,201,367	13
2.6	Bear right off jeep road	11,430	360.0	124.6	306,839	4,200,325	13
4.5	Reach high point on Jarosa Mesa	12,027	361.9	122.7	303,954	4,200,150	13
5.6	Go west at intersection	11,735	363.0	121.6	302,268	4,200,258	13
7.9	Go right onto single-track	12,018	365.3	119.3	299,464	4,199,593	13
8.7	Cross jeep road below yurt	11,713	366.1	118.5	298,954	4,198,589	13
9.2	Proceed right	11,924	366.6	118.0	299,194	4,197,912	13
9.5	Stay to left	12,040	366.9	117.7	298,901	4,197,793	13
14.4	Descend to saddle	12,880	371.8	112.8	294,095	4,193,852	13
15.6	CT highest point	13,271	373.0	111.6	293,620	4,192,498	13
16.0	Steep descent on jeep road	13,153	373.4	111.2	293,263	4,192,307	13
17.1	Turn right at intersection	12,297	374.5	110.1	291,865	4,192,390	13
17.2	End Segment 22	12,366	374.6	110.0	291,701	4,192,491	13

Segment 23: Carson Saddle to Stony Pass Trailhead

Segment 23 is nearly all above 12,000 feet.

PHOTO BY JULIE VIDA AND MARK TABB

Distance: 15.9 miles

Elevation gain: Approx. 3,515 feet

Elevation loss: Approx. 3,339 feet

USFS maps: Gunnison, Rio Grande, and San Juan National Forests, pages 236–237

The Colorado Trail Databook 6: pages 56–57

The CT Map Book: pages 53–55

National Geographic Trails Illustrated map: No. 141

Latitude 40° map: Southwest Colorado Trails

Jurisdiction: Gunnison and Divide Ranger Districts, Gunnison and Rio Grande National Forests

Access from Denver end:

Access from Durango end:

Availability of water:

Bicycling:

"Carson Saddle draws a surprising number of people in four-wheel-drive vehicles, which can be a shock after the previous isolation of the trail."

Enjoy the spectacular above-tree line views from the Continental Divide on this segment, but be cautious in conditions of poor visibility. A GPS receiver can be invaluable in locating the features noted in the Features Table.

Gudy's TIP

ABOUT THIS SEGMENT

Segment 23 is remote, high, physically demanding, and rewarding. The Colorado Trail leaves the popular motorized area at Carson Saddle and heads west on non-motorized single-track up the Lost Trail Creek watershed, passing fields of summer wildflowers and eventually reaching an unnamed pass that is often snowy until late June. While heading down the back side of the pass, Cataract Lake eventually comes into view below and the trail reaches a clearly marked junction that is the beginning of a major rerouting of the CT. The trail originally dropped into the Pole Creek drainage on a multi-use motorized trail, but now stays closer to the Continental Divide with its spectacular views. Authorities decided not to construct full-bench trail tread in this section, but volunteers have built huge rock cairns to mark the trail, and the cairns make the route easy to follow. This is one of the most remote segments of the CT and vehicle access to each end, especially Carson Saddle, can be quite challenging.

One of many striking views along Cataract Ridge.

PHOTO BY DEBBIE ABBOTT-BROWN

TRAILHEAD/ACCESS POINTS

Carson Saddle/Wager Gulch Trail Access: From Lake City, drive south on CO Hwy 149 about 1.5 miles to a Y in the road. The right branch leads to Lake San Cristobal. Follow this road for 9.3 miles to a turnoff on the left with a small parking area.

This is the beginning of Wager Gulch Road (BLM Rd 3308/FS Rd 568). This is not a road for the squeamish. It is very steep, rocky, and narrow, with many tight switchbacks and some significant exposure. In mid-summer, expect to encounter four-wheel-drives, ATVs, and motorcycles. Follow this road for about 5 miles to Carson Saddle, a low point on the Continental Divide about a mile above the abandoned mining town of Carson. Segment 23 begins at an intersection with a jeep trail here.

Stony Pass Trailhead:  See Segment 24 on page 238.

SERVICES, SUPPLIES, AND ACCOMMODATIONS

These amenities are available in Lake City; see Segment 22 on page 224.

TRAIL DESCRIPTION

Segment 23 begins at the jeep road intersection on Carson Saddle, **mile 0.0** (12,366). Go south on the jeep road and turn right on the single-track trail at **mile 0.5** (12,175). After a short climb, the trail bends to the west and crosses a small stream at **mile 1.2** (11,975). There is a good campsite about 50 feet below the trail. Begin a long climb up the Lost Trail Creek drainage, crossing a seasonal stream with campsite nearby at **mile 1.7**

A small pond offers a good spot to camp.

PHOTO BY ROGER FORMAN

Bighorn sheep look down from a ridgeline.
PHOTO BY PETE TURNER

(11,975) and a larger stream at **mile 2.4** (12,220). Reach a small, unnamed pass at **mile 3.7** (12,919) and drop into the Pole Creek drainage to the west.

The Colorado Trail continues straight at junction with West Lost Trail **mile 4.9** (12,420), then turns to the right at a junction with Pole Creek Trail at **mile 5.0** (12,389). This is the beginning of the Cataract Ridge reroute of the CT, which stays near the Divide and avoids old routing where motorized vehicles are allowed.

The trail heads west from here, then descends steeply to the north where it reaches a junction with Cataract Gulch Trail to the north at **mile 5.5** (12,246). Pass left along a small lake with several good campsites. There are also excellent campsites at Cataract Lake, about a quarter mile below the CT to the northeast. Follow the CT as it heads back west, passing several more potential campsites before crossing a stream at **mile 6.3** (12,350). After gaining the saddle at **mile 6.8** (12,673), the trail bears to the right and continues upward, crossing a wide field where elk are commonly seen. Contour along the north side of Peak 13164 and begin to follow a long string of cairns at **mile 7.8** (12,732), where the trail bends to the southwest. The cairns are tall and easy to follow.

Descend to a low saddle and junction with side trails at **mile 8.5** (12,356), then head up the other side in a westerly direction. Reach a small pass and cross the Continental Divide above Cuba Gulch at **mile 9.3** (12,722). From here, the trail contours above Cuba Gulch and continues straight at a trail junction at **mile 9.9** (12,538). A small grassy meadow, 300 feet below, makes a good campsite. A short distance ahead at **mile 10.2**

Volunteer-built cairns mark the trail to Stony Pass.

PHOTO BY MICK GIGONE

(12,650), water may be found in the headwaters of Cuba Creek.

The cairns continue to mark the trail as it climbs to another saddle at **mile 10.6** (12,909). Bear to the left at the pass. Note the distinctive Cuba Peak to the northeast. Cross the top of Minnie Gulch at **mile 11.4** (12,722) and go straight through the intersection with the Minnie Gulch Trail. Climb steeply to a high point on the ridge at **mile 11.6** (12,982). Bear left at **mile 11.9** (12,935) and continue to **mile 12.6** (12,541), where the CT continues straight ahead at the intersection with the Maggie Gulch Trail. The CT heads to the southwest, passing a small pond and potential campsite at **mile 13.5** (12,819), and then continues to a high point at **mile 13.7** (12,820). Descend to another well-marked trail intersection at **mile 13.9** (12,659) and go to the left (west) and begin traveling around Canby Mountain. Drop down to a creek at **mile 14.2** (12,450) and bear right at an intersection at **mile 14.6** (12,315), staying high on the hillside. The trail drops you down to the Stony Pass Road at **mile 15.5** (12,367). Take a right up the road to **mile 15.9** (12,524), where the trail leaves the road to the west at a trailhead sign 0.2 mile below the top of Stony Pass, the end of Segment 23.

The Stony Pass Road

The historic Stony Pass Road was constructed in 1879 as a means to transport supplies in and ore out of the booming Silverton mining district. For a few short years, it was a busy and important route for miners and others attracted by news of new-found wealth in the San Juans. After a couple years, however, the difficult route was eclipsed by the Denver and Rio Grande Western's rail route through Animas Canyon. The road quickly fell into a sorry state and gained a reputation as a "pretty rough ride."

Robert M. Ormes, of early guidebook fame, recalls struggling up it in his car, after being assured that the first car into Silverton came in this way. Finding it a lot more than his auto could handle, he encountered a man on the road who told him, "Sure it came in this way … but, it was in some wagons."

Stony Pass Road (left) beneath Canby Mountain divides Segments 23 and 24.
PHOTO BY JEFF SELLENRICK

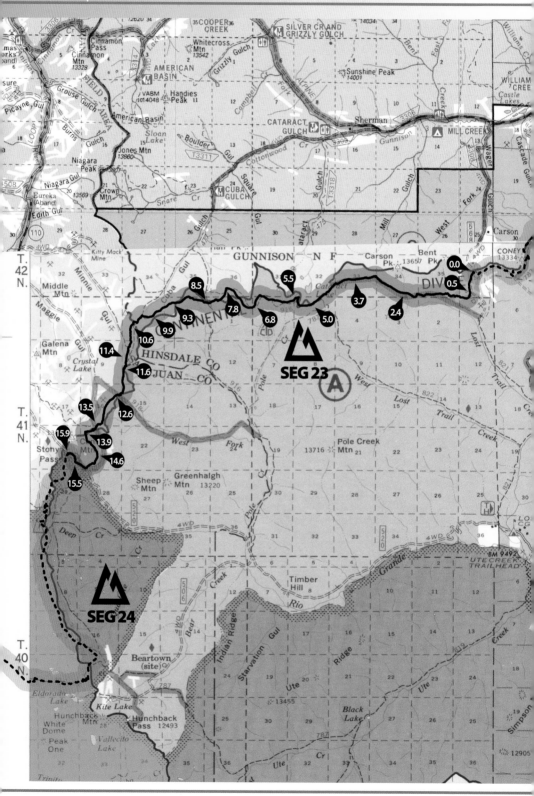

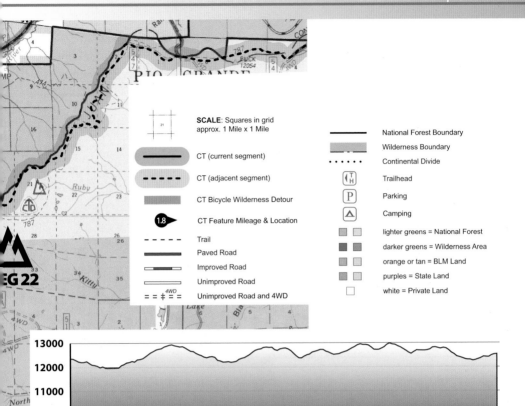

SEGMENT 23 FEATURES TABLE

Gunnison, Rio Grande, and San Juan National Forests

Mileage	Features & Comments	Elevation (feet)	Mileage from Denver	Mileage to Durango	UTM-E	UTM-N (NAD83)	Zone
0.0	Begin Segment 23	12,366	374.6	110.0	291,701	4,192,491	13
0.5	Leave road, right on single-track	12,175	375.1	109.5	291,567	4,191,739	13
3.7	Gain pass	12,919	378.3	106.3	287,126	4,192,297	13
5.0	Go right at intersection	12,389	379.6	105.0	285,439	4,191,420	13
5.5	Left along small lake	12,246	380.1	104.5	284,782	4,191,633	13
6.8	Gain saddle	12,673	381.4	103.2	283,195	4,191,411	13
7.8	Begin to follow cairns	12,732	382.4	102.2	282,113	4,192,071	13
9.3	Gain pass	12,722	383.9	100.7	280,050	4,191,571	13
9.9	Go straight at trail junction	12,538	384.5	100.1	279,268	4,191,105	13
10.6	Gain saddle	12,909	385.2	99.4	278,422	4,190,763	13
11.4	Go straight at junction	12,722	386.0	98.6	278,203	4,189,553	13
11.6	High point on ridge	12,982	386.2	98.4	278,100	4,189,155	13
12.6	Go straight at trails junction	12,541	387.2	97.4	277,777	4,188,191	13
13.5	Pass pond	12,819	388.1	96.5	277,038	4,187,096	13
13.9	Go left at intersection	12,659	388.5	96.1	276,514	4,186,805	13
14.6	Go right at intersection	12,315	389.2	95.4	276,984	4,185,969	13
15.5	Go right (uphill) on dirt road	12,367	390.1	94.5	276,114	4,185,742	13
15.9	End Segment 23	12,524	390.5	94.1	275,826	4,186,057	13

Segment 24: Stony Pass Trailhead to Molas Pass

Distance: 20.2 miles

Elevation gain: Approx. 3,475 feet

Elevation loss: Approx. 5,119 feet

USFS maps: Rio Grande and San Juan National Forests, pages 246–247

The Colorado Trail Databook 6: pages 58–59

The CT Map Book: pages 55–58

National Geographic Trails Illustrated map: No. 140

Latitude 40° map: Southwest Colorado Trails

Jurisdiction: Columbine and Divide Ranger Districts, San Juan and Rio Grande National Forests

Access from Denver end: 🏍

Access from Durango end: 🚗

Availability of water: ☕

Bicycling: 🚲 See page 244

CT Volunteer Adopter Jody Furtney carries a pulaski toward the next trail maintenance project.

PHOTO BY SETH FURTNEY

"Once over the Divide and into the Weminuche Wilderness Area, the Elk Creek drainage and its dramatic geologic walls are topped off with views of Arrow and Vestal peaks."

This short, impressive range of peaks is known as the Grenadiers. If you have time, the short (but steep) trail that begins at the beaver ponds (mile 11.6) is an interesting side trip. See if you can spot rock climbers on the famous Wham Ridge.

Gudy's TIP

ABOUT THIS SEGMENT

Segment 24 enters the Weminuche Wilderness Area just south of Stony Pass Road and follows the trail toward Arrow and Vestal Peaks, the two most prominent mountains ahead. The route is along the Continental Divide and is co-located with the CDNST. About 2 miles south of Stony Pass it passes out of the San Juan volcanic rocks and into 1.7 billion-year-old basement rocks and light- and dark-colored layered gneiss. After passing several small lakes, the trail follows a relatively flat plateau switching between double-track and single-track trail. Eventually the CT diverges from the CDNST and drops into the Elk Creek drainage on a series of impressive switchbacks. As it begins this descent, it suddenly enters completely different rocks, quartzite interleaved with thin layers of maroon to blue-gray slate, rocks that are part of the Uncompahgre Formation. Rocks like these are found nowhere else along the CT. They are metamorphic rocks, but they have never been subjected to the high temperatures like those that produced the other metamorphic basement rocks. They were clearly deposited as sandstone and shale after the 1.7 billion-year-old basement rocks were formed, but were lightly metamorphosed and squeezed into

Wildflowers in late July at 12,500 feet in the San Juan Mountains.

PHOTO BY SETH FURTNEY

Dramatic descent into Elk Creek from the Continental Divide.
PHOTO BY TODD WOLTER

a series of tight accordionlike folds before nearby bodies of 1.4 billion-year-old granite were injected into them. The towering peaks of the Grenadier Range that loom south of the trail are all carved from a thick north-sloping layer of the quartzite. Because the quartzite is particularly resistant to weathering, it preserves the smooth polished and striated rock outcrops shaped by the glacier that occupied this valley until about 12,000 years ago.

This is one of the most impressive sections of trail, descending a series of long switchbacks until reaching the headwaters of Elk Creek and the remnants of old mining operations below. The CT follows the creek down steeply at first, eventually reaching tree line and continuing generally westward until leaving the Weminuche Wilderness Area, crossing the train tracks for the Durango & Silverton Narrow Gauge Railroad, and passing over the Animas River on a good bridge.

As the CT climbs out of the canyon and approaches Molas Lake it passes out of quartzite and into nearly horizontal beds of early Paleozoic sandstone, shale, and limestone. From Molas Lake, access to Molas Pass, US Hwy 550, and Silverton is easy.

TRAILHEAD/ACCESS POINTS

Stony Pass Trailhead: 🚙 Drive northeast on Silverton's main, Greene Street. Before leaving town, turn right on County Road 2 and drive 4.1 miles (paved then gravel) to an area known as Howardsville. Turn right on the gravel County Road 4, also known as Forest Service Road 589, and drive uphill about 1.7 miles to a Y intersection. Veer left onto gravel County Road 3, also known as Forest Service Road 737, Stony Pass Road, and drive southeast 4.1 steep miles to the top. (Beyond the top, the FS Rd number changes to 520.) Continue driving southeast, now downhill, for 0.2 mile to a wide shoulder on the right with trail sign where CT Segment 24 single-track diverges to the south.

US Hwy 550–Molas Pass Trailhead: 🚗 See Segment 25 on page 248.

> Don't miss the turnoff point for the CT where it drops off the Continental Divide into Elk Creek Valley. Pay close attention.

SERVICES, SUPPLIES, AND ACCOMMODATIONS

These amenities are available in Silverton; see Segment 25, page 251.

TRAIL DESCRIPTION

Begin Segment 24 at the trail sign on the south side of Stony Pass Road, **mile 0.0** (12,524) and immediately enter the Weminuche Wilderness. (Cyclists diverge here onto the Weminuche Wilderness detour.) Follow the trail south, passing an old mine site and dropping to a small stream crossing at **mile 1.0** (12,524). Follow the trail back to the ridge and contour around Peak 12721. Descend to a small valley and cross the Highland Mary Lake Trail at **mile 1.8** (12,210).

The southbound CT diverges from the CDT in Segment 24.

PHOTO BY PATTY LAUSHMAN

Climb past a small knob to the west of the trail and stay left at an intersection at **mile 2.1** (12,137). Cross a small stream at **mile 2.6** (12,322) and a small lake and side trail at **mile 3.0** (12,547). Stay high as the trail closely follows the Divide for the next 2.3 miles. Stay to the left at an unmarked trail intersection at **mile 3.3** (12,589).

The trail follows a faint two-track trail, with several cairns marking the way, until reaching an intersection near several small lakes at **mile 5.3** (12,522) where the CT stays left. At **mile 5.8** (12,456) is a key, signed intersection. (This is where the CT and Continental Divide National Scenic Trail go their separate ways for good, after having been co-located for about 314 miles from Georgia Pass in Segment 6 by way of the CT Collegiate West.) Turn right (uphill) at this signed intersection. Stay to the left at the intersection at **mile 6.1** (12,657) and continue south enjoying one of the most memorable views on the entire CT. At **mile 6.4** (12,690), the CT turns to the right and drops down a steep hillside on a series of switchbacks into the Elk Creek drainage. Pass by an old mining shed at **mile 7.2** (12,105). At **mile 7.4** (11,795) cross to the south side of Elk Creek, then back north 0.2 mile farther.

Continue west and down as the canyon narrows. Be mindful of your footing as the trail drops steeply through a spectacular notch. Continue above the creek and, after entering the trees, drop back down to the creek and cross a side trail at **mile 9.0** (10,720)

Before ending Segment 24, southbounders look back on Elk Park and the Animas River with Mt. Garfield behind.
PHOTO BY JEFF MCGARVIN

Molas Lake and Campground near the end of Segment 24 where CT travelers might enjoy a shower.
PHOTO BY BILL BLOOMQUIST

that is used by climbers to access the saddle between Peak Two and Peak Three. There are good campsites here. Cross a side stream and then a second side stream with a trail to a hidden waterfall at **mile 9.6** (10,360). The canyon begins to widen out from here, with more campsites in the area.

Reach a pond at **mile 11.6** (9,994) with a classic view of Arrow and Vestal Peaks. There are good campsites on the east side of the pond, the last good ones until reaching the Animas River. Continuing west through thick forest, the trail traverses hillsides high above Elk Creek and then descends steeply to rejoin the creek. At **mile 14.4** (9,130), the CT leaves the gorge and wilderness, passing a trail register, interpretive sign, and wilderness boundary marker. Intersect a side trail at **mile 14.5** (9,122) that goes to the Elk Park loading and unloading point for passengers on the Durango & Silverton Narrow Gauge Railroad.

After descending a switchback, reach the railroad tracks next to the Animas River. Follow the tracks northwest for several hundred feet and cross the tracks at **mile 15.1** (8,930). Continue northwest and, after passing several potential campsites, cross the Animas River on a long bridge at **mile 15.2** (8,918). Looking downstream, the prominent peak is Mount Garfield. At **mile 15.4** (8,955), cross Molas Creek on a bridge built by CTF volunteers. Climb dozens of switchbacks and, at the top, bear right at an intersection with a horse trail at **mile 17.6** (10,280). Cross another horse trail at **mile 18.1** (10,246) and continue straight ahead. At **mile 18.4** (10,437), bear right at a third horse trail and go straight through the intersection with yet another horse trail at **mile 18.6** (10,504).

Take a left at the junction at **mile 18.7** (10,577) to stay on the CT. The right fork leads to Big Molas Lake. Cross Molas Creek again at **mile 19.1** (10,520) and continue to climb until reaching US Hwy 550 near the top of Molas Pass at **mile 20.2** (10,886). This is the end of Segment 24. Cyclists rejoin here after Weminuche Wilderness detour. There is a large parking area with toilets 300 feet to the south.

Weminuche Wilderness Bicycle Detour

This detour goes through Silverton, offering cyclists good opportunity to resupply. Begin at the division between Segments 23 and 24 at the Stony Pass Trailhead. Ride up the dirt road northwest 0.2 mile to the summit of the pass (12,588). Descend northwest to an intersection at **mile 2.8** (11,167) and turn left, continuing downhill. At **mile 4.4** (10,076), bear left, downhill. At another junction, **mile 4.9** (9,970), continue downhill onto Cunningham Gulch Rd, FS Rd 589. At **mile 5.9** (9,758) continue ahead at side road on the right. In the Animas River valley bottom at Howardsville, **mile 6.1** (9,678), turn left (southwest) onto County Rd 2, Engineer/Cinnamon Pass Rd (gravel then paved). Arrive in Silverton at **mile 10.8** (9,304). Pass through town southwest and continue straight onto US Hwy 550 (south) at **mile 11.4** (9,255). Pedal up the hill and, as you're nearing the top of Molas Pass, note the trail sign where the CT crosses the highway, **mile 17.5** (10,886). This is the start of Segment 25.

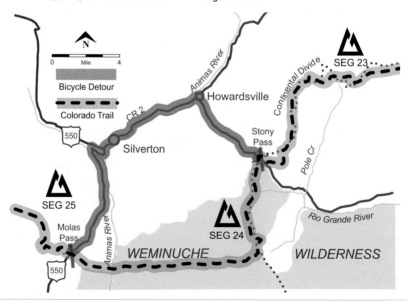

The Grenadiers

PHOTO BY JULIE MANCHESTER

Soaring faces of hard quartzite, tumbling brooks, and remote campsites characterize the beautiful Grenadier Range in the western portion of the Weminuche Wilderness Area. When the CT plunges off the Continental Divide into the Elk Creek Basin, it enters a world that is legendary with generations of Colorado mountaineers.

The Grenadiers were among the last high peaks in Colorado to be conquered; most were not climbed until the 1930s, on Colorado Mountain Club excursions and by members of the legendary San Juan Mountaineers group. They are unusual in that they are made up of quartzite, which is relatively rare in the Southern Rockies. Quartzite is a hard and resistant rock that weathers into clean, steep north faces that often require technical climbing with ropes. From the beaver ponds at mile 12.3 of Segment 24, there are excellent views of Arrow (13,803) and Vestal (13,864) Peaks, the most famous of the Grenadiers and members of Colorado's Highest Hundred (or hundred highest peaks). The climbers' trail begins here, ascending steeply into the basin beneath Wham Ridge, one of the most prized climbs in the state.

The western endpoint of the short but dramatic Grenadier Range is Mount Garfield (13,074). It looms 4,000 feet over the Animas River and Durango & Silverton Narrow Gauge Railroad tracks, and is a constant companion as you labor up the switchbacks to Molas Pass.

The Durango & Silverton Narrow Gauge train approaches the Elk Creek hiker stop.

PHOTO BY ERNIE NORRIS

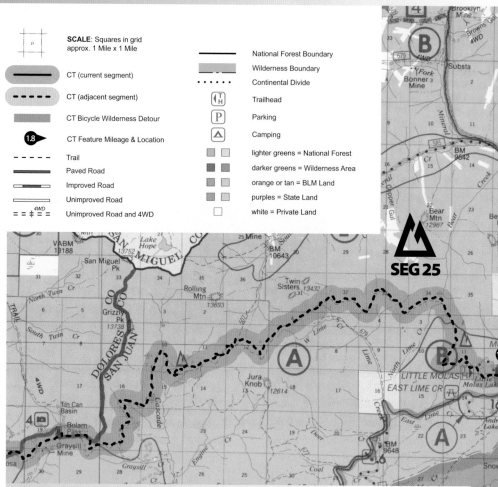

SCALE: Squares in grid approx. 1 Mile x 1 Mile

CT (current segment)

CT (adjacent segment)

CT Bicycle Wilderness Detour

1.8 CT Feature Mileage & Location

- - - - - Trail

Paved Road

Improved Road

Unimproved Road

= = ‡ = = Unimproved Road and 4WD

National Forest Boundary

Wilderness Boundary

Continental Divide

Trailhead

Parking

Camping

lighter greens = National Forest

darker greens = Wilderness Area

orange or tan = BLM Land

purples = State Land

white = Private Land

SEG 25

SEGMENT 24 FEATURES TABLE   San Juan National Forest

Mileage	Features & Comments	Elevation (feet)	Mileage from Denver	Mileage to Durango	UTM-E	UTM-N (NAD83)	Zone
0.0	Begin Segment 24, enter wilderness	12,524	390.5	94.1	275,826	4,186,057	13
1.8	Cross Highland Mary Lakes Trail	12,210	392.3	92.3	274,915	4,183,818	13
5.3	Bear left at intersection	12,522	395.8	88.8	275,888	4,179,087	13
5.8	Turn right at intersection	12,456	396.3	88.3	276,801	4,178,625	13
6.4	Turn right at intersection	12,690	396.9	87.7	276,472	4,177,596	13
7.4	Cross Elk Creek and then again	11,795	397.9	86.7	275,535	4,177,423	13
9.0	Pass side trail on left	10,720	399.5	85.1	273,836	4,177,766	13
11.6	Pass pond with classic view	9,994	402.1	82.5	270,110	4,178,016	13
14.4	Leave Weminuche Wilderness	9,130	404.9	79.7	266,337	4,178,801	13
15.2	Cross Animas River	8,918	405.7	78.9	265,505	4,179,581	13
17.6	Go right at intersection	10,280	408.1	76.5	264,687	4,180,604	13
18.4	Bear right at intersection	10,437	408.9	75.7	263,345	4,180,415	13
18.7	Bear left at intersection	10,577	409.2	75.4	263,152	4,180,893	13
19.1	Cross Molas Creek	10,520	409.6	75.0	262,839	4,180,625	13
20.2	End Segment 24	10,886	410.7	73.9	262,245	4,180,344	13

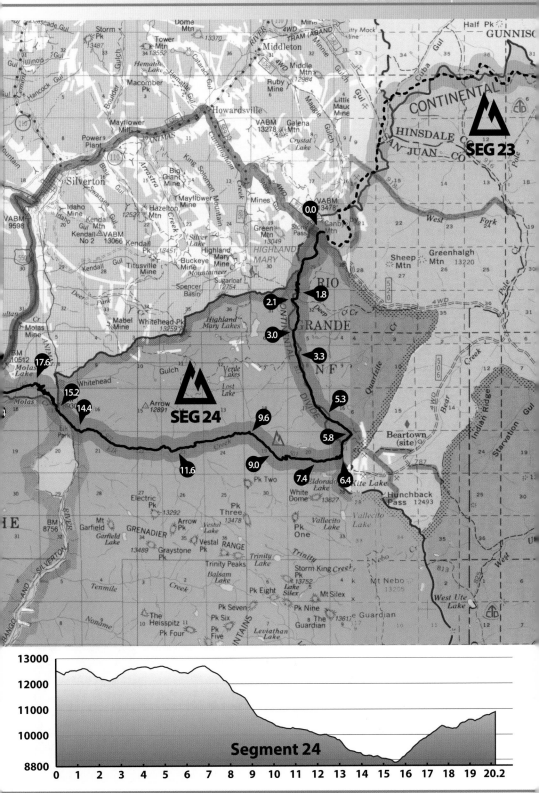

Segment 25: Molas Pass to Bolam Pass Road

Mid-segment descent beyond saddle near Rolling Mountain.

PHOTO BY KATIE QUINN

Distance: 20.9 miles

Elevation gain: Approx. 3,799 feet

Elevation loss: Approx. 3,578 feet

USFS map: San Juan National Forest, pages 254–255

The Colorado Trail Databook 6: pages 60–61

The CT Map Book: pages 58–60

National Geographic Trails Illustrated maps: Nos. 140, 141

Latitude 40° maps: Southwest Colorado Trails, Durango Trails

Jurisdiction: Columbine and Mancos/Dolores Ranger Districts, San Juan National Forest

Access from Denver end:

Access from Durango end:

Availability of water:

Bicycling: 🚲

"There is a campground at Molas Pass (by Big Molas Lake) that offers showers. Don't miss it. Between Little Molas Lake and Lime Creek, wildflowers grow knee high in a kaleidoscope of colors."

Big Molas Lake, east of the highway and north of the CT, has camping on private land. Little Molas Lake, west of the highway, has public camping.

Gudy's TIP

ABOUT THIS SEGMENT

The segment starts at US Hwy 550, just north of Molas Pass, and passes through a campground near Little Molas Lake. In this area the trail passes over gently inclined beds of gray shale, sandstone, and limestone of the Hermosa Formation, which was deposited in a shallow sea that flanked the rising Ancestral Rockies between 312 and 305 million years ago. The limestone layers contain abundant fossils.

After leaving the campground, the trail climbs to the Upper Lime Creek drainage, which was heavily forested until a fire roared through in 1879. The forest has not returned to this high-elevation area since then. In the summer months, when the wildflowers along the next few miles of trail are in full bloom, the CT is ablaze in various shades of yellows and purples. The views are second to none.

A cyclist enjoys a near perfect day.
PHOTO BY NATE HEBENSTREIT

Hikers have reported two places in this segment—at mileage points 10.2 and 12.9—where they have gotten off on the wrong trail. In both cases, they took off to the left because it appeared to be the more heavily traveled trail. At both spots the CT makes a sharp right turn!

At about mile 9 the trail crosses into redbeds of the Cutler Formation, deposited in lowlands flanking the Ancestral Rockies between 300 and 285 million years ago. The spectacular cliffs on the slopes above this part of the trail are conglomerate deposited on the post-Laramide land surface before the San Juan volcanic rocks, which cap the peaks and ridges, were erupted. Large blocks that have tumbled from the conglomerate layer are conspicuous in several places along this part of the trail. As the trail descends toward Cascade Creek it encounters an irregular body of light-colored granite and porphyry that makes up most of Grizzly Peak. A ledge of this rock forms a nice waterfall worth visiting uphill from the CT at mile 14.3, just before crossing Cascade Creek on a good bridge built by CT volunteers. After another climb, the distinctive Lizard Head Peak comes into view. The segment is largely above tree line, so travel during safe weather periods, trying to avoid the inevitable summer afternoon thunderstorms.

TRAILHEAD/ACCESS POINTS

US Hwy 550–Molas Trail Trailhead:  Segment 25 begins at a trail sign where the CT crosses Hwy 550 about 0.2 mile north of the Molas Pass summit and 7 miles south of Silverton. There is no parking where the trail crosses the highway. Close by at the pass summit, there is a scenic pullout, bathrooms, and ample daytime-only parking.

Cascade Creek.
PHOTO BY MORGAN AND ROBYN WILKINSON

About 1.5 miles north of the CT crossing, along the highway 5.5 miles south of Silverton, is the Molas Trail Trailhead where overnight parking is allowed. From this parking area, an old jeep track, the beginning of the Molas Trail, leads south about 0.2 mile and connects to the CT.

Little Molas Lake Trailhead: From Molas Pass on US Hwy 550, drive north 0.4 mile, turn left (west) on a dirt road, and continue 1 mile to the improved Little Molas Lake parking area. There are bathrooms and camping spots here. The CT passes on the south and west sides of the lake.

Bolam Pass Trail Access: See Segment 26 on page 256.

SERVICES, SUPPLIES, AND ACCOMMODATIONS – SILVERTON

Silverton is approximately 7 miles north of Molas Pass on US Hwy 550. Molas Lake Campground, near Molas Lake Trailhead, offers hot showers but no longer carries grocery items nor does it have postal delivery. CT travelers have arranged for campground delivery of their resupply box by contacting the Town of Silverton at (970) 387-5522.

Distance from CT: 7 miles
Elevation: 9,318 feet
Zip code: 81433
Area code: 970

Dining
Several locations in town

Gear (including fuel canisters)
Outdoor World
1234 Greene St.
(970) 387-5628

Groceries
Silverton Grocery
717 Greene St.
(970) 387-5652

Info
Chamber of Commerce
414 Greene St.
(970) 387-5654

Laundry
A & B RV Park
1445 Mineral St.
(970) 387-5347

Lodging
Several locations in town

Medical
Silverton Clinic
1450 Greene St.
(970) 387-5354

Post Office
Silverton Post Office
138 W. 12th St.
(970) 387-5402

Train Depot
Durango & Silverton Narrow Gauge Railroad
Blair and W. 12th streets
(970) 387-5416
(888) 872-4607

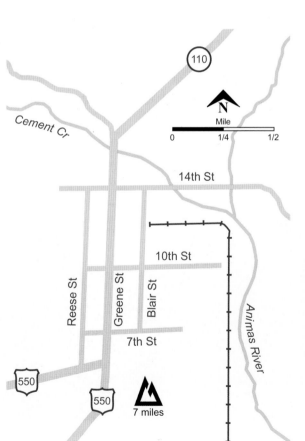

TRAIL DESCRIPTION

Segment 25 begins on the west side of US Hwy 550 at a large Colorado Trail interpretive sign 0.2 mile north of the Molas Pass summit. Because there's no parking here, some hikers take off from nearby parking locations, including the scenic pullout at the Molas Pass summit, the Molas Trail Trailhead, or Little Molas Lake Trailhead and Campground.

After crossing US Hwy 550, **mile 0.0** (10,886), pass under a power line at **mile 0.3** (10,955) and then around the west shore of Little Molas Lake where a side trail to the lake and campground intersects the CT at **mile 0.7** (10,927). The trail heads northwest, passes through the campground, then bends to the southwest. Stay right on old road at **mile 1.6** (11,097). At **mile 2.0** (11,205), turn right (northeast) at an intersection of two old roads. Continue to climb, turning left (northwest) and joining a single-track trail at **mile 3.0** (11,626).

Reach a saddle between Peak 12764 and Peak 12849 at **mile 3.9** (11,525). The trail turns to the west here and eventually reaches an overlook at **mile 5.0** (11,537) with a campsite near ponds 0.2 mile to the south. The Colorado Trail crosses a tributary stream to Lime Creek on a wet ledge at **mile 5.3** (11,573) with a campsite 0.4 mile ahead. Cross Lime Creek at **mile 6.1** (11,392) with possible small campsite. Continue generally westward, passing a campsite at **mile 8.0** (11,578) with water 0.1 mile farther. At **mile 9.6** (11,920),

Saddling up after a day of trail work.

PHOTO BY PETE TURNER

In July much of the CT is an alpine garden.

PHOTO BY ROGER FORMAN

on the right just 0.1 mile off the trail, is a campsite at a small lake. The trail reaches small lakes and comes to a T intersection with the Engineer Mountain Trail at **mile 10.2** (12,125). Go to the right at this marked intersection and pass between lakes. Climb up the rocky (and sometimes snowy) trail and join the Rico-Silverton Trail at **mile 11.0** (12,344). Bear left here, eventually reaching a series of switchbacks that gains the saddle south of Rolling Mountain at **mile 11.2** (12,500).

Descend from the saddle. At **mile 12.7** (11,640), bear to the left at an intersection with a side trail that goes to a nearby campsite at a small lake. Intersect the White Creek Trail at **mile 12.9** (11,452) and go to the right. Continue downhill crossing streams at **mile 13.2** (11,440) and **mile 14.2** (11,236) with an impressive cascade just uphill from the trail. Cross Cascade Creek on a bridge at **mile 14.8** (10,852) near a refreshing waterfall. There is a good campsite 200 feet from the bridge on the east side of the creek. From here, head south then climb, bending to the west and then crossing a creek at **mile 17.0** (11,162). The trail turns south again to a junction with side trail at **mile 17.3** (11,252) that connects to FS Rd 579. Continue right, passing good campsites near seasonal streams in the next two miles.

At **mile 19.1** (11,761), the CT crosses a saddle in a large meadow with views of Lizard Head Peak ahead and Engineer Mountain behind. Go left on dirt FS Rd 578B at **mile 20.1** (11,293) then leave road left onto single-track at **mile 20.7** (11,135). Pass through a forested area and reach Bolam Pass Road (FS Rd 578) near Celebration Lake at **mile 20.9** (11,094). This is the end of Segment 25.

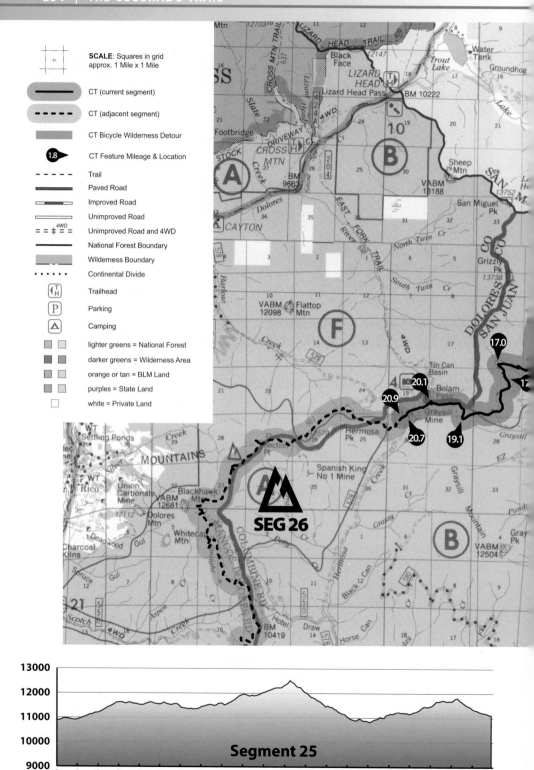

SCALE: Squares in grid approx. 1 Mile x 1 Mile

CT (current segment)

CT (adjacent segment)

CT Bicycle Wilderness Detour

1.8 CT Feature Mileage & Location

- - - - Trail

Paved Road

Improved Road

Unimproved Road

= = ‡ = = Unimproved Road and 4WD

National Forest Boundary

Wilderness Boundary

• • • • • • Continental Divide

Trailhead

Parking

Camping

lighter greens = National Forest

darker greens = Wilderness Area

orange or tan = BLM Land

purples = State Land

white = Private Land

SEG 26

Segment 25

SEGMENT 25 FEATURES TABLE San Juan National Forest

Mileage	Features & Comments	Elevation (feet)	Mileage from Denver	Mileage to Durango	UTM-E	UTM-N (NAD83)	Zone
0.0	Begin Segment 25	10,886	410.7	73.9	262,245	4,180,344	13
1.6	Go right at intersection	11,097	412.3	72.3	260,785	4,181,175	13
2.0	At junction go right northeast	11,205	412.7	71.9	260,128	4,180,933	13
3.0	Join single-track trail to left	11,626	413.7	70.9	260,414	4,181,971	13
3.9	Reach saddle	11,525	414.6	70.0	259,693	4,183,401	13
5.3	Cross creek	11,573	416.0	68.6	258,281	4,183,308	13
6.1	Cross Lime Creek	11,392	416.8	67.8	257,366	4,183,709	13
10.2	Right at Engineer Mtn Trail	12,125	420.9	63.7	252,838	4,181,383	13
11.0	Left join Rico Silverton Trail	12,344	421.7	62.9	251,950	4,181,899	13
11.2	Gain saddle	12,500	421.9	62.7	251,843	4,181,740	13
12.9	Right at White Crk Tr on left	11,452	423.6	61.0	250,381	4,180,897	13
14.8	Cross Cascade Creek	10,852	425.5	59.1	249,046	4,181,555	13
17.3	Straight at side trail on left	11,252	428.0	56.6	247,641	4,179,279	13
19.1	Gain saddle	11,761	429.8	54.8	246,169	4,177,932	13
20.1	Left onto dirt FS Rd 578B	11,293	430.8	53.8	245,102	4,178,509	13
20.7	Leave road, left on single-track	11,135	431.4	53.2	244,274	4,178,139	13
20.9	End Segment 25	11,094	431.6	53.0	244,068	4,177,965	13

Segment 26: **Bolam Pass Road to Hotel Draw Road**

Distance: 10.9 miles

Elevation gain: Approx. 1,827 feet

Elevation loss: Approx. 2,551 feet

USFS map: San Juan National Forest, pages 262–263

The Colorado Trail Databook 6: pages 62–63

The CT Map Book: pages 60–61

National Geographic Trails Illustrated maps: Nos. 141, 144

Latitude 40° maps: Southwest Colorado Trails, Durango Trails

Jurisdiction: Mancos/Dolores Ranger District, San Juan National Forest

Access from Denver end: 🚙

Access from Durango end: 🚙

Availability of water: ☕

Bicycling: 🚲

Ascending to Blackhawk Pass.

PHOTO BY NATE HEBENSTREIT

"The north side of Blackhawk Pass is a valley of enchantment with vast herds of elk."

Verdant alpine meadows near the pass, filled with lush mid-summer growth, attract wildlife—elk and mule deer, marmots and pika —and hikers drawn by the wildflowers and lovely vistas. Have your camera ready. Famous Lizard Head Peak is in view near the pass.

Gudy's TIP

ABOUT THIS SEGMENT

This segment follows the high ground between the Hermosa Creek drainage to the south and east and the Dolores River drainage to the north and west. The trail here is largely in flat-lying beds of the Cutler Formation, cut by dikes and sills of light-colored porphyry. This segment feels very remote, descending and ascending forested ridges until climbing to Blackhawk Pass just east of Blackhawk Mountain. The views from here are outstanding. The CT then drops into the Straight Creek watershed below. There are several potential campsites after entering the forest with good access to the creek. The second crossing of Straight Creek is the last reliable water for the next 22 miles. Be sure to fill your water bottles here!

TRAILHEAD/ACCESS POINTS

Bolam Pass Road (FS Rd 578) Trail Access: There are two ways to drive to this access point, both requiring a four-wheel-drive vehicle: from US Hwy 550 through Purgatory Resort (formally Durango Mountain Resort) and from CO Hwy 145, south of Lizard Head Pass and just north of Rico. For the US Hwy 550 approach, drive approximately 28 miles north of Durango to the main entrance to Purgatory Resort on the west

Cornhusk lily.
PHOTO BY NATE HEBENSTREIT

side of the road. At the upper parking area, bear right onto FS Rd 578. Drive on gravel, staying on FS Rd 578, west then north about 10 miles to a ford of Hermosa Creek. Continue about 5 miles farther to Celebration Lake where the CT crosses the road. For the approach from CO Hwy 145, drive 6 miles north of Rico and turn right onto FS Rd 578 and drive about 7 miles along Barlow Creek. At a Y intersection, take the left branch to Celebration Lake and the CT access point.

> ! Scrutinize the depth of the Hermosa Creek ford and the optimal line before driving into it.

Hotel Draw Trail Access:

SERVICES, SUPPLIES, AND ACCOMMODATIONS

There is no convenient resupply point for this segment.

TRAIL DESCRIPTION

Segment 26 begins at the southwest edge of Celebration Lake on Bolam Pass Road (FS Rd 578), where The Colorado Trail crosses the road from the northeast, **mile 0.0** (11,094 feet). There is a small parking lot and hard-packed camping area here. Cross a small stream flowing out of the south end of the lake and begin a climb reaching seasonal

The CT is well signed in most places, but using this guide will help ensure you keep on track.
PHOTO BY NATE HEBENSTREIT

A marmot at full alert.

PHOTO BY ERNIE NORRIS

springs at **mile 0.1** (11,100) and **mile 0.6** (11,400). Continue climbing to **mile 0.9** (11,532), where the trail gains a saddle on the east side of Hermosa Peak. The trail contours beneath the peak to the north and passes a spring with a good campsite at **mile 1.3** (11,452). Turn left at a T intersection onto a jeep road at **mile 1.6** (11,565) and head southwest. Cross a small stream at **mile 1.8** (11,486), where there is potential camping, and continue to **mile 3.0** (11,561), where the trail leaves the road to the right.

At a small saddle at **mile 3.9** (11,814), turn left at a junction with the old Circle Trail coming up from Silver Creek and Rico at **mile 4.1** (11,761). Pass over a small knob and down several switchbacks. The trail contours around the valley ahead and begins to climb at **mile 6.0** (11,511). From here, pass a small stream at **mile 6.3** (11,600) and a larger stream at **mile 6.4** (11,611). Gain Blackhawk Pass at **mile 6.9** (11,985) and descend to the headwaters of Straight Creek at **mile 7.5** (11,468). There is a good campsite 0.1 mile to the south. Continue heading downhill through the forest, crossing to the east side of Straight Creek at **mile 8.4** (11,032). Fill your water bottles, as this is the last reliable water source for the next 22 miles. Continue southeast, passing several potential campsites over the next 2.5 miles. At **mile 10.0** (10,668) join an old road on the ridge and reach the end of Segment 26, 50 feet before Hotel Draw Road at **mile 10.9** (10,385).

Thru-hikers should be aware that the Straight Creek crossing at mile 8.4 is the last reliable water source before reaching Taylor Lake, some 22 miles away over Indian Trail Ridge.

Biking

A popular local mountain bike ride utilizes CT Segment 26, often as part of a loop using Hermosa Creek Road (FS Rd 578) and Hotel Draw Road (FS Rd 550). Riders enjoy the high elevation, views, flowers, and the challenge of Blackhawk Pass.

Maintaining the Trail: CTF Volunteers

Maintaining all 567 miles of The Colorado Trail is an immense undertaking, requiring the efforts of hundreds of dedicated CTF Trail Crew and Adopt-A-Trail volunteers each year.

Every summer, The Colorado Trail Foundation organizes around 15 volunteer trail crews. The efforts vary from one-day to weeklong, with 20 to 25 volunteers on each. CT crews work on trail improvement projects including bridge installation, retaining walls, trail reroutes, rebuilding tread, and constructing water diversions. Volunteers receive training on trail work, tool use, and safety. They value spending time in the outdoors and "giving back" to The Colorado Trail. Volunteers enjoy camping in the Colorado mountains, learning, group meals, and building friendships. Trail crews are rewarding work and a lot of fun.

Adopters and their helpers are the trail's frontline volunteers, keeping the CT passable and reporting trail conditions to the CT Foundation. Approximately 80 adopters care for their 5- to 15-mile section by removing fallen trees, maintaining water diversions, and replacing CT signage. Adopters are responsible individuals, representing a family group, Scout troop, hiking club, mountain bike group, horse users, or simply a group of friends. Adopters often stick with the task for many years, even decades, finding outdoor fun and a sense of accomplishment in keeping their adopted section in good shape for trail users.

If you are interested and would like more

CTF volunteers ready to make trail improvements.
PHOTO BY COLIN MCKENNA

information on CTF trail crews or Adopt-A-Trail, please visit ColoradoTrail.org.

Reconstructing tread.

PHOTO BY LISA TURNER

Volunteer with a Pulaski and a smile.

PHOTO BY BILL BLOOMQUIST

Teamwork is key to improving the trail.

PHOTO BY BILL BLOOMQUIST

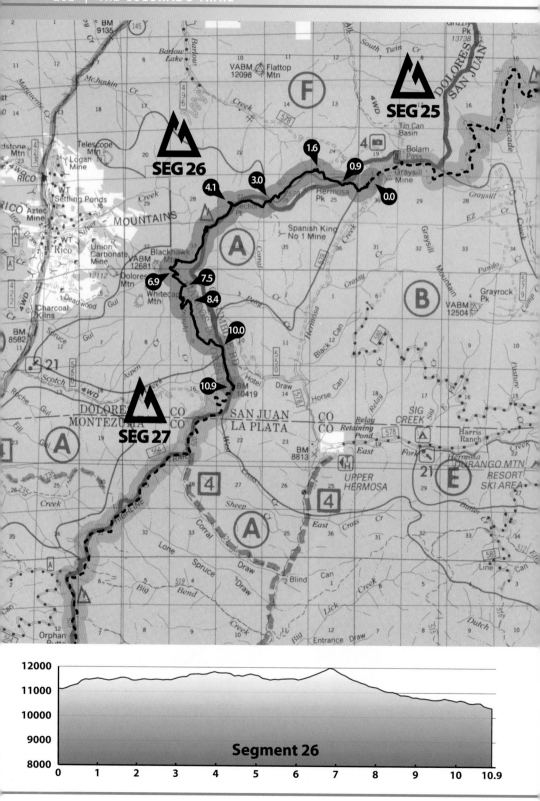

Segment 26

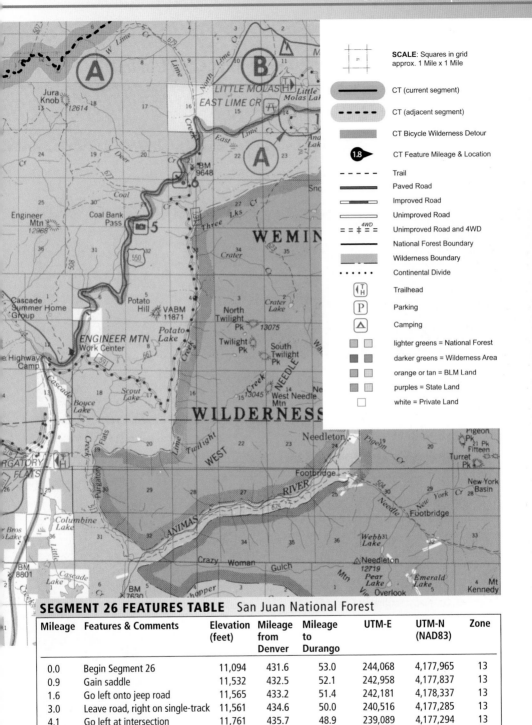

SCALE: Squares in grid approx. 1 Mile x 1 Mile

CT (current segment)

CT (adjacent segment)

CT Bicycle Wilderness Detour

1.8 ▸ CT Feature Mileage & Location

Trail

Paved Road

Improved Road

Unimproved Road

Unimproved Road and 4WD

National Forest Boundary

Wilderness Boundary

Continental Divide

Trailhead

Parking

Camping

lighter greens = National Forest

darker greens = Wilderness Area

orange or tan = BLM Land

purples = State Land

white = Private Land

SEGMENT 26 FEATURES TABLE San Juan National Forest

Mileage	Features & Comments	Elevation (feet)	Mileage from Denver	Mileage to Durango	UTM-E	UTM-N (NAD83)	Zone
0.0	Begin Segment 26	11,094	431.6	53.0	244,068	4,177,965	13
0.9	Gain saddle	11,532	432.5	52.1	242,958	4,177,837	13
1.6	Go left onto jeep road	11,565	433.2	51.4	242,181	4,178,337	13
3.0	Leave road, right on single-track	11,561	434.6	50.0	240,516	4,177,285	13
4.1	Go left at intersection	11,761	435.7	48.9	239,089	4,177,294	13
6.9	Gain Blackhawk Pass	11,985	438.5	46.1	237,186	4,174,993	13
7.5	Cross Straight Creek	11,468	439.1	45.5	237,433	4,174,469	13
8.4	Cross Straight Creek	11,032	440.0	44.6	237,642	4,173,999	13
10.9	End Segment 26	10,385	442.5	42.1	239,125	4,171,049	13

Segment 27: Hotel Draw Road to Kennebec Trailhead

Looking south toward the La Plata Mountains.

PHOTO BY NATE HEBENSTREIT

Distance: 20.6 miles

Elevation gain: Approx. 4,186 feet

Elevation loss: Approx. 2,922 feet

USFS map: San Juan National Forest, pages 270–271

The Colorado Trail Databook 6: pages 64–65

The CT Map Book: pages 61–64

National Geographic Trails Illustrated map: No. 144

Latitude 40° maps: Southwest Colorado Trails, Durango Trails

Jurisdiction: Columbine Ranger District, San Juan National Forest

Access from Denver end:

Access from Durango end:

Availability of water:

Bicycling:

"From Indian Trail Ridge, a crest of cascading wildflowers and the views of Hermosa Valley and the La Plata Mountains are extraordinary."

This segment features sweeping vistas, culminating in a dramatic, 5-mile walk atop an alpine ridge at more than 12,000 feet. Wildflower enthusiasts find the incredible displays at their peak starting in mid-July.

Gudy's TIP

ABOUT THIS SEGMENT

The first 9 miles of Segment 27 encounter several infrequently used Forest Service roads and closed logging roads. For the most part the trail stays near the ridgeline, here chiefly made up of rocks of the Cutler Formation, then it climbs as it leaves the roads and logged forests behind. At mile 4 it crosses into red sandstone shale and siltstone of the Dolores Formation, deposited by streams, lakes, and winds between about 230 and 200 million years ago, after destruction of the Ancestral Rockies. As The Colorado Trail climbs toward the Cape of Good Hope it passes into still younger rocks, sandstone, shale, and limestone deposited shortly before the inundation by the Cretaceous Seaway.

Once the trail passes the junction with the Grindstone Trail, it enters the tundra and traverses Indian Trail Ridge, which is made up of a thick layer of sandstone that belongs to this group of younger rocks. From here, there are fantastic views of the surrounding mountains and drainages below. It is common to see large herds of elk below the ridge to the west. Between miles 15.5 and 19.4, the trail is sometimes rocky and precipitous, where horseback riders will want to be especially cautious. The CT stays above tree line, with no easy means of escape from sudden storms. All travelers will want to watch the weather patterns before committing to this section. Taylor Lake at mile 19.4 is a great sight from above for southbound hikers who have covered the last 22 miles with no reliable water sources.

Taylor Lake is a welcome sight at the south end of Indian Trail Ridge.
PHOTO BY BEN KRAUSHAAR

TRAILHEAD/ACCESS POINTS

There are three ways to drive to the beginning of Segment 27. Two require a four-wheel-drive vehicle: from US Hwy 550 through Purgatory Resort (formally Durango Mountain Resort) and from CO Hwy 145, south of Lizard Head Pass and just south of Rico. The two-wheel-drive approach via FS Rds 435/564/550 is much longer but usually accessible by regular passenger cars.

US Hwy 550 Access (Hotel Draw): Drive approximately 28 miles north of Durango to the main entrance of Purgatory Resort on the west side of the road. At the upper parking area, bear right onto FS Rd 578. Follow this road for approximately 8 miles along the East Fork of Hermosa Creek, continuing west past Sig Creek Campground and on to the main channel of Hermosa Creek, then north along the main channel and through a ford. About a mile after the ford, make a sharp left turn onto the Hotel Draw Road (FS Rd 550). After about 3.5 miles, at the top of the ridge, the CT comes down from the north and intersects the Hotel Draw Road.

CO Hwy 145 Access: Drive 2 miles south of Rico and turn left onto Scotch Creek Road (FS Rd 550). Proceed about 5 miles to an intersection near the top of the ridge and turn left, continuing to the top of the ridge where the CT comes down the ridge on the road from the north.

FS Rds 435/564/550 Access: Drive 9 miles south of Rico and turn east onto FS Rd 435. After 6 miles, make a sharp left turn onto FS Rd 564. Continue for about 15 miles to its terminus at FS Rd 550. Follow FS Rd 550 for 1.3 miles to the beginning of the segment. FS Rd 564 intersects with the CT several times before reaching its terminus at FS Rd 550.

Kennebec Trailhead: See Segment 28 on page 272.

Scrutinize the depth of the Hermosa Creek ford and the optimal line before driving into it.

SERVICES, SUPPLIES, AND ACCOMMODATIONS

There is no convenient resupply point for this segment.

TRAIL DESCRIPTION

Segment 27 begins 50 feet north of a small parking area on Hotel Draw Road (FS Rd 550) at **mile 0.0** (10,385). The first 9 miles of this segment pass through and along a maze of old logging trails. Much of the CT follows these old cuts. There are numerous intersections, but thanks to both CTF volunteers and US Forest Service personnel, they are marked well by wooden posts, signs, or confidence markers.

Just before reaching the parking area, thru-hikers will turn right and head southwest on single-track that parallels the road. In 300 feet, turn right on a closed logging road, then bear left at a fork a few hundred feet farther. At **mile 0.7** (10,408), the CT continues on another logging road that turns sharply to the left (south) and uphill. A few hundred feet farther, continue straight past another logging road. Turn right at a Y intersection onto FS Rd 550 at **mile 1.2** (10,444). Turn left onto FS Rd 564 at **mile 1.3** (10,415). Leave FS Rd 564 and turn left onto trail at **mile 1.4** (10,408). Climb a forested ridge with good views to the south before reaching the top of the ridge at **mile 2.6** (10,907).

Continue southwest passing the junction with Corral Draw Trail on the left at **mile 2.9** (10,828). Stay high on the ridge, passing several potential campsites before meeting a dirt road (FS Rd 564) at **mile 4.0** (10,760). Follow it to the left. The trail leaves the road but crosses back over it several times in the next 2 miles. CT confidence markers are clearly posted throughout. At **mile 6.5** (10,617), reach the Big Bend Trail and signs, where water might be found via a faint trail 200 yards downhill (southeast) in the trees. Pass just south of FS Rd 564 at **mile 7.0** (10,710). Users may find water flowing from a piped spring west on the road (south side) 0.1 mile. The trail joins a logging road at **mile 7.1** (10,762) and turns sharply to the south. Continuing south, meet and follow the co-located Salt Creek Trail at **mile 7.2** (10,780) and diverge from it at **mile 7.9** (10,851). Continue heading toward Orphan Butte, the bald knob to the south. After passing to the east of Orphan Butte and crossing two more logging roads, the trail becomes more straightforward as the logging roads are left behind.

> Indian Trail Ridge can be dangerous during afternoon thunderstorms.

Begin a steady climb up the ridge at **mile 11.3** (10,818). Seasonal springs exist in the area of **mile 11.9** (11,120). Look for on-trail water trickles and, at the south end of a talus slope and bottom of switchbacks, look 100 feet below the CT for higher volume water and a possible campsite. At **mile 12.3** (11,331) the trail tops out at a sign for scenic view where there's a side trail on the right to a bench,

Looking north along Indian Trail Ridge.
PHOTO BY DEAN KRAKEL

views, and campsite. The trail continues left (northwest) from here, passing a seasonal spring along the trail. The CT bends sharply at **mile 12.5** (11,432) to resume its southward bearing. Encounter a junction with Cape of Good Hope Trail on the left and a wood sign identifying the co-located Highline Trail at **mile 13.3** (11,617). At **mile 14.1** (11,450) there is a faint side trail on the right that leads to a seasonal seep. Turn left at an intersection with the Grindstone Trail at **mile 15.0** (11,686), the last downhill exit from high ridge for more than 3.5 miles.

Enter tundra at **mile 15.5** (11,821) and begin very exposed sections of Indian Trail Ridge. At **mile 17.1** (11,863) there is a side trail that leads east to a pond and campsite 700 feet and 0.6 mile below the CT. Climb to a high point on the ridge at **mile 18.3** (12,310) and reach a second, lower summit at **mile 18.7** (12,258). After a brief descent along the ridge from the second summit, turn left and head downhill toward Cumberland Basin and Taylor Lake below. After a steep, rocky descent particularly troublesome for horse-back riders, pass a side trail leading to Taylor Lake on the right at **mile 19.4** (11,642). Southbound hikers will appreciate this water source after 22 miles of dry trail. Continue to the southeast, eventually reaching the Kennebec Trailhead parking area and the end of Segment 27 at **mile 20.6** (11,642).

Trail Photo Tips

The Colorado Trail is a spectacular but challenging environment to take photographs in, especially photographs that capture the beauty and uniqueness of your trip.

▲ The most important thing is to take your time. TAKE YOUR TIME. Most hikers snap shoot. Go beyond that by investing a minute or two in making your photographs.

▲ Think about what you're taking a picture of and why. What attracted your attention? Compose the frame so that element is the most important part of the image.

▲ When something catches your attention, whether it's the scenic beauty or a camp moment, stop whatever you're doing and take the photo.

▲ Take more than one shot. Take lots of pictures. Take risks. Experiment with exposure. Shoot even when you don't think there's any chance of a frame coming out.

▲ Shoot in rain and snow. Use boulders and trees to steady your hands. Change lenses. Zoom in and out.

▲ Use the light. Morning and evening light is best, but even in direct sunlight there's a way to find light that will enhance your subject. Shoot the quiet before the sunrise and the twilight after the sunset.

▲ Never pass by something you want to photograph just because the light is poor or because you think you'll see another similar scene or object on down the trail. When something catches your eye, take the picture. Make the best use of what's available.

▲ Change your point of view. Walk a few feet or yards off the trail. Lie down. Bend over. Squat. Stand up on something or get beneath something. Don't shoot everything from eye level.

▲ Keep your camera handy. If you're not wearing it around your neck stow it within easy reach in a pocket or pouch. Then, when a spectacular ray of light touches the peaks or a moose strolls onto the trail, you won't have to fumble around and miss the moment.

▲ Photograph people as well as the scenery. Candid photos and portraits add human interest to the photo report. Act naturally when you're being photographed, candid and cool. If you're photographing people, don't become a director. Natural moments are the best.

▲ I like to keep my pack light and camera gear to a minimum. My main trail camera is an Olympus TG-4 weatherproof point-and-shoot. But good photography, on the trail or off, isn't a matter of what kind of camera you carry. Making good photographs is up to the photographer.

A hiker against the sky, Collegiate West near Cottonwood Pass.
PHOTO BY DEAN KRAKEL

Hiker shadows and trail marker, Camp Hale, Segment 8.
PHOTO BY DEAN KRAKEL

Columbines, Kennebec Pass, Segment 28.
PHOTO BY DEAN KRAKEL

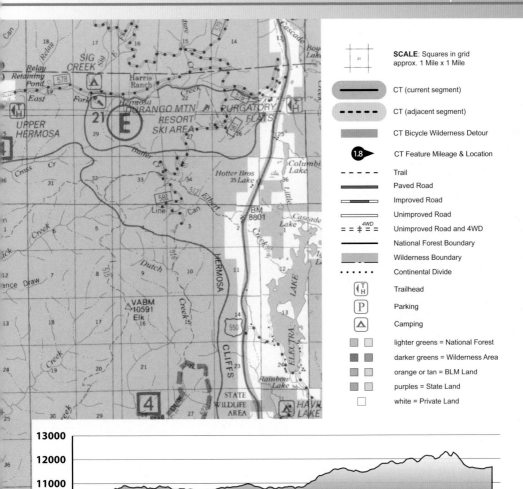

SCALE: Squares in grid approx. 1 Mile x 1 Mile

CT (current segment)

CT (adjacent segment)

CT Bicycle Wilderness Detour

1.8 CT Feature Mileage & Location

Trail

Paved Road

Improved Road

Unimproved Road

Unimproved Road and 4WD

National Forest Boundary

Wilderness Boundary

Continental Divide

Trailhead

Parking

Camping

lighter greens = National Forest

darker greens = Wilderness Area

orange or tan = BLM Land

purples = State Land

white = Private Land

SEGMENT 27 FEATURES TABLE San Juan National Forest

Mileage	Features & Comments	Elevation (feet)	Mileage from Denver	Mileage to Durango	UTM-E	UTM-N (NAD83)	Zone
0.0	Begin Segment 27	10,385	442.5	42.1	239,125	4,171,049	13
0.7	Continue on logging road	10,408	443.2	41.4	238,476	4,170,721	13
1.2	Turn right at intersection	10,444	443.7	40.9	238,460	4,170,120	13
2.9	Pass Corral Draw Trail on left	10,828	445.4	39.2	237,013	4,168,800	13
4.0	Left on FS Rd 564 short distance	10,760	446.5	38.1	235,789	4,167,690	13
6.5	Cross Big Bend Trail	10,617	449.0	35.6	763,576	4,165,143	12
7.9	Salt Creek Trail diverges left	10,851	450.4	34.2	763,298	4,163,430	12
12.3	Left for CT or right for view	11,331	454.8	29.8	762,217	4,158,197	12
15.0	Go left at Grindstone Trail	11,686	457.5	27.1	761,759	4,154,954	12
18.3	Reach high point	12,310	460.8	23.8	762,350	4,150,637	12
19.4	Left for CT or right for lake	11,642	461.9	22.7	762,709	4,149,685	12
20.6	End Segment 27	11,642	463.1	21.5	764,382	4,149,157	12

Segment 28: Kennebec Trailhead to Junction Creek Trailhead

Gudy's Rest at mile 17.4 honors Gudy Gaskill.

PHOTO BY JULIE VIDA AND MARK TABB

Distance: 21.5 miles

Elevation gain: Approx. 1,897 feet

Elevation loss: Approx. 6,557 feet

USFS map: San Juan National Forest, pages 280–281

The Colorado Trail Databook 6: pages 66–67

The CT Map Book: pages 64–67

National Geographic Trails Illustrated map: No. 144

Latitude 40° maps: Southwest Colorado Trails, Durango Trails

Jurisdiction: Columbine Ranger District, San Juan National Forest

Access from Denver end:

Access from Durango end:

Availability of water:

Bicycling:

"If you didn't stop for a shower in one of the falls in Junction Canyon, grab one at the rec center, just north of where the Junction Creek Road dead-ends into Main Avenue in Durango."

Durango has a large, modern recreational center three blocks north of Junction Creek Road and Main Avenue, where hikers and riders can get a hot shower. There is bus service along Main Avenue.

Gudy's TIP

ABOUT THIS SEGMENT

The final segment of The Colorado Trail begins at the Kennebec Trailhead, climbs to Kennebec Pass, and then descends thousands of feet to the Junction Creek Trailhead near Durango. It is an incredibly diverse segment, starting above tree line, passing through stands of spruce, fir, and pine, and crossing Junction Creek at its headwaters and again where there are sturdy bridges. There is dense vegetation in the Junction Creek drainage, which stands in sharp contrast to the alpine basin filled with summer wildflowers at the beginning of the segment. The views are magnificent from Kennebec Pass, but quickly disappear as the trail enters the narrow canyon below. Around Kennebec Pass and along the trail as it descends to the creek, rocks of the Dolores and Cutler Formations are cut by numerous dikes, sills, and irregular bodies of white porphyry that were emplaced during the Laramide Orogeny. Trail users pass several mines and prospects that explored mineral deposits related to the porphyry.

Camping is NOT allowed beyond mile 16.9 of this segment (except at Junction Creek Campground, less than a half mile from CT mile 20.3).

Campsites are limited in this segment. There is plenty of water when first entering the canyon, but flat spots for camping are rare. Later in the segment, when the CT climbs out of the canyon, there are flat spots but water is scarce. Camping is not permitted after mile 16.9, prohibited by authorities because this area is heavily used and easily accessible from Durango and beyond. To reduce frustration, plan your trip down this segment carefully and stop early before all the best camping sites are taken.

Trailhead sign below Kennebec Pass.
PHOTO BY LAWTON "DISCO" GRINTER

Kennebec Trailhead is at the intersection of four-wheel-drive FS Rd 171 and The Colorado Trail where there is a large trailhead sign and ample parking. Kennebec Pass is on the CT, 0.7 mile east and above. Beyond the pass, the CT descends a section of "slide rock." This steep hillside is most impressive and constantly changing under natural forces including gravity. CTF volunteers work every year to rebuild the trail bench and reestablish it as user friendly.

This segment of the CT has the most vertical travel of any segment of the trail: more than 6,500 feet of vertical in one direction and nearly 1,900 feet in the other. Tired muscles from big elevation are often forgotten during celebrations upon completion of The Colorado Trail.

East of Kennebec Pass and the Sliderock section, these cyclists push uphill.
PHOTO BY ADAM LISONBEE

TRAILHEAD/ACCESS POINTS

Kennebec Trailhead: 🏍 From Durango, drive west on US Hwy 160 about 13 miles (0.5 mile beyond the village of Hesperus). Turn right on La Plata County Rd 124 (paved), which eventually becomes FS Rd 498 (gravel) and then FS Rd 571 (4WD), until reaching the Kennebec Trailhead. The last 2 miles are rough and steep, a section where a four-wheel-drive vehicle is strongly recommended.

Junction Creek Trailhead: 🚗 Drive on north Main Avenue in Durango to 25th Street and turn west. After a couple of blocks the street bears right and becomes Junction Creek Road (La Plata County Rd 204). Follow it for 3 miles and take the left branch. Continue another 0.4 mile to a cattle guard and a San Juan National Forest sign. On the left is a 19-car Forest Service parking lot and toilet. This is the Junction Creek Trailhead and southern terminus of The Colorado Trail. The road continues as FS Rd 171. In about another mile there is a switchback with seven more parking spaces and a 100-yard-long trail connector to the CT.

Sliderock Trail Access Point:  The CT can be accessed by two-wheel-drive vehicles at mile 2.4 of this segment. From the Junction Creek Trailhead previously described, continue on the gravel-improved FS Rd 171 for 17.5 miles to a side road on the left. Turn left and proceed 0.7 mile on this more rugged road to where the CT crosses. To the right, uphill, the CT leads 1.7 miles to Kennebec Pass via the Sliderock portion of this segment. To the left, downhill, the CT leads to Junction Creek Trailhead, 19.1 miles away.

Thru-hikers celebrating their CT completion on the Durango end.
PHOTO COURTESY OF ALICIA AND TOM BLANK

TRAIL DESCRIPTION

Segment 28 begins at the Kennebec Trailhead, **mile 0.0** (11,642); pay attention to the signs and landscape to ensure you're on the CT as it diverges east on trail closed to vehicles. (Avoid the jeep road that leads to a notch in the ridge above; it dead ends and is not the CT.) Climb through a meadow with seasonal seeps at **mile 0.3** (11,680). After

A miner's cabin sits atop redbeds of the Cutler Formation opposite a large talus slope known as Sliderock.
PHOTO BY ROGER FORMAN

SERVICES, SUPPLIES, AND ACCOMMODATIONS – DURANGO

Durango, an old railroad town and now the commercial center for southwestern Colorado, is approximately 3.5 miles from the Junction Creek Trailhead. The town is connected to Denver via airline and bus service, and to Silverton by the Durango & Silverton Narrow Gauge Railroad.

Distance from CT: 3.5 miles
Elevation: 6,512 feet
Zip code: 81301
Area code: 970

Bus
Durango Transit Center
250 W. 8th St.
(970) 259-2755

Dining (several)
Carver Bakery & Brewing Co.
1022 Main Ave.
(970) 259-2545

Gear (including fuel canisters)
Backcountry Experience
120 Camino del Rio
(970) 247-5830

Gardenswartz Outdoors
863 Main Ave.
(970) 259-6696

Pine Needle Mountaineering
835 Main Ave.
(970) 247-8728

Groceries (several)
City Market
South 6 Town Plaza
(970) 247-4475

Info
Chamber of Commerce
111 S. Camino del Rio
(970) 247-0312

Laundry (several)
North Main Laundry
2980 Main Ave.
(970) 247-9915

Lodging (several)
Check rates etc. online; consider options on N. Main Ave.

Medical
Durango Urgent Care
2577 N. Main Ave.
(970) 247-8382

Mercy Regional Medical Center
1010 Three Springs Blvd.
(970) 247-4311

Post Office
Durango Post Office
222 W. 8th St.
(970) 247-3968

Showers
Durango Recreation Center
2700 Main Ave.
(970) 375-7300

Train Depot
Durango & Silverton Narrow Gauge Railroad
479 Main Ave.
(888) 872-4607

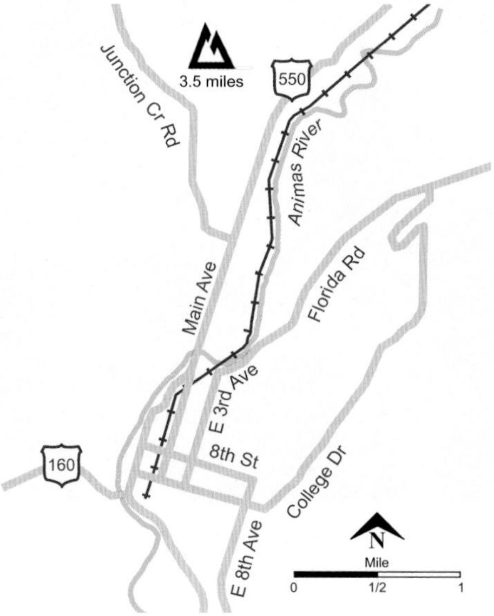

gaining Kennebec Pass at **mile 0.4** (11,700), head downhill then left at junction at **mile 0.7** (11,713). The trail crosses a large talus slope beginning at **mile 1.1** (11,336) appropriately named the Sliderock. Below, enter a spruce forest and descend switchbacks until reaching Champion Venture Mine Road, a spur of FS Rd 171, at **mile 2.4** (10,351). Cross the road, pass a dry campsite, and continue heading downhill into Fassbinder Gulch. There is a seasonal creek at **mile 3.7** (10,003). Then at **mile 4.0** (9,800) the CT leaves the gulch and crosses two small tributaries in the next half mile with a stream at **mile 4.7** (9,483). Camping in this area is generally poor due to thick vegetation.

Pass by the Gaines Gulch waterfall at **mile 5.4** (9,250). Cross Flagler Fork of Junction Creek at **mile 5.7** (9,029) and cross Junction Creek three more times; there are no bridges here. Pass campsite, fill up water bottles, and cross again at **mile 7.1** (8,522) on a volunteer-rebuilt bridge.

Begin the last notable climb on The Colorado Trail after crossing the bridge. This 4-mile climb gains more than 1,000 feet through beautiful, rugged terrain, with steep slopes dropping into the Junction Creek gorge. Water flow in the side canyons is variable, but in the canyon south of Chicago Gulch, First Trail Canyon, and Sliderock Canyon, trail users find flows all season. Where the trail reaches a ridge at **mile 8.0** (8,974), there

Cyclists at Champion Venture Road.
PHOTO BY BILL MANNING

is a good campsite with a small creek 0.2 mile farther. The trail begins following an old mining road at about **mile 11.0** (9,516), then reaches the top of the climb at **mile 11.2** (9,557). From here the trail begins its final descent toward the Junction Creek Trailhead near Durango.

At a sharp left bend in the trail at **mile 11.5** (9,415), there is an excellent small campsite on a bench above the trail and water in a small stream 200 feet below the trail. Continue downhill and pass through a Forest Service gate at **mile 14.4** (8,676). There are two more gates to pass through in the next mile and a half. Just after the first gate, take a left when the CT intersects with the Dry Fork Trail at **mile 14.6** (8,606). At **mile 16.9** (8,210), there are small campsites and possible spring water from pipe, though this area is often used heavily by cows. This is the last campsite, as camping is prohibited beyond here. (Off-trail, fee camping is available at the Junction Creek Campground, 1.5 miles east of the intersection of FS Rd 171 and the CT at mile 20.3.)

Kennebec Pass is at far right beneath Cumberland Mountain.
PHOTO BY CARL BROWN

At junction with Hoffheins Trail at **mile 17.2** (7,997), bear left and continue to Gudy's Rest at **mile 17.4** (7,970). This is a scenic overlook with a bench placed in honor of Gudy Gaskill, the remarkable woman who made The Colorado Trail a reality. After descending a series of switchbacks, travel over Junction Creek on Ted's Crossing bridge at **mile 18.9** (7,431). Stay right at a trail junction at **mile 20.3** (7,183). (Going left on this connector trail leads 100 yards to FS Rd 171/Junction Creek Rd.) Continue on the CT down the narrow canyon paralleling the stream, eventually reaching the Junction Creek Trailhead and the southern terminus of The Colorado Trail at **mile 21.5** (6,983). The trailhead is about 3.5 miles on paved road from Durango's Main Avenue and 25th Street where there are several motels nearby. Downtown Durango is south on Main about one mile.

Camping is NOT allowed beyond mile 16.9 of this segment (except at Junction Creek Campground, a mile and a half off the trail).

Viewing Dippers

A chunky, drab, wrenlike bird, the water ouzel, or dipper, would hardly attract anyone's attention if not for its unusual manner of earning a living. Dippers reside along rushing mountain streams, often perched atop a rock in the foaming center of the torrent. From this vantage point, it constantly bobs up and down, looking for aquatic insects or even small fish to eat. Spotting a tasty morsel, it then dives headlong into the water, opens its wings, and "flies" or walks submerged through the flow. Birds stake out a 75- to 200-yard length of stream for their territory, rarely venturing far from its banks.

When disturbed, dippers fly low and rapidly up and down the stream, sounding a high, ringing alarm. During winter, they move to lower levels. Their nests are a bulky ball of moss open on one side, built just above the waterline in inaccessible places such as on a rock wall or behind a waterfall.

Dippers can be found along the streams and rivers throughout western Colorado. In Segment 28, you are as likely to spot one along the lush banks of little Quinn Creek as perched on a boulder in the middle of the Animas River in downtown Durango.

American dipper.
PHOTO BY DAN GARBER

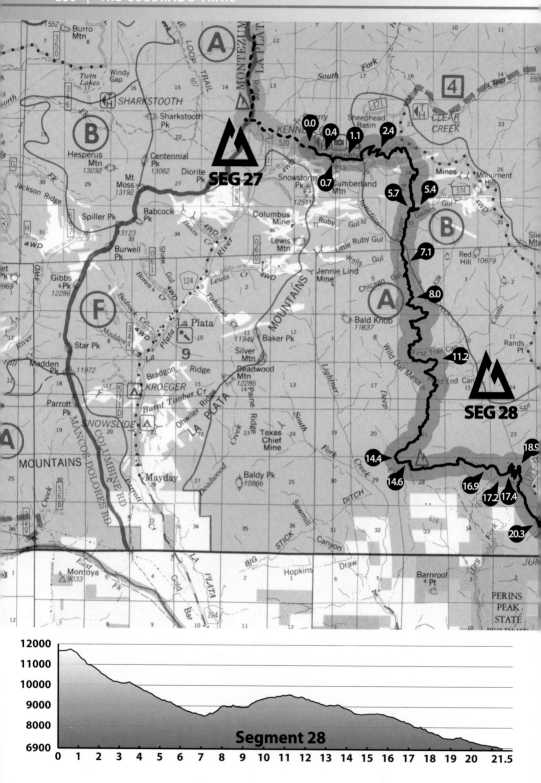

Segment 28

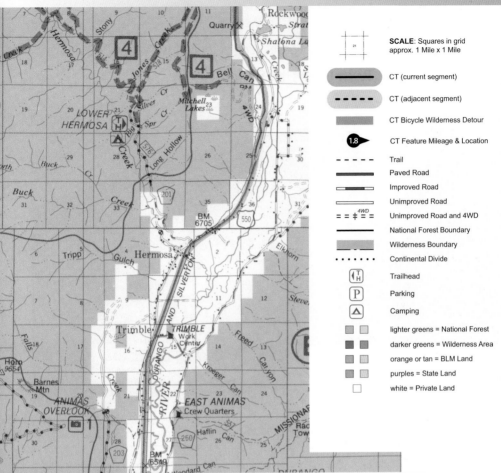

SEGMENT 28 FEATURES TABLE San Juan National Forest

Mileage	Features & Comments	Elevation (feet)	Mileage from Denver	Mileage to Durango	UTM-E	UTM-N (NAD83)	Zone
0.0	Begin Segment 28	11,642	463.1	21.5	764,382	4,149,157	12
0.4	Gain Kennebec Pass	11,700	463.5	21.1	764,995	4,148,913	12
0.7	Go left at intersection	11,713	463.8	20.8	765,209	4,148,699	12
1.1	Cross Sliderock talus slope	11,336	464.2	20.4	234,955	4,148,718	13
2.4	Reach spur of FS Rd 571	10,351	465.5	19.1	236,016	4,149,026	13
5.4	Pass waterfall	9,250	468.5	16.1	237,369	4,147,064	13
5.7	First crossing of Junction Creek	9,029	468.8	15.8	237,102	4,147,083	13
7.1	Last crossing of Junction Creek	8,522	470.2	14.4	236,896	4,145,211	13
11.2	Reach top of climb	9,557	474.3	10.3	237,868	4,141,920	13
14.4	Pass through gate	8,676	477.5	7.1	236,420	4,138,600	13
14.6	Turn left at Dry Fork Trail	8,606	477.7	6.9	236,793	4,138,500	13
16.9	Spring, no camping beyond	8,210	480.0	4.6	239,600	4,138,215	13
17.2	Stay left at Hoffheins Trail	7,997	480.3	4.3	240,015	4,137,998	13
17.4	Gudy's Rest overlook	7,970	480.5	4.1	240,329	4,138,070	13
18.9	Bridge over Junction Creek	7,431	482.0	2.6	240,682	4,138,256	13
20.3	Right for CT left for road	7,183	483.4	1.2	241,314	4,136,340	13
21.5	End Segment 28	6,983	484.6	0.0	242,827	4,135,585	13

Collegiate West, Twin Lakes to S. Fooses Ridge (Segments CW01–CW05)

Segment CW01: Twin Lakes to Sheep Gulch

Southbound beneath Hope Pass.

PHOTO BY ROGER O'DOHERTY

Distance: 9.8 miles

Elevation Gain: Approx. 3,606 feet

Elevation Loss: Approx. 2,644 feet

USFS Map: San Isabel National Forest, pages 288–289

The Colorado Trail Databook 6: pages 68–69

The CT Map Book: pages 68–69

National Geographic Trails Illustrated maps: Nos. 110, 127, 129, 148

Latitude 40° Map: Salida Buena Vista Trails

Jurisdiction: Leadville Ranger District, San Isabel National Forest

Access from Denver end:

Access from Durango end:

Availability of water: 🍵

Bicycling:

"Even though it can be a strenuous climb and descent, Hope Pass is a delight with wildflowers, elevation variety, spectacular views, and the sense of accomplishment. Slowing your pace a little and 'taking it all in' will heighten your enjoyment."

CT travelers in this segment share the route with hardy runners training for, and partici-pating in, the Leadville 100, a torturous mountain ultramarathon held each year.

Gudy's TIP

ABOUT THIS SEGMENT

The 83.2-mile Collegiate West route was added to The Colorado Trail in 2012. The route is co-located with the Continental Divide National Scenic Trail. Together with the Collegiate East route it creates the 160-mile Collegiate Loop, a multi-day hike that is growing in popularity in part because it doesn't require shuttling of vehicles. Users can park anywhere with access to the loop and return to the same spot upon completion.

The beginning of Segment CW01 generally parallels the southern shoreline of Twin Lakes Reservoir through a forest of evergreens and aspen. The historic Interlaken Resort (see page 285) is less than a mile from the beginning of the segment. Several of the resort's original buildings, dating to the late 19th century, are in various states of preservation. Wandering through them takes one back to an earlier era when tourists arrived, not by automobile, but by train and stagecoach.

For another 2 miles the trail passes through gently rolling sagebrush-covered hills before beginning a challenging 3.5-mile, 3,500-plus-foot ascent to 12,548-foot Hope Pass, nestled between Mount Hope and Quail Mountain. The trail then descends nearly 2,400 feet in 2.5 miles to the end of the segment at the trail intersection toward the ghost town of Winfield, now the site of several summer homes and a campground.

From Hope Pass, begin descending into Sheep Gulch and the Clear Creek valley.
PHOTO BY ROGER O'DOHERTY

Reaching timberline, high above Twin Lakes.
PHOTO BY BILL MANNING

TRAILHEAD/ACCESS POINTS

Interlaken Trailhead: 🚗 The northern terminus of the Collegiate West section of The Colorado Trail can be accessed from a parking area at the southeast corner of Twin Lakes and a trail walk of 1.1 miles. From Leadville to the north, take US Highway 24 south about 15 miles to the Twin Lakes turnoff and turn west onto Colorado 82. About 0.6 mile past the turnoff, take a left on the gravel County Rd 25 about 1 mile to a parking lot and the Interlaken Trailhead. From Buena Vista to the south, drive north on US 24 about 19.5 miles and turn west on Colorado 82. During the summer, when Independence Pass is open, Twin Lakes and the trailhead are accessible from Aspen on Colorado 82.

Sheep Gulch Trailhead: 🚗 See Segment CW02 on page 290.

TRAIL DESCRIPTION

Segment CW01 starts on the southeastern edge of Twin Lakes Reservoir at a Segment 11 trail junction not accessible by vehicle. To reach the start of CW01, begin at the Interlaken Trailhead parking area near mile 12.2 of Segment 11 and travel west to and along the CT about 1.5 miles to mile 13.7 of Segment 11. At this well-marked trail junction, the fork to the left continues on Segment 11 and the traditional Collegiate East route. The right fork marks the northern terminus of the CT Collegiate West, CW01, **mile 0.0** (9,222).

The trail generally follows the shoreline west for slightly more than a mile. Cross a small creek, where water may be available, on a bridge at **mile 0.5** (9,215). At **mile 0.7** (9,219) is an intersection. The right fork is what most CT users choose because it goes

The Legacy of the Interlaken Resort

Seemingly isolated and forgotten today, it's hard to imagine that one of the most popular tourist destinations in Colorado before the twentieth century was Interlaken, nestled on the shores of the present-day Twin Lakes. The complex was started in 1879 and enlarged after James V. Dexter bought the lakeside resort and grounds in 1883 and transformed it into a popular summer retreat. Visitors rode the train to a nearby stop, then took the short carriage ride to the south shore location.

The Interlaken Hotel boasted some of the best amenities of the time, with comfortable rooms and expansive views of the surrounding mountains and lakes. There was a tavern, pool hall, barns and stables, and a unique six-sided outdoor privy. An icehouse, granaries, and laundry rounded out the facility. Guests came to fish, hunt, ride horses, or just plain relax. Dexter built his own private cabin reflecting his nautical interests, including a cupola atop the second story with views in all directions.

Unfortunately, the resort fell into rapid

decline after the turn of the century when the Twin Lakes were enlarged to serve irrigation interests. The entrance road was inundated and the large, but now shallow lakes, were less attractive to nature lovers. Eventually, the place was abandoned and the buildings began to deteriorate.

In 1979, as the reservoir was enlarged further, the Bureau of Reclamation stepped in and began to record and stabilize the historic district. Buildings that were to be inundated by the new dam were moved slightly uphill and extensively repaired. For CT hikers, a short side trip to the site provides a glimpse at a slice of Colorado history.

Restored history at Interlaken.

PHOTO BY BILL MANNING

Beneath Mount Hope (13,933 feet) north of the pass.

PHOTO BY MARY AND MARC PARLANGE

through the historic Interlaken Resort (see description on page 285). The left fork is a slightly shorter alternative that bypasses Interlaken.

After having passed Interlaken, at an intersection at **mile 1.2** (9,220), turn left and continue to another intersection at **mile 1.9** (9,280). Continue right. Cross a dry creek on a bridge at **mile 2.3** (9,271). Here the trail begins veering southwest from Twin Lakes Reservoir.

Water may be available at the Boswell Creek crossing at **mile 2.9** (9,254). Take an abrupt left at an intersection at **mile 3.5** (9,287), where the trail joins an old jeep road. This is where the trail begins climbing toward Hope Pass, a gain of nearly 3,000 feet over the next 3.8 miles. Switchback to the left at **mile 3.9** (9,590), where the road is blocked.

At a trail junction at **mile 4.2** (9,873), continue straight ahead. In 0.1 mile pass by a bridge at another intersection, continuing straight ahead. At **mile 4.7** (10,301), at an intersection with Willis Gulch Trail, bear left into Little Willis Gulch. Cross the dry Cache Creek Ditch at **mile 4.8** (10,479). In an avalanche meadow at **mile 5.6** (10,970) there is a campsite and water available. There is a picturesque old cabin 0.2 mile farther up the trail and another good water stop at **mile 6.4** (11,668). Timberline is reached at approximately **mile 6.8** (11,959). There is a campsite with water nearby.

Hope Pass, another half-mile up the trail at **mile 7.3** (12,548), is rewarding and offers spectacular views of the Collegiate Range north and south. Mount Elbert, the highest point in Colorado and second highest in the Continental United States, towers to the northwest. Another Fourteener, La Plata Peak, is almost due west, and to the south, from east to west, are fellow Fourteeners Mount Oxford, Mount Belford, Missouri Mountain, and Huron Peak.

From the pass, descend more than 2,300 feet in 2.5 miles to the end of CW01. There is a dry campsite at **mile 8.3** (11,642) and two small seasonal streams at a rockslide at **mile 8.8** (11,281). Water may also be available at a small spring at **mile 9.3** (10,716). The segment ends at a three-way trail intersection at **mile 9.8** (10,177). The CT continues to the right. Sheep Gulch Trailhead along County Rd 390 is left, 0.2 mile and 250 feet downhill on trail. A major side trip is possible from here to climb Mount Oxford, Mount Belford, and Missouri Mountain.

Hope Pass, a rewarding climb.

PHOTO BY ALICIA BLANK

SERVICES, SUPPLIES, AND ACCOMMODATIONS

There are full services and accommodations available in Leadville and Buena Vista and limited amenities in Twin Lakes. See Segment 10 (page 139) for Leadville services, Segment 11 (page 148) for Twin Lakes, and Segment 13 (page 163) for Buena Vista.

Reflection of Mount Elbert, Colorado's highest peak, in Twin Lakes.

PHOTO BY JIM RAHTZ

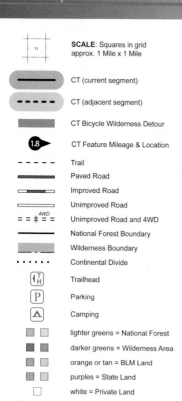

SCALE: Squares in grid approx. 1 Mile x 1 Mile

CT (current segment)

CT (adjacent segment)

CT Bicycle Wilderness Detour

1.8   CT Feature Mileage & Location

Trail

Paved Road

Improved Road

Unimproved Road

Unimproved Road and 4WD

National Forest Boundary

Wilderness Boundary

Continental Divide

Trailhead

Parking

Camping

lighter greens = National Forest

darker greens = Wilderness Area

orange or tan = BLM Land

purples = State Land

white = Private Land

COLLEGIATE WEST 01 FEATURES TABLE   San Isabel National Forest

Mileage	Features & Comments	Elevation (feet)	Mileage from Denver	Mileage to Durango	UTM-E	UTM-N (NAD83)	Zone
0.0	Collegiate West start (Seg 11 mi 13.7) right for CW (co-loc CDT)	9,222	183.0	306.7	384,754	4,325,974	13
0.5	Cross small creek on bridge	9,215	183.5	306.2	384,018	4,326,240	13
0.7	Right to historic Interlaken Resort buildings	9,219	183.7	306.0	383,791	4,326,199	13
1.2	Turn left	9,220	184.2	305.5	383,111	4,326,320	13
1.9	Continue right	9,280	184.9	304.8	382,154	4,326,320	13
2.3	Cross dry creek on bridge	9,271	185.3	304.4	381,607	4,325,597	13
2.9	Cross Boswell Creek no bridge	9,254	185.9	303.8	380,898	4,325,215	13
3.5	Abrupt left join old jeep road	9,287	186.5	303.2	380,080	4,324,834	13
4.2	Continue straight ahead	9,873	187.2	302.5	379,856	4,323,919	13
4.3	Pass bridge continue straight	9,951	187.3	302.4	379,835	4,323,827	13
4.7	Bear left into Little Willis Gulch	10,301	187.7	302.0	379,695	4,323,199	13
4.8	Cross Cache Creek Ditch (dry)	10,479	187.8	301.9	379,736	4,322,970	13
6.4	Good water stop	11,668	189.4	300.3	378,770	4,320,970	13
6.8	Treeline (approx)	11,959	189.8	299.9	378,493	4,320,418	13
7.3	Hope Pass	12,548	190.3	299.4	378,360	4,319,922	13
8.3	Dry campsite	11,642	191.3	298.4	378,511	4,319,067	13
8.8	Two small streams at rockslide	11,281	191.8	297.9	378,440	4,318,754	13
9.3	Small spring	10,716	192.3	297.4	378,524	4,318,131	13
9.8	CW01 ends continue CT West (right) or South (down 0.2 mi) to Sheep Gulch Trailhead	10,207	192.8	296.9	378,510	4,317,559	13

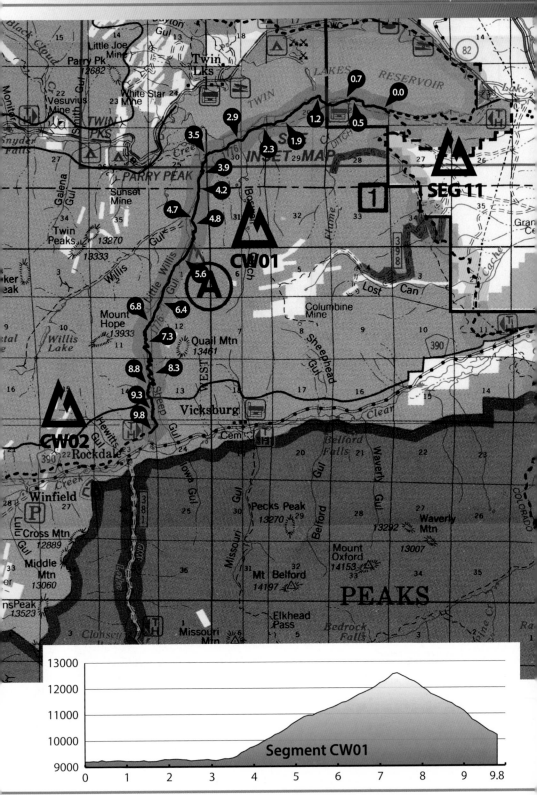

Segment CW02: **Sheep Gulch to Cottonwood Pass Trailhead**

The Three Apostles lie ahead of southbound travelers in Segment CW02. PHOTO BY SAM PARKS

Distance: 25.9 miles

Elevation Gain: Approx. 6,122 feet

Elevation Loss: Approx. 4,163 feet

USFS Map: San Isabel and Gunnison National Forests, pages 296–297

The Colorado Trail Databook 6: pages 70–71

The CT Map Book: pages 69–72

National Geographic Trails Illustrated maps: Nos. 129, 148

Latitude 40° Map: Salida Buena Vista Trails

Jurisdiction: Leadville, Salida, and Gunnison Ranger Districts, San Isabel and Gunnison National Forests

Access from Denver end:

Access from Durango end:

Availability of Water:

Bicycling: 🚲

"Volunteers and the U.S. Forest Service have accomplished wonderful segment CW02 reroutes in recent years, moving lengthy sections off of motorized routes. The single-track on the first 5 miles is an example and, compared to the road walk before, travels a more tranquil setting with stunning views of the Three Apostles."

There is more of this volunteer and USFS rerouting planned, a hardcore endeavor to move the co-located CT and CDT off the Timberline Motorcycle Trail.

Gudy's TIP

ABOUT THIS SEGMENT

Segment CW02 passes in and out of the heart of the Collegiate Peaks Wilderness Area, which contains more Fourteeners and high peaks than any other designated wilderness area in Colorado and the rest of the lower 48 states. The trail crosses the Continental Divide at the rocky and windswept Lake Ann Pass. Huron and La Plata Peaks, both Fourteeners, are directly accessible from the trail, as are a host of Thirteeners, including the Three Apostles east of Lake Ann Pass. Lake Ann itself is one of the jewels in the Collegiate West crown.

There are several stream crossings and many year-round water sources all along this segment, including the lovely beaver-damned streams and ponds in the Texas Creek Basin.

The newest part of the Collegiate West trail, known informally as the "High 23," begins in this segment. This 23-mile stretch between Texas Creek and Tincup Road was completed in 2013 and was officially opened to trail users in 2014. The multi-year project, accomplished by crews including Southwest Conservation Corps, Continental Divide Trail Alliance (now Coalition), Volunteers for Outdoor Colorado, Buena Vista Correctional Facility, and The Colorado Trail Foundation enhanced the trail by

> Parts of the Collegiate West alternative hold deep snowpack into July and are among the last places on the CT to melt off and become passable.
>
> The steep rock slope beneath Lake Ann Pass in CW02 is typically a snowfield until early- or mid-July, as are parts of CW03.

Lake Ann from above.

PHOTO BY DAVID DOLTON

constructing almost 16 miles of new, spectacular single-track tread, moving it off motor-cycle track and forest roads.

TRAILHEAD/ACCESS POINTS

Sheep Gulch Trailhead: 🚗 The northern terminus of this segment is at a three-way trail intersection 0.2 trail mile above the trailhead, between the old mining towns of Vicksburg and Winfield. The trailhead is accessible by driving US Highway 24 about 19 miles south of Leadville or 15 miles north of Buena Vista. Turn west on the graveled Clear Creek Road (County Road 390) and drive about 9.5 miles to the Sheep Gulch Trailhead on the right.

Cottonwood Pass Trailhead: 🚗 See Segment CW03 on page 298.

TRAIL DESCRIPTION

Begin this segment at a 3-way trail junction, 0.2 mile on trail uphill and north of Sheep Gulch Trailhead along County Rd 390. From the junction, **mile 0.0** (10,177), head southwest. Cross a small creek at **mile 0.7** (10,096), where water may be available. The trail passes through aspen groves and clearings with two high peaks visible in the distance to the south. It reaches a large dry gulch at **mile 1.8** (10,366) and continues through groves of aspen and pine to a big rise and another gulch. Winfield and Virginia Peaks rise to the west.

Clear Creek near Winfield, Collegiate West, Segment CW02.
PHOTO BY DAVE ANKENBAUER

Cross another small seasonal stream at **mile 2.5** (10,519). Pass through more tall aspen groves and meadows before entering the pines. At **mile 3.1** (10,397) the trail intersects with Forest Service Road 390-A. (Those wishing to climb La Plata Peak can diverge from the trail here, following the road west for about a mile, then a faint and difficult trail for 2 miles and 4,100 feet to the top of the 14,361-foot peak.) At **mile 3.2** (10,370) the trail crosses the North Fork Clear Creek on a bridge. Water is generally available here year-round. There is camping possible between the road and the river crossing.

Deer in South Fork Texas Creek, Collegiate Peaks Wilderness.

PHOTO BY CORNELIUS FRIESEN

Continuing south, trail users are treated to views of the jagged mountains known as the Three Apostles, including Ice Mountain, which is 13,951 feet high. The trail enters the Collegiate Peaks Wilderness Area at **mile 5.0** (10,630) and then passes through a clearing surrounded by aspen. Looking back to the north, there is a good view of La Plata Peak. There are also great views ahead of Granite Mountain to the south and Huron Peak to the southeast. About a tenth of a mile before crossing Silver Creek on a bridge at **mile 5.7** (10,620), the trail intersects with a trail to Silver Basin. Cross South Fork Clear Creek on a bridge at **mile 5.8** (10,590). Both creeks are reliable water sources.

After crossing South Fork Clear Creek, the trail exits the Collegiate Peaks Wilderness for about a half-mile. At **mile 5.9** (10,614), turn right onto an old roadbed. (From here, those wishing to climb 14,003-foot Huron Peak can depart the trail and head northeast for 0.3 mile to a parking area and the beginning of the 2.3-mile, 3,400-foot climb to the top of the peak.)

At **mile 6.4** (10,680), reenter the Collegiate Peaks Wilderness at a stream crossing, and begin the increasingly steep climb toward Lake Ann Pass. There are campsites to the west in the trees on the eastern slope of Granite Mountain. Take a right at the junction with Apostle Basin Trail at **mile 7.1** (10,830) and cross South Fork Clear Creek on a bridge. There is a campsite nearby.

The trail crosses a seasonal stream at **mile 7.4** (10,959) and the cascading South Fork Clear Creek at **mile 8.5** (11,496). The trail breaks out of the forest before reaching an intersection at **mile 8.9** (11,776). Bear right to stay on the trail. The path to the left leads to Lake Ann, 0.2 mile below, where there is camping and water. In the next mile the trail switchbacks 800 feet through tundra and talus, where marmots scramble and squeak, to 12,588-foot Lake Ann Pass, **mile 9.8,** atop the Continental Divide, with its sweeping vistas of the Collegiate Peaks Wilderness and beyond.

Collegiate Peaks Wilderness Area.
PHOTO BY BILL MANNING

The trail descends more than 1,400 feet over the next 2 miles on switchbacks and meandering tread, with expansive views of the Taylor Park area to the west, and exits the Collegiate Peaks Wilderness at an intersection at **mile 11.9** (11,156). Turn left onto the Timberline Trail, a multiple-use route on which motorcycles are allowed. Cross a seasonal stream at **mile 12.9** (11,230). Continue straight at **mile 13.8** (11,031) at an intersection with the old Gunnison Spur. At one time this was part of The Colorado Trail, taking trail users toward the town of Gunnison. Cross Illinois Creek. There are campsites over the next 0.1 mile.

The trail undulates over the next 3 miles, crossing seasonal streams at **mile 14.0** (11,088), **mile 15.3** (11,414), and **mile 17.0** (10,875), before dropping into forested Prospector Gulch to the southeast and descending more than 800 feet. At an intersection with the end of Texas Creek Road (Forest Service Road 755), **mile 18.6** (10,007), leave the Timberline Trail and head east on Texas Creek Trail 416. There is a big meadow with a pond, stream, and possible campsites nearby.

A pond midway in South Fork Texas Creek makes for good camping.
PHOTO BY TIM BURROUGHS

Climbing south toward the end of Segment CW02 at Cottonwood Pass.
PHOTO BY BILL MANNING

Reenter the Collegiate Peaks Wilderness. For the next couple of miles, the trail generally parallels Texas Creek and a series of small beaver ponds. At **mile 19.3** (10,010), there is an intersection with the Waterloo Gulch Trail, which heads north. Cross the stream, where water is available, and continue straight. There is an open meadow nearby, where camping is possible. At **mile 20.6** (10,160), cross North Texas Creek, a good water source. Take a right, heading due south, onto South Texas Creek Trail 417 at **mile 21.4** (10,345) and ford Texas Creek. There is a campsite nearby. There is another stream crossing at **mile 21.9** (10,540). After a nearly 1,000-foot elevation gain, there is a small pond to the right of the trail at **mile 23.4** (11,500), with camping on the north side. This is the last on-trail, year-round water until Segment CW03 mile 7.0, over 9 miles farther.

Continue gaining elevation. There are two more seasonal stream crossings at **mile 23.8** (11,650), on the edge of a meadow, and **mile 24.3** (11,730). It's a steep climb to the top of a saddle at **mile 25.6** (12,180). Turn northwest and climb a bit higher along the ridge before descending to Cottonwood Pass at **mile 25.9** (12,142), the southern terminus of Segment CW02. Cross to the parking area at the top of the pass to pick up Segment CW03. There is an exposed campsite near a pond 0.1 mile and 100 feet below the pass to the west.

SERVICES, SUPPLIES, AND ACCOMMODATIONS

Buena Vista, approximately 19 miles from Cottonwood Pass, offers full services. See Segment 13 (page 163) for a more complete description. The Taylor Park Trading Post, about 15 miles west of the pass, offers limited services.

SCALE: Squares in grid approx. 1 Mile x 1 Mile

CT (current segment)

CT (adjacent segment)

CT Bicycle Wilderness Detour

(1.8) CT Feature Mileage & Location

- - - - - Trail

Paved Road

Improved Road

Unimproved Road

== ‡ == Unimproved Road and 4WD

National Forest Boundary

Wilderness Boundary

Continental Divide

Trailhead

Parking

Camping

COLLEGIATE WEST 02 FEATURES TABLE San Isabel and Gunnison National Forests

Mileage	Features & Comments	Elevation (feet)	Mileage from Denver	Mileage to Durango	UTM-E	UTM-N (NAD83)	Zone
0.0	Start CW02 continue CT West	10,207	192.8	296.9	378,510	4,317,559	13
0.7	Cross small creek	10,096	193.5	296.2	377,609	4,317,010	13
2.5	Cross small creek	10,506	195.3	294.4	375,248	4,316,489	13
3.1	Cross FS Rd 390A	10,397	195.9	293.8	374,292	4,316,240	13
3.2	Cross N Fk Clear Creek (bridge)	10,370	196.0	293.7	374,298	4,316,121	13
5.0	Enter Collegiate Peaks Wilderness	10,630	197.8	291.9	373,266	4,313,953	13
5.7	Cross Silver Creek on bridge	10,620	198.5	291.2	372,999	4,312,968	13
5.8	Cross creek exit Wilderness	10,590	198.6	291.1	373,177	4,312,841	13
5.9	Turn right onto old roadbed	10,614	198.7	291.0	373,269	4,312,834	13
6.4	Cross stream enter Wilderness	10,680	199.2	290.5	373,416	4,312,132	13
7.1	Right at Apostle Basin Trail cross S Fork Clear Crk (bridge)	10,830	199.9	289.8	373,758	4,311,197	13
7.4	Cross a stream	10,959	200.2	289.5	373,643	4,310,690	13
8.5	Cross South Fork Clear Creek	11,496	201.3	288.4	372,885	4,309,502	13
8.9	Right for CT left for Lake Ann	11,776	201.7	288.0	372,856	4,309,018	13
9.8	Top of Lake Ann Pass	12,588	202.6	287.1	372,639	4,308,098	13
11.9	Exit Wilderness then turn left	11,156	204.7	285.0	371,524	4,307,650	13
12.9	Cross stream	11,230	205.7	284.0	372,324	4,306,608	13
13.8	Straight then cross Illinois Creek	11,031	206.6	283.1	372,662	4,306,027	13
14.0	Cross stream	11,088	206.8	282.9	372,663	4,305,718	13
15.3	Cross stream	11,414	208.1	281.6	373,863	4,305,262	13
17.0	Cross/follow Prospector Gulch	10,875	209.8	279.9	374,933	4,304,916	13
18.6	Intersect road go East on Texas Crk Tr 416 enter Wilderness	10,007	211.4	278.3	376,242	4,303,666	13
19.3	Continue straight cross stream	10,010	212.1	277.6	377,125	4,303,995	13
20.6	Cross North Texas Creek	10,160	213.4	276.3	378,737	4,304,219	13
21.4	Right onto S Texas Crk Tr 417 and ford where trail crosses	10,345	214.2	275.5	379,848	4,303,571	13
21.9	Cross stream	10,540	214.7	275.0	379,598	4,303,080	13
23.4	Side trails right to small pond	11,500	216.2	273.5	379,534	4,301,205	13
23.8	Cross stream	11,650	216.6	273.1	379,025	4,300,734	13
24.3	Cross stream	11,730	217.1	272.6	378,788	4,300,166	13
25.6	Ridgetop turn right up then down	12,180	218.4	271.3	378,176	4,298,506	13
25.9	End CW02 at Cottonwood Pass	12,142	218.7	271.0	377,654	4,298,614	13

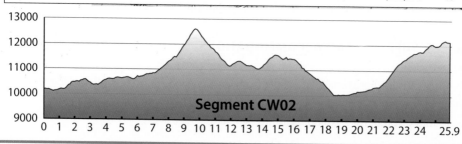

Segment CW02

lighter greens = National Forest
darker greens = Wilderness Area
orange or tan = BLM Land
purples = State Land
white = Private Land

Segment CW03: Cottonwood Pass Trailhead to Tincup Pass Road

From Cottonwood Pass looking north at the Divide, including the Three Apostles.

PHOTO BY MIKE FIFE

Distance: 15.9 miles

Elevation Gain: Approx. 3,532 feet

Elevation Loss: Approx. 4,591 feet

USFS Map: San Isabel and Gunnison National Forests, pages 304–305

The Colorado Trail Databook 6: pages 72–73

The CT Map Book: pages 72–74

National Geographic Trails Illustrated maps: Nos. 129, 130, 148

Latitude 40° Map: Salida Buena Vista Trails

Jurisdiction: Salida and Gunnison Ranger Districts, San Isabel and Gunnison National Forests

Access from Denver end:

Access from Durango end:

Availability of Water:

Bicycling:

"Carefully plan your travel timing in the above-timberline CW03 to be well situated for any storms. The first 5.6 miles is quite exposed, but it generally faces west, allowing users to monitor incoming weather and reformulate plans."

South of 5.6 miles, the trail is east of (and well below) the Divide. This part of the segment is not as exposed but users are less able to see and gauge approaching storms.

Gudy's TIP

ABOUT THIS SEGMENT

This entire segment is part of the "High 23," which was officially opened to trail users in 2014, a substantial reroute that moved the combined CT/CDT off of motorized routes. (See description on page 291.) As befitting its name, it is the highest segment in the Collegiate West, staying above 12,000 feet—and reaching nearly 13,000 feet—for most of its length before dropping some 1,800 feet in the final 3.7 miles

Even above timberline, Mother Nature is hearty.
PHOTO BY CORNELIUS FRIESEN

as it descends toward the segment's southern terminus at Tincup Pass Road. Because of camping and water limitations, consider completing this segment in a single day.

The trail begins climbing immediately from Cottonwood Pass Road on the Continental Divide, reaching a ridgeline overlooking Taylor Park to the west and the imposing profiles of several Fourteeners to the north and east.

Because much of this segment is well above timberline, users are encouraged to

Midway in Segment CW03 is South Mineral Basin looking ahead to Emma Burr Mountain.
PHOTO BY RICK STOCKWELL

Midway in Segment CW03 is Mineral Basin and stunning scenery.
PHOTO BY MAL SILLARS

avoid exposure to the Colorado high country's frequent and unpredictable lightning storms by hiking early in the day and moving lower as clouds roll in. It is not unusual to encounter cold rain, sleet, heavy fog, and hail—all in the span of a single day—even in the heart of the summer trail season. Take precautions, especially when lightning is present.

Although this segment does not pass through designated wilderness, it nevertheless is closed to bicycles.

TRAILHEAD/ACCESS POINTS

Cottonwood Pass Trailhead: Cottonwood Pass, the northern terminus of CW03, can be reached from the east and west on Cottonwood Pass Road. From the center of Buena Vista, take Colorado 306 west about 19 miles to the top of the pass. From Gunnison, it is approximately 50 miles east on County Roads 742 and 209, passing by Taylor Park Reservoir along the way. Go southwest on the trail to begin Segment CW03.

Tincup Pass Road: See Segment CW04 on page 306.

TRAIL DESCRIPTION

The segment begins on the southwest side of Cottonwood Pass, **mile 0.0** (12,126). There is an exposed campsite near a pond 0.1 mile and 100 feet below the pass to the west.

Segment CW03 south of Cottonwood Pass feels like the top of the world.
PHOTO BY MIKE FIFE

Ascend more than 400 feet to a high point at **mile 0.9** (12,558) before beginning a descent south to some ridgetop meadows. This is a great spot to take photos of the surrounding Collegiate Peaks and Taylor Park to the west. At **mile 2.1** (12,450), Lost Lake lies 0.3 mile and 700 feet below the trail. Reaching the lake requires off-trail hiking down a steep but straightforward slope and the climb out, but there is camping there and reliable water. Past the Lost Lake divergent point, the trail climbs and then descends for a couple of miles. A stand of trees at a low point, **mile 4.2** (12,000), offers the possibility of shelter in bad weather, but camping is problematical because of the steepness of the slope.

Co-located CT and CDNST in Segment CW03 with Mounts Harvard (left) and Columbia (middle) in the far background.
PHOTO BY MAL SILLARS

Indian paintbrush.

Over the next mile and a half or so the trail ascends more than 700 feet to gain the Sanford Saddle, and the Continental Divide, at **mile 5.6** (12,750). Stay to the right (south) of any remaining snow while descending the other side. Descend into Mineral Basin and cross a seasonal stream (the headwaters of South Cottonwood Creek) at **mile 6.2** (12,440). During the descent, there are some small grassy areas where camping is possible.

There is a year-round stream at **mile 7.0** (11,879). Continue straight at a signpost at **mile 7.8** (11,980). Diverge left and bushwhack 0.2 mile and 200 feet below the trail for possible camping, if not too soggy, and water.

There is a seasonal stream crossing at **mile 8.8** (12,090). Over the next 1.5 miles climb about 700 feet through a talus field and a high mountain

The off-trail descent to Lost Lake for water and camping.

Hiking ridgeline meadows south of Cottonwood Pass.
PHOTO BY TIM BURROUGHS

meadow to the top of a ridge below Emma Burr Mountain at **mile 10.2** (12,780). There are spectacular 360-degree views at the top, including the trail as it drops nearly 600 feet into a valley before beginning to climb again. There is a stream crossing at **mile 11.4** (12,184). Signage nearby discourages camping in the area due to sensitive wildlife habitat.

From the stream, the trail ascends nearly 700 feet in less than a mile before topping out at **mile 12.2**. At 12,860 feet, it is the highest point on the Collegiate West route, offering great views. The trail now descends into the Woodchopper Creek drainage. At **mile 13.4** (12,490), diverge off trail, downhill (northeast) 0.4 mile to a pair of small lakes for water and camping.

The final 2.5 miles of the segment descend steadily toward Tincup Pass Road (Forest Service Road 267) at **mile 15.9** (11,070). There is camping here and water available from nearby North Fork Chalk Creek.

SERVICES, SUPPLIES, AND ACCOMMODATIONS

Full services are available in Buena Vista (see page 163). Limited services are available at Mount Princeton Hot Springs and Taylor Park Trading Post.

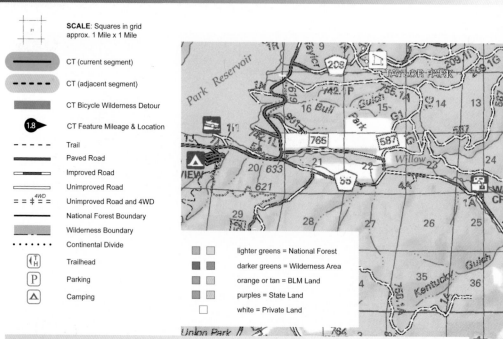

SCALE: Squares in grid approx. 1 Mile x 1 Mile

CT (current segment)

CT (adjacent segment)

CT Bicycle Wilderness Detour

1.8 ▶ CT Feature Mileage & Location

- - - - - Trail

Paved Road

Improved Road

Unimproved Road

= = ‡ = = 4WD Unimproved Road and 4WD

National Forest Boundary

Wilderness Boundary

· · · · · · · Continental Divide

Trailhead

Parking

Camping

lighter greens = National Forest

darker greens = Wilderness Area

orange or tan = BLM Land

purples = State Land

white = Private Land

COLLEGIATE WEST 03 FEATURES TABLE San Isabel and Gunnison National Forests

Mileage	Features & Comments	Elevation (feet)	Mileage from Denver	Mileage to Durango	UTM-E	UTM-N (NAD83)	Zone
0.0	Begin CW03 at Cottonwood Pass (segment closed to bicycles)	12,126	218.7	271.0	377,654	4,298,614	13
0.9	High point good for photos	12,558	219.6	270.1	377,098	4,298,215	13
2.1	For water and camping diverge off trail downhill to Lost Lake	12,450	220.8	268.9	376,703	4,296,545	13
4.2	Low point in trees (shelter)	12,000	222.9	266.8	376,547	4,294,336	13
5.6	Continental Divide high point	12,750	224.3	265.4	377,120	4,292,877	13
6.2	Cross South Cottonwood Creek	12,440	224.9	264.8	377,237	4,292,239	13
7.0	Cross stream	11,879	225.7	264.0	377,655	4,291,393	13
7.8	Continue straight at signpost	11,980	226.5	263.2	377,966	4,290,556	13
8.8	Cross tributary	12,090	227.5	262.2	377,330	4,289,607	13
10.2	Ridgetop below Emma Burr Mtn	12,780	228.9	260.8	377,717	4,288,329	13
11.4	Cross stream and begin climb	12,184	230.1	259.6	377,592	4,286,976	13
12.2	Top of ridge	12,860	230.9	258.8	377,220	4,286,361	13
13.4	For water and camping diverge off trail to pair of small lakes	12,490	232.1	257.6	376,725	4,285,057	13
15.9	End CW03 at Tincup Pass Rd 267	11,070	234.6	255.1	377,014	4,283,592	13

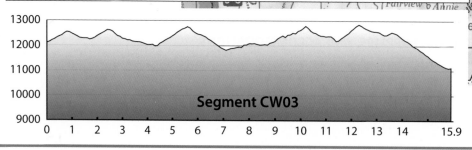

Segment CW03

Segment CW04: Tincup Pass Road to Boss Lake Trailhead

Hancock Lake and Chalk Creek Pass.

PHOTO BY CORNELIUS FRIESEN

Distance: 15.9 miles

Elevation Gain: Approx. 2,738 feet

Elevation Loss: Approx. 3,389 feet

USFS Map: San Isabel National Forest, pages 312–313

The Colorado Trail Databook 6: pages 74–75

The CT Map Book: pages 74–76

National Geographic Trails Illustrated maps: No. 130

Latitude 40° Map: Salida Buena Vista Trails

Jurisdiction: Salida Ranger District, San Isabel National Forest

Access from Denver end:

Access from Durango end:

Availability of Water:

Bicycling: 🚲

"Users in Collegiate West Segment 04 will enjoy reading the interpretive signs about the Alpine Tunnel, an ideal chance to reflect on Colorado mountain history. Traveling along the old railroad grade is a welcome, gentle grade break to steeper routings else- where."

You'll be on this old grade for almost 3 miles, a stretch popular with dayhikers and families. Meeting them can be fun and sometimes visiting can lead to an offer for a ride to, say, Mount Princeton Hot Springs.

Gudy's TIP

ABOUT THIS SEGMENT

There is nothing subtle about this segment, which climbs steadily some 1,250 feet over the first 3.5 miles before descending about an equal amount over the next 4.5 miles. The pattern repeats itself with another long ascent to Chalk Creek Pass and descent to the Boss Lake Trailhead.

Along the way, trail users encounter remnants of Colorado's mining history, particularly the Alpine Tunnel, an 1,800-foot engineering marvel built in the 1880s for the narrow-gauge Denver, South Park and Pacific Railroad's route from Denver to Gunnison. At an elevation of more than 11,500 feet, it was the first tunnel constructed under the Continental Divide in Colorado. According to the U.S. Forest Service, it "remains the highest railroad tunnel and the longest narrow-gauge tunnel in North America." Completed in 1882, it was abandoned in 1910 after minor damage wasn't deemed worth repairing due to the lack of traffic. It is now sealed at both ends. Historical markers at the tunnel's east entrance and farther down the trail built on the old railroad grade recount the history of the tunnel and of the Denver, South Park and Pacific Railroad.

TRAILHEAD/ACCESS POINTS

Tincup Pass Road: The intersection of the Collegiate West trail and Tincup Pass Road can be reached via county and Forest Service roads from Mount Princeton Hot

Segment CW04 begins by crossing this bridge over North Fork Chalk Creek.
PHOTO BY BILL MANNING

CTF volunteer trail crew working to relocate more trail off of roads. PHOTO BY CORNELIUS FRIESEN

Springs. Take Chalk Creek Drive (County Road 162) west about 11 miles to the intersection with Forest Service Road 267 at the ghost town of St. Elmo. Continue west on the increasingly rough FS 267, paralleling North Fork Chalk Creek, for another 4 miles to the intersection with the trail.

Hancock Trailhead: 🚗
From Mount Princeton Hot Springs, take Chalk Creek Drive (County Road 162) west about 11 miles to where it intersects with Hancock Road (County Road 295) near the ghost town of St. Elmo and turn left. Continue south about 6 miles to the Hancock Trailhead.

Looking north at Hancock Lakes below, CT segment CW04.
PHOTO BY CORNELIUS FRIESEN

The old railroad grade makes for a friendly path in Tunnel Gulch. Some old ties remain, foreground.
PHOTO BY BILL MANNING

Boss Lake Trailhead: 🚙 See Segment CW05 on page 314.

TRAIL DESCRIPTION

From Tincup Pass Road, **mile 0.0** (11,070), diverge west onto the trail along North Fork Chalk Creek. At **mile 0.3** (11,113), cross the creek on a bridge and enter some trees. After a 600-foot gain through a pine forest there is another stream crossing at **mile 1.6** (11,726). Emerge into a meadow and continue climbing another 375 feet to a high point above Wildcat Gulch to the east at **mile 2.7** (12,100). Enjoy a slight elevation loss to a possible spring at **mile 2.9** (11,954) before ascending 325 feet through alpine tundra to a pass above Tunnel Lake at **mile 3.6** (12,326). The lake itself comes into view shortly after crossing the pass.

Begin descending toward Hancock Trailhead, passing through some willows. At **mile 4.1** (12,048), cross a seasonal stream that feeds Tunnel Lake below. There is another seasonal stream crossing at **mile 4.5** (11,971). Turn left (north) at **mile 4.9** (11,925) and switchback down a scree-covered slope into Tunnel Gulch. The abandoned Alpine Tunnel lies beneath the trail. At **mile 5.4** (11,556), turn right onto an old railroad grade. (Left 200 yards near the tunnel's blocked east entrance is a sign describing the history of the tunnel.)

Up close detail is stunning, often worth an extra minute.

PHOTO BY BILL MANNING

There are multiple small campsites below the cliffs along the railroad grade between **mile 5.6** and **mile 6.2** (11,480).

Cross a seasonal stream at **mile 6.5** (11,342) and enter a pine forest. There is more historical signage at **mile 7.2** (11,202) about the Denver, South Park and Pacific Railroad, which once passed over the old grade. At **mile 7.5** (11,160), continue southeast on the railroad grade (or, if signed as open, take the newly con-structed single-track alternative to near Hancock Lake). Proceed straight onto a road at **mile 7.7** (11,134) and bear south-east. There is a trail register at **mile 7.9** (11,063). Continue bearing southeast and arrive at Hancock Trailhead on County Road 295 at **mile 8.1** (11,048). There is water available at Chalk Creek beneath a bridge 100 feet northeast of the trailhead.

Go south on County Road 295 and begin ascending. There is a campsite at **mile 8.7** (11,270) and other possibili-ties elsewhere along the road. At **mile 9.7** (11,636), after a climb of nearly 600 feet from the trailhead, continue beyond the end of the road and join the trail in a large, open, willow-covered valley. After passing Hancock Lake, where camping is possible, cross Chalk Creek at **mile 10.3** (11,701). Shortly after the crossing, reach an intersection with a trail to Upper Hancock Lake. Continue on the main trail and switchback 400 feet to Chalk Creek Pass at **mile 10.8** (12,105). To the left of the pass, there is often a small pond fed by a snow-field. Looking back, there are great views of Hancock and Upper Hancock Lakes. The view ahead overlooks the Middle Fork South Arkansas River valley surrounded by a host of 12,000- and 13,000-foot peaks.

Descend nearly 500 feet in the next 0.6 mile to a pond on the Middle Fork South Arkansas River at **mile 11.4** (11,628). The trail reenters the trees and continues losing elevation, crossing a seasonal stream at **mile 12.2** (11,270). At **mile 12.7** (11,230), veer left at a trail junction. (Right 50 yards to the end of the Middle Fork Road and a short distance beyond, is the river, where water is available and camping a possibility.) Cross two small seasonal streams at **mile 13.3** (11,170). Have a camera ready to photograph the Rocky

Sunrise from a campsite near Tincup Pass Road.
PHOTO BY BILL MANNING

Mountain bristlecone pine on the left at **mile 13.6** (11,080). This hardy, slow-growing, long-lived tree species is resistant to even the harshest weather conditions and can grow in very poor soil.

At **mile 14.0** (10,800), take a left onto a road (Forest Service Road 230) and hike 0.1 mile to where the trail diverges to the left and proceeds uphill. Cross a small stream at **mile 14.7** (10,920), then another close by that usually has a better flow. The trail emerges again onto FS 230 at **mile 15.7** (10,480). Cross the road and continue south toward Boss Lake. (The road itself continues southwest for 1.5 miles to US Highway 50 and the small town of Garfield, where there are some services available, possibly including mail drop.) At **mile 15.9** (10,420), stay right. The Boss Lake Trailhead is on the left. There is water available nearby at the Middle Fork South Arkansas River.

SERVICES, SUPPLIES, AND ACCOMMODATIONS

Services are available at Mount Princeton Hot Springs, 15 miles east of the Tincup Pass Road Trailhead and about 17 miles northeast of the Hancock Trailhead. Limited services are available at Garfield on US Highway 50, about 1.5 miles from the Boss Lake Trailhead.

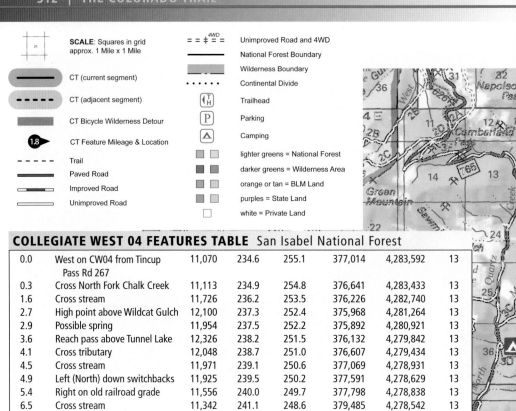

SCALE: Squares in grid approx. 1 Mile x 1 Mile

CT (current segment)

CT (adjacent segment)

CT Bicycle Wilderness Detour

1.8 CT Feature Mileage & Location

Trail

Paved Road

Improved Road

Unimproved Road

Unimproved Road and 4WD

National Forest Boundary

Wilderness Boundary

Continental Divide

Trailhead

Parking

Camping

lighter greens = National Forest

darker greens = Wilderness Area

orange or tan = BLM Land

purples = State Land

white = Private Land

COLLEGIATE WEST 04 FEATURES TABLE San Isabel National Forest

0.0	West on CW04 from Tincup Pass Rd 267	11,070	234.6	255.1	377,014	4,283,592	13
0.3	Cross North Fork Chalk Creek	11,113	234.9	254.8	376,641	4,283,433	13
1.6	Cross stream	11,726	236.2	253.5	376,226	4,282,740	13
2.7	High point above Wildcat Gulch	12,100	237.3	252.4	375,968	4,281,264	13
2.9	Possible spring	11,954	237.5	252.2	375,892	4,280,921	13
3.6	Reach pass above Tunnel Lake	12,326	238.2	251.5	376,132	4,279,842	13
4.1	Cross tributary	12,048	238.7	251.0	376,607	4,279,434	13
4.5	Cross stream	11,971	239.1	250.6	377,069	4,278,931	13
4.9	Left (North) down switchbacks	11,925	239.5	250.2	377,591	4,278,629	13
5.4	Right on old railroad grade	11,556	240.0	249.7	377,798	4,278,838	13
6.5	Cross stream	11,342	241.1	248.6	379,485	4,278,542	13
7.2	Pass historical signage	11,202	241.8	247.9	380,386	4,278,442	13
7.5	Continue Southeast	11,160	242.1	247.6	380,669	4,278,060	13
7.7	Straight (Southeast) onto road	11,134	242.3	247.4	380,894	4,277,689	13
8.1	Hancock "Alpine Tunnel" Trailhead along County Rd 295	11,048	242.7	247.0	381,483	4,277,637	13
8.7	Possible campsites on jeep road	11,270	243.3	246.4	381,555	4,276,857	13
9.7	End road join trail South	11,636	244.3	245.4	382,021	4,275,415	13
10.3	Creek beyond Hancock Lake	11,701	244.9	244.8	382,108	4,274,415	13
10.8	Reach Chalk Creek Pass	12,105	245.4	244.3	382,376	4,273,971	13
11.4	Pond Middle Fk S Arkansas River	11,628	246.0	243.7	382,676	4,273,206	13
12.2	Cross stream	11,270	246.8	242.9	383,321	4,272,118	13
12.7	Left for CT or right for road end	11,230	247.3	242.4	383,499	4,271,485	13
13.3	Cross 2 small streams	11,170	247.9	241.8	383,962	4,270,708	13
14.0	Left on road (for short distance)	10,800	248.6	241.1	384,636	4,269,961	13
14.1	Leave road turn left uphill	10,760	248.7	241.0	384,807	4,269,816	13
14.7	Cross small stream then another	10,920	249.3	240.4	385,063	4,269,884	13
15.7	Cross road	10,480	250.3	239.4	385,404	4,269,276	13
15.9	End CW04 at Boss Lake Trailhead	10,420	250.5	239.2	385,475	4,269,228	13

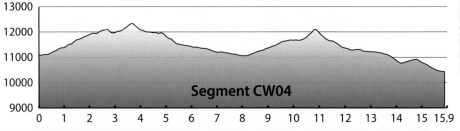

Segment CW04

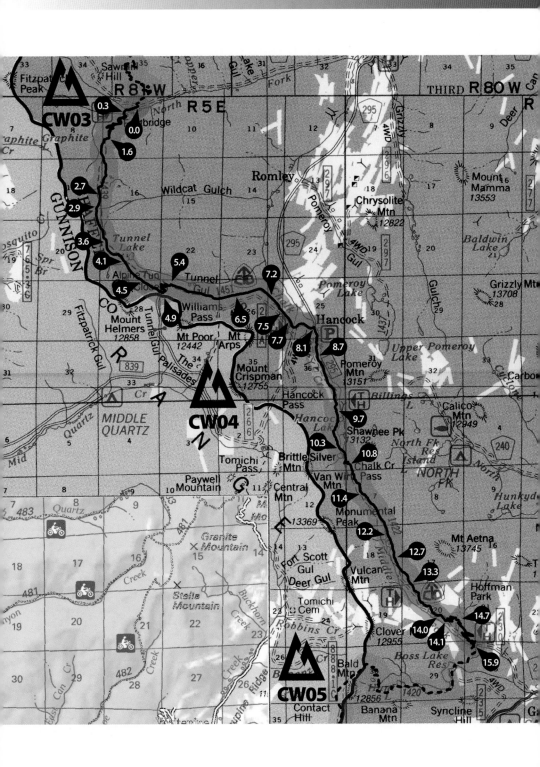

Segment CW05: Boss Lake Trailhead to Ridge Above South Fooses Creek

Evening light hits Mount Aetna and skips off Hunt Lake, Segment CW05. PHOTO BY DEAN KRAKEL

Distance: 15.7 miles

Elevation Gain: Approx. 3,750 feet

Elevation Loss: Approx. 2,271 feet

USFS Map: San Isabel and Gunnison National Forests, pages 320–321

The Colorado Trail Databook 6: pages 76–77

The CT Map Book: pages 76–77

National Geographic Trails Illustrated maps: Nos. 130, 139

Latitude 40° Map: Salida Buena Vista Trails

Jurisdiction: Salida and Gunnison Ranger Districts, San Isabel and Gunnison National Forests

Access from Denver end:

Access from Durango end: No road access

Availability of Water:

Bicycling:

"Travelers in segment CW05 have an opportunity to resupply at the Souvenir Store at the top of Monarch Pass. Selections are limited to snacks and water. Thankfully, store personnel invite trail users to phone ahead and make advanced arrangements for a mail drop."

Calling ahead to prospective businesses about package delivery and holding is essential, giving both parties an opportunity to formulate a plan for success. It will help ensure that your resupply box is waiting for you.

Gudy's TIP

ABOUT THIS SEGMENT

This segment features a climb of more than 2,000 feet to the Continental Divide, before descending to Monarch Pass and continuing along a ridgeline to the intersection with the Collegiate East trail above South Fooses Creek. It skirts Boss and Hunt Lakes, presents spectacular views from on and near the Divide, passes through the Monarch Mountain Ski Area, and crosses the only true thoroughfare on the entire Collegiate West route, US Highway 50. Though it is south of most the Collegiate Range's Fourteeners, it is surrounded by a host of impressive 12,000- and 13,000-foot peaks that repeatedly draw the eye upward.

At its endpoint on the Monarch Crest above South Fooses Creek, trail users can choose to continue in the direction of Durango and the western terminus of The Colorado Trail, or to turn back north toward Twin Lakes, where they can complete the 160-mile Collegiate Loop, an option that continues to grow in popularity.

Gaining the Continental Divide in Segment CW05 is breathtaking.
PHOTO BY DEAN WAITS

Boss Lake is good for camping or a day outing, great for fishing, and offers access by 4WD vehicles.

PHOTO BY SOPHIE PENNIMAN

TRAILHEAD/ACCESS POINTS

Boss Lake Trailhead: The trailhead is about 1.5 miles northwest of US Highway 50 on the Middle Fork Road (Forest Service Road 230) that begins at Garfield, a small community sometimes referred to as Monarch. The road is rocky and steep and lends itself best to a four-wheel-drive vehicle with high clearance and low range, though it's not uncommon to see lesser vehicles at the trailhead.

Monarch Pass: From the north, the Collegiate West trail intersects with US Highway 50 about a quarter-mile southwest of Monarch Pass. Southbound, it picks up again at the pass on a service road between the concession building and the aerial tramway. Monarch Pass is 22 miles west of Salida and 42 miles east of Gunnison.

TRAIL DESCRIPTION

At the west end of Boss Lake Trailhead, **mile 0.0** (10,428), take the trail south and cross the river on a bridge. There is camping nearby. The trail climbs very steeply before reaching Boss Lake dam at **mile 0.6** (10,819). Turn left on the dam and cross a bridge at the lake outlet at **mile 0.7** (10,819). There is water available below the bridge, but it can be difficult to access. Continue south with Boss Lake on the right. There is camping along the lake.

At **mile 0.9** (10,897), turn right onto a road and continue south for 0.1 mile. At **mile 1.0** (10,943), leave the road and turn right (west) toward Hunt Lake. There are campsites just south of Boss Lake near the inlet stream. After a 500-foot-plus climb, reach Hunt Lake at **mile 2.1** (11,470), where there is a campsite.

Emerge from the trees and onto a large rocky area. There is another small lake, 450 feet higher, at **mile 2.7** (11,922). This is the last reliable water source before reaching Monarch Pass, 8 miles ahead. In 0.7 mile and another 550-foot elevation gain, reach the

Continental Divide at a large cairn at **mile 3.4** (12,472). Here, and on the side of Bald Mountain, **mile 4.2** (12,515), are good places to photograph some of the most scenic views along the Collegiate West trail.

A rock helps steady the camera for a self-timer shot.
PHOTO BY BILL MANNING

As the trail descends, closely following the Continental Divide, pass a large cairn at **mile 4.7** (12,258) and a small power line at **mile 5.5** (12,074). At **mile 6.2** (11,741), there is a historical marker recounting how prehistoric tribes built a system of low boulder walls and ambush pits in this area to divert big game herds to awaiting hunters. Evidence suggests this "game drive" was used for thousands of years, perhaps from as early as 3000 B.C. to A.D. 1800. Remnants of the walls are still visible. This is another good photo opportunity.

At **mile 7.0** (11,638), turn right onto a road approaching the Monarch Mountain Ski Area. At another intersection at **mile 7.3** (11,494), take a right, staying close to the

Cyclists enjoy Monarch Crest in CW05 south of Highway 50.
PHOTO BY RAVI NAGARAJAN

Enjoying a well-deserved rest at the top after a big climb from the lakes below.

PHOTO BY BILL MANNING

Continental Divide. Reach a high point on the Divide at **mile 7.8** (11,773), where there is a picnic table at the top of a ski lift, before beginning the descent toward Monarch Pass. At **mile 7.9** (11,700), there is a directional marker to the right of the trail that can be rotated to identify various peaks visible on the horizon. Continue underneath a power line at **mile 8.6** (11,517). Pass gates and a large sign at **mile 8.9** (11,356) and turn right on the Old Monarch Pass Road. At the top of Old Monarch Pass, **mile 9.1** (11,386), diverge left and up onto the trail.

At **mile 10.5** (11,260), emerge onto US Highway 50. Go uphill (left) toward Monarch Pass at **mile 10.8** (11,300). A souvenir store at the pass offers a limited number of items plus they have a hydration station inside. During the trail season, the store is open during the day only. Those arriving late will be disappointed to find no outdoor water sources and none for the next several miles.

The trail continues on a service road between the concessions building and the

On the Divide, above (and in) the clouds.

PHOTO BY RICK STOCKWELL

A cairn near the Continental Divide on the Collegiate West, Segment CW05.
PHOTO BY GIFF KRIEBEL

chairlift. Turn right onto the Monarch Crest Trail at **mile 11.0** (11,378). Beware that this trail is popular with mountain bikers, especially on weekends, so be on the lookout and ready to share the tread. Motorcycles are also allowed here and in places ahead.

Turn right and uphill onto an old road at **mile 11.7** (11,383), then right underneath some old power lines onto single-track trail at **mile 12.3** (11,616). There is a dry campsite at **mile 12.7** (11,658). Beyond this point, the trail opens up, offering some great views. Because of the exposure, however, keep an eye on the weather.

At **mile 15.7** (11,909), reach the southern terminus of the Collegiate West at a junction with the Collegiate East trail, which is mile 8.6 of Segment 15. Turn left (north) to continue on Collegiate East. Continue straight (southwest) to pick up Segment 15 as it heads toward its terminus at the Marshall Pass Trailhead in 5.7 miles.

SERVICES, SUPPLIES, AND ACCOMMODATIONS

There are full services available in Salida, 22 miles east of Monarch Pass, and Gunnison, 42 miles to the west. Limited selections are available at the souvenir shop at Monarch Pass. Lodging and a restaurant are available at Garfield, about 5.5 miles northeast of Monarch Pass on US Highway 50, or 1.5 miles from the Boss Lake Trailhead on the Middle Fork Road (Forest Service Road 230).

SCALE: Squares in grid approx. 1 Mile x 1 Mile

CT (current segment)

- - - - - CT (adjacent segment)

CT Bicycle Wilderness Detour

1.8 CT Feature Mileage & Location

- - - - Trail

Paved Road

Improved Road

Unimproved Road

= = ‡ = = Unimproved Road and 4WD

National Forest Boundary

Wilderness Boundary

· · · · · · · Continental Divide

TH Trailhead

P Parking

A Camping

lighter greens = National Forest

darker greens = Wilderness Area

orange or tan = BLM Land

purples = State Land

white = Private Land

COLLEGIATE WEST 05 FEATURES TABLE San Isabel and Gunnison National Forests

Mileage	Features & Comments	Elevation (feet)	Mileage from Denver	Mileage to Durango	UTM-E	UTM-N (NAD83)	Zone
0.0	Boss Lake Trailhead start CW05 South cross stream (bridge)	10,428	250.5	239.2	385,475	4,269,228	13
0.6	Left along Boss Lake dam	10,819	251.1	238.6	385,026	4,268,700	13
0.7	Cross bridge over lake outlet	10,819	251.2	238.5	385,029	4,268,617	13
0.9	Right on road continue South	10,897	251.4	238.3	384,949	4,268,297	13
1.0	Leave road turn right (West)	10,943	251.5	238.2	384,954	4,268,080	13
2.1	Pass Hunt Lake	11,470	252.6	237.1	383,557	4,268,089	13
2.7	Pass by small lake	11,922	253.2	236.5	383,006	4,268,151	13
3.4	Continental Divide large cairn	12,472	253.9	235.8	382,674	4,268,689	13
4.2	Side of Bald Mountain	12,515	254.7	235.0	381,906	4,267,893	13
4.7	Cairn	12,258	255.2	234.5	381,961	4,267,132	13
5.5	Small power line	12,074	256.0	233.7	381,872	4,265,944	13
6.2	Signs near prehistoric walls	11,741	256.7	233.0	382,606	4,265,154	13
7.0	Right onto road	11,638	257.5	232.2	382,764	4,264,035	13
7.3	Right on road stay high (South)	11,494	257.8	231.9	382,578	4,263,488	13
7.8	Top of ski lift high point	11,773	258.3	231.4	382,705	4,262,830	13
8.6	Pass under power line	11,517	259.1	230.6	383,297	4,262,257	13
8.9	Gates/large sign right on road	11,356	259.4	230.3	383,419	4,262,153	13
9.1	Old Monarch Pass, leave road left (South) uphill	11,386	259.6	230.1	383,364	4,261,910	13
10.5	Left onto US Hwy-50 uphill	11,260	261.0	228.7	384,291	4,261,386	13
10.8	Monarch Pass along Hwy 50 go South on chairlift road	11,300	261.3	228.4	384,456	4,261,703	13
11.0	Leave road turn right onto trail	11,378	261.5	228.2	384,791	4,261,379	13
11.7	Right uphill on old road	11,383	262.2	227.5	385,800	4,260,933	13
12.3	Right onto single-track	11,616	262.8	226.9	385,848	4,260,246	13
12.7	Dry campsite	11,658	263.2	226.5	385,787	4,259,662	13
15.7	South end Collegiate West and junction with Collegiate East (Seg 15 mi 8.6) stay right	11,909	266.2	223.5	388,571	4,257,020	13

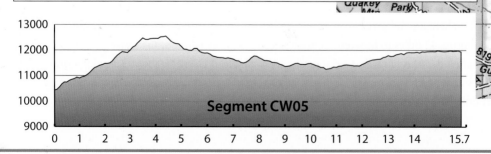

Segment CW05

Forest Service Offices

United States
Forest Service
Rocky Mountain Regional Office
740 Simms St.
Golden, CO 80401-4720
(303) 275-5350

Gunnison
National Forest
Gunnison Ranger District
216 N. Colorado St.
Gunnison, CO 81230
(970) 641-0471

Pike
National Forest
South Park Ranger District
320 US Hwy 285, Box 219
Fairplay, CO 80440
(719) 836-2031
South Platte Ranger District
19316 Goddard Ranch Ct.
Morrison, CO 80465
(303) 275-5610

Rio Grande
National Forest
Divide Ranger District
3rd and Creede Ave., Box 270
Creede, CO 81130
(719) 658-2556
Saguache Ranger District
46525 CO Hwy 114, Box 67
Saguache, CO 81149
(719) 655-2547

San Isabel
National Forest
Leadville Ranger District
810 Front St.
Leadville, CO 80461
(719) 486-0749
Salida Ranger District
5575 Cleora Road
Salida, CO 81201
(719) 539-3591

San Juan
National Forest
Columbine District
367 S. Pearl St., Box 439
Bayfield, CO 81122
(970) 884-2512
Dolores District
29211 CO Hwy 184, Box 210
Dolores, CO 81323
(970) 882-7296

White River
National Forest
Dillon Ranger District
680 Blue River Parkway,
Box 620
Silverthorne, CO 80498
(970) 468-5400
Holy Cross Ranger District
24747 US Hwy 24, Box 190
Minturn, CO 81645
(970) 827-5715

Useful Phone Numbers

The Colorado Trail Foundation
(303) 384-3729

Colorado Division of Wildlife
(303) 297-1192

To activate a rescue group, contact the nearest county sheriff:
Seg. 1–3   Jefferson (303) 277-0211
Seg. 4–6   Park (719) 836-2494
Seg. 7–8   Summit (970) 453-2232
Seg. 8   Eagle (970) 328-8500
Seg. 9–11   Lake (719) 486-1249
Seg. 12–15   Chaffee (719) 539-2596

Seg. 16–20   Saguache (719) 655-2525
Seg. 21   Mineral (719) 658-2600
Seg. 22–23   Hinsdale (970) 944-2291
Seg. 24–25   San Juan (970) 387-5531
Seg. 26   Dolores (970) 677-2257
Seg. 27–28   La Plata (970) 385-2900
Seg. CW01   Lake (719) 486-1249
Seg. CW02–CW05 Chaffee (719) 539-2596

Leave No Trace

Aspen grove found in Segment 11.
PHOTO BY JULIE VIDA AND MARK TABB

The **Leave No Trace** (LNT) program is a message to promote and inspire responsible outdoor recreation through education, research, and partnerships. Managed as a nonprofit educational organization and authorized by the U.S. Forest Service, LNT is about enjoying places like The Colorado Trail, while traveling and camping with care and preserving these places for the future. The seven Leave No Trace principles of outdoor ethics are:

• PLAN AHEAD AND PREPARE

Know the regulations and special concerns for the area you'll visit.
Prepare for extreme weather, hazards, and emergencies.
Schedule your trip to avoid times of high use.
Visit in small groups when possible. Consider splitting larger groups into smaller groups.
Repackage food to minimize waste.
Use a map and compass to eliminate the use of marking paint, rock cairns, or flagging.

• TRAVEL AND CAMP ON DURABLE SURFACES

Durable surfaces include established trails and campsites, rock, gravel, dry grasses, or snow.

Protect riparian areas by camping at least 200 feet from lakes and streams.

Good campsites are found, not made. Altering a site is not necessary.

In popular areas:

Concentrate use on existing trails and campsites.

Walk single file in the middle of the trail, even when wet or muddy.

Keep campsites small. Focus activity in areas where vegetation is absent.

In pristine areas:

Disperse use to prevent the creation of campsites and trails.

Avoid places where impacts are just beginning.

• DISPOSE OF WASTE PROPERLY

Pack it in, pack it out. Inspect your campsite and rest areas for trash or spilled foods.

Pack out all trash, leftover food, and litter.

Deposit solid human waste in catholes dug 6 to 8 inches deep at least 200 feet from water, camp, and trails. Cover and disguise the cathole when finished.

Pack out toilet paper and hygiene products.

To wash yourself or your dishes, carry water 200 feet away from streams or lakes and use small amounts of biodegradable soap. Scatter strained dishwater.

• LEAVE WHAT YOU FIND

Preserve the past: examine, but do not touch, cultural or historic structures and artifacts.

Leave rocks, plants, and other natural objects as you find them.

Avoid introducing or transporting non-native species.

Do not build structures, furniture, or dig trenches.

• MINIMIZE CAMPFIRE IMPACTS

Campfires can cause lasting impacts to the backcountry. Use a lightweight stove for cooking and enjoy a candle lantern for light.

Where fires are permitted, use established fire rings, fire pans, or mound fires.

Keep fires small. Only use sticks from the ground that can be broken by hand.

Burn all wood/coals to ash, put out campfires completely, then scatter cool ashes.

• RESPECT WILDLIFE

Observe wildlife from a distance. Do not follow or approach them.

Never feed animals. Feeding wildlife damages their health, alters natural behaviors, and exposes them to predators or other dangers.

Protect wildlife and your food by storing rations and trash securely.

Control pets at all times, or leave them at home.

Avoid wildlife during sensitive times: mating, nesting, raising young, or winter.

• BE CONSIDERATE OF OTHER VISITORS

Respect other visitors and protect the quality of their experience.

Be courteous. Yield to other users on the trail.

Step to the downhill side of the trail when encountering pack stock.

Take breaks and camp away from trails and other visitors.

Let nature's sounds prevail. Avoid loud voices and noises.

Leave No Trace publishes an educational booklet, *Outdoor Skills and Ethics*, that specifically covers backcountry recreation in the Rocky Mountains. To obtain a copy of this, or for more information about the LNT program, contact:

Leave No Trace, Inc.
P.O. Box 997
Boulder, CO 80306
(800) 332-4100
LNT.org
info@LNT.org

Aconitum columbianum monkshood.
PHOTO BY LORI BRUMMER

INDEX

Snow remains in late July on Segment 8 near Searle Pass.
PHOTO BY LEN GLASSNER

Sunset over the San Juan Mountains.
PHOTO BY LEN GLASSNER

Get Outside.

Become a CMC Member, today!

Explore the mountains and meet new people with the Colorado Mountain Club. Join us for trips, hikes, and activities throughout the state! Join today and save with special membership promotions for our readers: www.cmc.org/readerspecials

The Colorado Mountain Club is the state's leading organization dedicated to adventure, recreation, conservation, and education. Founded in 1912, the CMC acts as a gateway to the mountains for novices and experts alike, offering an array of year-round activities, events, and schools centered on outdoor recreation.

When you join the Colorado Mountain Club, you receive a variety of member benefits including:

- 20% member discount on CMC Press books
- 15% member discount on CMC hats, t-shirts, and hoodies
- 40% off admission to the American Mountaineering Museum
- Discounts at various outdoor retailers
- Subscription to *Trail & Timberline* magazine
- FREE signups to over 3,000 mountain adventures annually
- Access to courses, classes, and seminars throughout the state
- Adventure Travel opportunities to take you to the world's great destinations